AUTODESK® REVIT®
ARCHITECTURE 2016

ESSENTIALS

AUTODESK® REVIT® ARCHITECTURE 2016

ESSENTIALS

Ryan Duell

Tobias Hathorn

Tessa Reist Hathorn

AUTODESK.
Official Press

SYBEX®
A Wiley Brand

Acquisitions Editor: Stephanie McComb
Development Editor: Alexa Murphy
Technical Editors: Jon McFarland, Keith Reicher
Production Editor: Rebecca Anderson
Copy Editor: Judy Flynn
Editorial Manager: Mary Beth Wakefield
Production Manager: Kathleen Wisor
Associate Publisher: Jim Minatel
Book Designer: Happenstance Type-O-Rama
Proofreader: Rebecca Rider
Indexer: Johnna VanHoose Dinse
Project Coordinator, Cover: Brent Savage
Cover Designer: Wiley
Cover Image: Jeffrey A. Pinheiro

For Stacey, Lucely, and Nathaniel—more
caffeine, less snow please!
—Ryan
For RoMBIS, BoBTech, Reviteers,
FormIteers, and TNT!
—Tobias
For T and N, my two sidekicks.
—Tessa

ACKNOWLEDGMENTS

This has been an extraordinary year of change. I would like to first thank all of the family members who assisted us in transitioning out of our condominium and into our new home—it would not have been possible without your assistance. I would like to thank my wife, Stacey, for always being understanding about the crazy things I get myself involved in. I would like to give a huge round of thanks to everyone at Autodesk. From the QA guild to my agile team, your continued support, humor, and depth of knowledge is second to none. I couldn't ask for a better group of individuals to work (or share a beer) with. Next, Wiley—this book would have never been possible without your talented staff, editing, and support, so thank you. And Tobias and Tessa, thank you for the solid teamwork and dedication getting another edition wrapped!

—Ryan

Thanks to the lovely city of Boulder, Colorado, for the exciting year. The Boulder ADSK office especially has been great to work with—the team is brilliant and expedient. Thanks to my family for the support and bike ride destinations. Also, to Wiley, for making this book happen. Thanks to Ryan, for the solid, ahead-of-schedule work. Thanks to Tessa, for *everything still*. Thanks to Noelle, for the inspirational chatter.

—Tobias

Thank you to Fänas Architecture for showing me how to have a career and be a mom. You *can* have it all. Thank you to my cowriters: to Ryan, for always (again) being one step ahead of the game, and Tobias, for your great dedication and sense of humor. We did it again! Thanks also to our technical editor, Jon McFarland, for keeping us on our toes. And an enormous thanks to our team at Wiley—Stephanie McComb, Alexa Murphy, and the rest of the editorial staff—for making everything behind the scenes happen.

—Tessa

About the Authors

 Ryan Duell is a principal quality assurance analyst for Revit at Autodesk. He holds a bachelor's degree in design computing from Boston Architectural College. He started his career with cbt Architects in Boston, Massachusetts, working on a variety of project teams ranging from single-family residential to large commercial projects. Ryan transitioned into the BIM manager role, focusing on Autodesk® AutoCAD® Architecture and Autodesk® Revit® Architecture standards along with contributing assistance to project teams. At Autodesk, he spent several years in the product support organization providing Revit support for end users and enterprise accounts. In addition to working at Autodesk, Ryan teaches Revit at the Boston Architectural College and contributes to the Revit Clinic blog.

 Tobias Hathorn is a licensed architect and user experience designer for Autodesk. He holds a bachelor's degree in architecture from Kansas State University. He started his career at BNIM Architects in Kansas City, Missouri, working on a one-million-square-foot IRS paper-processing center in Revit Architecture. After working as a liaison between BNIM and Moshe Safdie and Associates on the Kansas City Performing Arts Center, Tobias moved to Boston to join the Revit product team in Waltham, Massachusetts. Tobias has honed his knowledge and experience with Revit, especially the graphics and rendering features, over the past seven years in the quality assurance and user experience groups. He is currently working on Autodesk® FormIt®, a conceptual design tool to aid in the early stages of a BIM workflow. In his free time, he likes to bicycle and play Tetris.

 Tessa Reist Hathorn is a licensed architect and a LEED Accredited Professional with 10 years of experience in architecture using Autodesk® Revit®. After starting her career at BNIM Architects working on historic renovations and the renowned Kauffman Center for the Performing Arts, she eventually moved to Boston, Massachusetts, to work with Moshe Safdie and Associates, working on high-profile international projects, and later worked with Austin Architects in Cambridge, Massachusetts. Tessa currently works as an architect in Boulder, Colorado, at Fänas Architecture, specializing in custom homes.

Contents at a Glance

CONTENTS

CHAPTER 3   Floors, Roofs, and Ceilings   59

CHAPTER 4   Stairs, Ramps, and Railings   95

CHAPTER 5   Adding Families   123

CHAPTER 6   Modifying Families   149

CHAPTER 7   **Schematic Design**   **189**

CHAPTER 8   **Rooms and Color Fill Plans**   **203**

CHAPTER 9   **Materials, Visualization, Rendering**   **221**

CHAPTER 10   **Worksharing**   **239**

CHAPTER 11   **Details and Annotations**   **261**

CHAPTER 14   Repetition in Revit   335

APPENDIX   Autodesk Revit Architecture 2016 Certification   357

FOREWORD

Congratulations on choosing Autodesk® Revit® software to be your BIM authoring tool! To prepare you for the journey of learning Revit, there are three major phases you should be aware of: the challenges, the benefits, and the guru. Let's look at each.

The Challenges

Revit is hard, but don't let it scare you. Revit is a dialogue-heavy database with a graphic front end. If you have no idea what the last sentence means, don't worry; you don't need to understand it! My point is, you will not understand everything inside of Revit. I have been using Revit for over seven years and I still don't understand everything!

The first phase in your learning process will be the challenges. You *will* get stuck. You *will* break things. This is all part of the process. Don't let it stop you. Many of the little tips, tricks, and techniques I publish were discovered when I was stuck or broke something. Welcome the challenges with open arms instead of frustration.

The Benefits

Once you have accepted and conquered the aforementioned challenges, you will enter the benefits phase. In the benefits phase you will begin to understand the power of Revit. You will begin creating construction documents faster than ever, your callouts will be automatically coordinated, and you'll have a greater understanding of your buildings than ever before.

This phase will make you smile. You are now beginning to see the "BIM light" at the end of the tunnel and it excites you! But don't stop there!

The Guru

The benefits phase has such a positive effect on you that you just *have* to expand your knowledge. If you can double your productivity with the essentials put forth in this book, imagine what you can do beyond the essentials!

The guru phase is the final phase on your journey. You'll know you are in the guru phase because you are no longer afraid of the program and it has become part of your workflow. You are reaping the benefits of BIM and forgot what life was like before it. Now, you want to push the program to its limits and become an elite user. Embrace this phase. You've earned it.

I began my Revit journey reading a book just like this one. Let this book be your guide and help you through the challenges. Keep it on your desk for reference as you reap the benefits. Finally, pass it on to a new user when you are a guru. Who knows, maybe you will be asked to write the foreword one day...

Jeffrey A. Pinheiro, AIA
"The Revit Kid"

BIM After Dark.com
@TheRevitKid

INTRODUCTION

Welcome to Autodesk Revit Architecture 2016 Essentials, based on the Autodesk® Revit® Architecture 2016 software release.

We continually shape the focus and content of our book from our diverse experience as Revit teachers, writers, users, support specialists, designers, and testers. We have tailored the content to what we think is the most valuable combination of topics and generated exercise files that target these topics. Because we teach Revit Architecture to first-time users, we feel this book's content is of most value to our students learning the program for the first time. This book should benefit new Revit Architecture users as well as long-term users who may not use every aspect of the program on a daily basis and could benefit from revisiting exercises as needed.

Revit Architecture 2016 includes several new valuable tools. While each tool may not be considered "essential," we have made an effort to mix new tools, tips, and tricks, along with established features, into the context of the text and supporting exercises. For this book, many of the existing exercises have been revisited, and we've included new exercises meant to further your knowledge of Revit. The book follows real-life workflows and scenarios and is full of practical examples that explain how to leverage the tools within Revit Architecture. We hope you find that the topics in this book are beneficial and contribute to your continual Revit development.

Who Should Read This Book

This book is written for architects, designers, students, and anyone else who needs their first exposure to Revit Architecture or has had an initial introduction and wants a refresher on the program's core features and functionality. We've designed the book to follow real project workflows and processes to help make the tools easy to learn, and the chapters are full of handy tips to make it easy to leverage Revit Architecture. This book can also be used to help prepare for Autodesk's Certified User and Certified Professional exams. For more information on certification, please visit www.autodesk.com/certification.

What You Will Learn

This book is designed to help you grasp the basics of Revit Architecture using real-world examples and techniques you'll use in everyday design and documentation. We'll explain the Revit Architecture interface and help you find the tools you need as well as help you understand how the application is structured. From there we'll show you how to create and modify the primary components in a building design. We'll show you how to take a preliminary model and add layers of intelligence to help analyze and augment your designs. We'll demonstrate how to create robust and accurate documentation and then guide you through the construction process. Whenever possible, we will both teach you how to use Revit and show you how to put those newfound skills to use in focused exercises.

As you are already aware, building information modeling (BIM) involves more than just a change in software; it also represents a change in architectural workflow and culture. To take full advantage of both BIM and Revit Architecture in your office, you'll have to make some changes to how you work. We've designed the book around an ideal, integrated workflow to aid in this transition.

What You Will See

The screen captures and other graphics in this book are based on Revit 2016, which combines the architectural, structural, and MEP disciplines and tools into a single application. If you notice small differences based on the exact version of Revit you have installed, we apologize, but it would be very confusing to base the book on all versions of the application, noting all the small differences along the way. However, whichever version you have, you'll be able to follow the lessons and chapter exercises of this book with ease.

What You Need

To leverage the full capacity of this book, we highly recommend you have a copy of Revit installed on a computer strong enough to handle it. To download the trial version of Revit (offered as Revit 2016), go to www.autodesk.com/ revitarchitecture, where you'll also find complete system requirements for running the application.

From a software standpoint, the exercises in this book are designed to be lightweight and not computationally intensive. This way, you avoid long wait times to open and save files and perform certain tasks. That said, keep in mind that the Autodesk-recommended computer specs for Revit Architecture are far more than what you need to do the exercises in this book but are *exactly* what you need to work on a project using Revit Architecture.

FREE AUTODESK SOFTWARE FOR THE EDUCATION COMMUNITY

The Autodesk Education Community is an online resource with more than five million members that enables the education community access to download—for free (see website for terms and conditions)—the same software used by professionals worldwide. You can also access additional tools and materials to help you design, visualize, and simulate ideas. Connect with other learners to stay current with the latest industry trends and get the most out of your designs. Get started today at www.autodesk.com/joinedu.

What Is Covered in This Book

Revit Architecture is a building information modeling (BIM) application that has emerged as the forerunner in the design industry. In this book, we'll focus on using real-world workflows and examples to guide you through learning the basics of Revit Architecture 2016—the *essentials*.

Autodesk Revit Architecture 2016 Essentials is organized to provide you with the knowledge needed to gain experience in many different facets of the software. The book is broken down into the following 14 chapters, which also contain numerous exercise files:

Chapter 1, "Introducing the Autodesk Revit Architecture Interface," introduces you to the user interface and gets you acquainted with the tools and technology—the workflow—behind the software.

Chapter 2, "Walls and Curtain Walls," helps you build on that initial knowledge by establishing some of the basic building blocks in architecture: walls.

Chapter 3, "Floors, Roofs, and Ceilings," introduces you to the other basic building blocks: floors, roofs, and ceilings. By the end of the first three chapters you will begin to see how easy it is to create the core elements of your building.

Chapter 4, "Stairs, Ramps, and Railings," explains the basics of stairs, ramps, and railings. These core components are versatile, and using them can be a bit tricky, so we'll guide you through the process of creating several types of stairs and railings.

Chapter 5, "Adding Families," shows you how to add a core element to your project: families. You use families to create most of your content, and Revit Architecture by default comes with a robust supply.

Chapter 6, "Modifying Families," shows you how to take these families and modify them or create your own, making the library of your content limitless.

Chapter 7, "Schematic Design," introduces you to conceptual design workflows using Autodesk® FormIt™ software and Autodesk® Sketchbook® Pro software to generate design sketches. Using those sketches, you can take the building design and model it in Revit Architecture.

Chapter 8, "Rooms and Color Fill Plans," shows you how to add room elements to your spaces, assign information to them, and create colorful diagrams based on space, department, or any other variable you need.

Chapter 9, "Materials, Visualization, Rendering," introduces you to visualization tools and techniques. You prepare presentation-quality views of your design in elevation, axonometric, and perspective views.

Chapter 10, "Worksharing," discusses how to take your Revit Architecture file into a multiperson working environment. Worksharing allows several people within your office or project team to work on the same Revit Architecture file simultaneously.

Chapter 11, "Details and Annotations," focuses on adding annotation to explain your designs. You'll learn how to add detail to your model in the form of dimensions, text, keynotes, and tags and how to embellish your 3D model with additional detailing.

Chapter 12, "Drawing Sets," shows you how to take all this information and place those drawings and views onto sheets so they can be printed and distributed to your project stakeholders.

Chapter 13, "Workflow and Site Modeling," provides the basics on how to take your office from a CAD environment to one that works with BIM. This chapter explores tools for every level of the project team—from the new staff to project managers. Understanding the process and workflow will be key to the success of your first Revit Architecture project.

Chapter 14, "Repetition in Revit," covers the primary methods to repeat geometry in Revit. This chapter explores several approaches, focusing on the primary benefits of each tool. Wrapping up the chapter are some tips and shortcuts to utilize on your own projects.

The Essentials Series

The Essentials series from Sybex provides outstanding instruction for readers who are just beginning to develop their professional skills. Every Essentials book includes these features:

▶ Skill-based instruction with chapters organized around projects rather than abstract concepts or subjects.

▶ Digital files (via download) so you can work through the project tutorials yourself. Please check the book's web page at www.sybex.com/go/revit2016essentials for the companion downloads.

At the book's web page, you'll also find a special bonus file full of suggestions for additional exercises related to each chapter, so you can practice and extend your skills.

 NOTE Should you choose to browse the book's companion web page, it will look like a site to purchase the book, which it is. But if you pan down just a bit, you'll see three gray tabs. The third one is the book's companion downloads.

Contacting the Authors

We welcome your feedback and comments. You can find the three of us on Facebook at Mastering Revit. We hope you enjoy the book.

CHAPTER 1

Introducing the Autodesk Revit Architecture Interface

After more than a decade of use in the architecture, engineering, and construction (AEC) industry, Autodesk® Revit® Architecture software continues to be unique in its holistic building information modeling (BIM) approach to design. There are other tools that allow you to design in 3D, and 10 years ago 3D might have been a differentiator, but today 3D is the standard. BIM is quickly becoming the standard as well.

Revit Architecture provides the unique ability to design, update, and document your project information from within a single file — something no other BIM tool allows you to do. Because all of your data resides in a single project file, you can work in any view to edit your model—plan, section, elevation, 3D, sheets, details, even a schedule—and then watch as your file updates in all views automatically. To begin your journey of learning Revit Architecture, we'll help you become comfortable with the user interface and the basic steps of the Revit Architecture workflow.

In this chapter, you'll learn to:

▶ **Use the Properties palette**

▶ **Use the Project Browser**

▶ **Use the View Control Bar**

▶ **Navigate with the ViewCube®**

▶ **Create floors, walls, and levels**

▶ **Change a wall type**

▶ **Place doors and windows**

▶ **Space elements equally**

Understanding the User Interface

The user interface (UI) of Revit Architecture is similar to other Autodesk products, such as the Autodesk® AutoCAD®, Autodesk® Inventor, and Autodesk® 3ds Max® products. You might also notice that it's similar to Windows-based applications such as Microsoft Word. All of these applications are based on the "ribbon" concept: tools are placed on panels organized on tabs in a *ribbon* across the top of the screen. The ribbon is contextually updated based on the elements you have selected. We'll cover the most critical aspects of the UI in this section, but we won't provide an exhaustive review of all tools and commands. You'll gain experience with a variety of tools as you read the chapters and go through the exercises in this book.

Figure 1.1 shows the Revit Architecture UI with labels illustrating the major UI elements. Four project views are tiled to display at the same time: plan, elevation, 3D, and perspective camera.

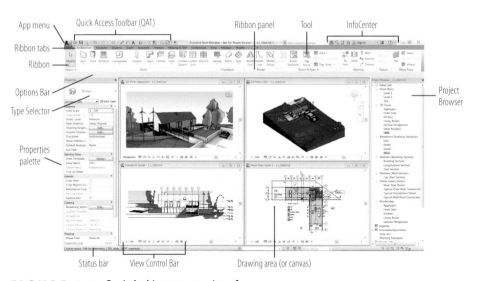

F I G U R E   1 . 1   Revit Architecture user interface

Exercise 1.1: Use the Properties Palette to See Dynamic Updates of Properties

The Properties palette is a floating palette that remains open while you work in the model. The palette dynamically updates to show the properties of the element you have selected. If you have nothing selected, then the view's properties are displayed.

To begin, go to the book's web page at www.sybex.com/go/revit2016essentials, download the files for Chapter 1, and open the file c01-ex-01.1start .rvt. You can open a Revit Architecture project file by dragging it directly into the application or by using the Open command from the Application menu (also known as the App menu).

1. Go to the Modify tab of the ribbon, find the Properties panel on the far left side of the ribbon, and click the Properties button. This button will open or close the Properties palette. Leave the Properties palette open.

2. Go to the View tab of the ribbon, find the Windows panel to the far right, click the User Interface button, and uncheck or check the Properties option. This will also open or close the Properties palette. Leave the Properties palette open. This is how to turn on UI elements that you accidentally turn off!

3. Move your mouse into the drawing area, or canvas, and then right-click with the mouse; this will bring up a context menu. Click the word *Properties* near the bottom of the list. This will also open or close the Properties palette.

4. You can also toggle the visibility of the Properties palette by pressing Ctrl+1 on your keyboard.

5. The palette can be docked on either side of your screen or it can float in your canvas. To move the palette, just click the Properties palette header and drag it with your mouse. You will see an outline preview of the palette to aid you in placement; release the mouse button to place the palette.

6. To dock the palette back to the left side of the screen, click and drag the mouse *all the way* to the left side of the screen, until the preview outline spans the entire height of the screen. The Properties palette may be up against the Project Browser. See Figure 1.2. You will move the browser to the right side of the screen in the next exercise.

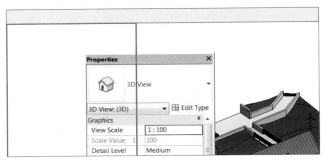

FIGURE 1.2   Preview of docking the Properties palette to the left side

The Properties palette can be pulled outside the Revit application frame. This is especially helpful if you have a second monitor. You can move the palette to a second screen for maximum Revit canvas space on the primary screen.

7. Make sure you don't have any elements selected; look in the Properties palette and notice that it displays the properties of the active view, the 3D view. Use the scroll bar on the right side of the Properties palette to find the Extents group of properties. Check the Crop View option. You don't need to use the Apply button to commit the change; instead, just move your mouse into the canvas to automatically apply your changes.

8. Select the red roof in the 3D view. Notice that the Properties palette updates to show the properties of the current selection, the Basic Roof SG Metal Panels roof. Any changes to these properties will affect this Roof element only.

9. While you still have the roof selected, click the Type Selector drop-down at the top of the Properties palette. Choose the Warm Roof - Timber option from the list. Click your mouse off into space to deselect the roof. You'll notice that the roof is no longer red. When you choose another type from the list, you are swapping the current roof type for another roof with different *type properties*, but the *element properties* stay the same!

The Properties palette displays element properties. Changes made in the Properties palette will affect only the currently selected elements. Changes made in the Type Properties dialog (found by clicking the Edit Type button, below the Type Selector) will affect all elements of the type currently displayed in the Type Selector, whether they are selected or not!

This concludes Exercise 1.1. You can compare your results with the sample file c01-ex-01.1end.rvt, available in the files you downloaded for this chapter.

Exercise 1.2: Explore the Content of Your Project with the Project Browser

The Project Browser (refer back to Figure 1.1) is a table of contents for your project. The structure of the browser is a tree consisting of all the views, legends, schedules, renderings, sheets, families, groups, and links in your Revit Architecture project.

To begin the next exercise, open the file c01-ex-01.2start.rvt.

The Project Browser can also be dragged outside the Revit canvas. This comes in very handy if you are using multiple monitors and want to maximize your drawing area.

1. Much like the Properties palette, the Project Browser can be docked on either side of the Revit canvas. Follow steps 5 and 6 in the previous exercise, but drag the Project Browser *all the way* to the right of the canvas as in Figure 1.1.

2. The Project Browser is set up as a tree view with + and − icons to expand or collapse the nodes of the tree structure. Find the very top node of the browser named Views (All). Click the − icon found to the left of the Views (All) node.

3. Now click the − icon next to the other top-level nodes: Legends, Schedules/Quantities, Sheets (All), Families, Groups, and Revit Links. Now your Project Browser looks very small, but in reality there are many pieces of content loaded in the current project.

4. Expand the Families node. Find the Planting folder and expand that. Then expand the RPC Tree - Deciduous folder.

5. Find the Hawthorn - 25′ family. Click the text, and drag your mouse onto the canvas. Release the mouse button, and you will see an outline preview to help you place the tree. Hover your mouse anywhere on the green landscape, and click again to place the tree. The browser allows this nice drag-and-drop workflow for placing content! Make sure to click the Esc key to clear the tool before the next step.

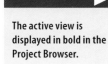

The active view is displayed in bold in the Project Browser.

6. The Project Browser has a search utility as well. If you right-click any element in the browser, you will see a Search option at the bottom of the context menu. Click Search, and in the dialog that appears, type **Kitchen**; then click the Next button. The search utility opens folders to find any project content with the word *Kitchen* in the title. Keep clicking Next until you find the Rendering: Kitchen view under Sheets (All) ➤ A001 - Title Sheet (Figure 1.3).

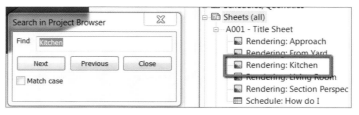

FIGURE 1.3 Project Browser search results for *Kitchen*

By default, the Project Browser displays all of your content; you can filter and customize what you see in the browser. Right-click Views (All) at the top of the browser; then select Browser Organization.

7. Once you've found the Rendering: Kitchen view, close the Search In Project Browser dialog and open the Rendering: Kitchen view by double-clicking the view name in the Project Browser. A very nice rendering opens; read Chapter 9 to learn how to use Revit's rendering features.

This concludes Exercise 1.2. You can compare your results with the sample file c01-ex-01.2end.rvt, included with the files you downloaded for this chapter.

Exercise 1.3: Use the View Control Bar to See Frequently Used View Properties

The View Control Bar is at the bottom-left corner of every view. It is a shortcut for frequently used view properties. In most cases you can find the same parameter in the Properties palette for the current view. It is important to note that these commands affect only the currently active view (Figure 1.4).

FIGURE 1.4 The View Control Bar for a 3D view

Open the file c01-ex-01.3start.rvt to begin this exercise.

1. Hover your mouse over the icons on the View Control Bar to see a tooltip, which displays the name of the specific tool. The first item is View Scale (1:100), and the second is Detail Level; we won't be changing these view properties in this exercise.

2. The third icon is a cube called Visual Style; click this icon and choose Realistic from the list that pops up. Note that you now see material textures on the walls and site (if you zoom in closely). Also, the trees look more realistic.

3. Click the Visual Style icon again; this time click Hidden Line from the list. This is a more traditional black-and-white style for viewing your 3D model.

4. The next icon on the View Control Bar is Sun Path; skip this one. The next icon is Shadows; click this icon and you should see shadows render in your scene.

5. The next icon is a teapot, and it launches the Rendering dialog. The rendering workflow is covered in Chapter 9. Click the teapot icon again to close the Rendering dialog.

6. The next icon is Crop View. This is a very important tool, so click it now. You should see parts of your model around the corners disappear! The model is not deleted, only the view is cropped.

7. The next icon on the View Control Bar is Show Crop Region. Click this to see the crop box for the view. Now that you see it, select it and use the blue grips that appear to adjust your crop as you desire. See Figure 1.5 for an example.

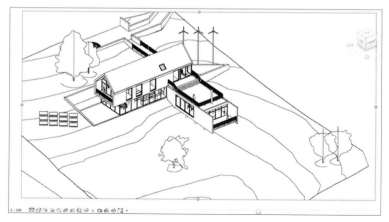

FIGURE 1.5 The Show Crop Region tool and the View Control Bar

8. The next icon allows you to lock your 3D view. This option is available only in 3D views. The command is helpful if you ever add text to a 3D view and you don't want the viewpoint to change.

9. The next icon looks like sunglasses. The Temporary Hide/Isolate tool is very useful as your project grows more complex. Select the roof in your project, and then click the sunglasses. Choose the option Isolate Element from the list. Notice that all other elements in the view are hidden so you can focus on the roof only. Click the sunglasses again, and choose Reset Temporary Hide/Isolate. Now your view is back to normal.

10. The next icon in the View Control Bar is the light bulb, for Reveal Hidden Elements mode. Click the light bulb and a magenta border surrounds your view. Any element that is hidden, or turned off, will also be displayed with magenta lines. This viewing mode will prove very helpful in locating elements that appear in some views but not your current view. Click the light bulb on the View Control Bar again to return to your normal working mode.

11. Finally, there are four additional icons for specialized view modes related to more advanced workflows. Temporary View Properties is useful when you have a view template applied to the view and you need to adjust view properties temporarily. Hide Analytical Model is useful if you're working with Structural elements and their analytical visualization. Highlight Displacement Sets is related to exploded views, covered more in Chapter 9. Finally, there is the Reveal Constraints mode, similar to Reveal Hidden Elements covered in step 10; this is a useful setting in plan views to see what "invisible" constraints might keep you from making the types of changes you want to make.

This concludes Exercise 1.3. You can compare your results with the sample file `c01-ex-01.3end.rvt`, available with the files you downloaded previously.

Exercise 1.4: Navigate with the ViewCube

As one of several navigation aids in Revit Architecture, the ViewCube is located in the upper-right corner of 3D views. This is a familiar UI element that appears in many Autodesk products.

To begin this exercise, open the file c01-ex-01.4start.rvt.

1. Click the face of the ViewCube that is labeled Front. The view dynamically orbits to show a straight-on, elevation-style view of your project—and it will automatically fit the view to the entire model.

2. Move your mouse over the ViewCube. As you hover the mouse, arrows appear on each side of the Front face. Click the arrow to the left of the Front face. The view will dynamically orbit to the Left elevation of your project.

3. Hover your mouse over the ViewCube again; this time click the arrow above the ViewCube. This will take you to a Top view, or plan view orientation, of your project.

4. Hover your mouse over the lower-right corner of the ViewCube top. Click this corner and the view will dynamically orbit back to the 3/4 corner view you started out in.

5. Now click your mouse anywhere on the ViewCube and drag the mouse. This is a custom orbit, not a predefined angle like Front, Left, or Top. Notice that the word PIVOT appears at the center of the model. Release the mouse when you like your camera angle. The model does not zoom to fit with this type of orbiting.

If you've zoomed in too far and want to zoom to fit, double-click the middle mouse button. You can use the keyboard shortcut ZE to apply Zoom To Fit to the current view or ZA to apply Zoom All To Fit (if you have many views open).

6. Select one of the trees in the model; then click and drag the ViewCube again. Notice that the green Pivot icon is now in the middle of the selected element. This is a very useful technique for navigating large models if you're editing a specific element.

7. If you are using a mouse, then the scroll wheel is ideal for zooming in and out. If you don't have a mouse, the zoom controls are all under the magnifying glass near the ViewCube. The default zoom tool when you click this icon is Zoom In Region, which allows you to choose a rectangle you'd like to examine closer.

8. Once you've navigated the view and you're satisfied with the camera angle, it is important to save the current viewpoint. Hover your mouse anywhere over the ViewCube and right-click. Select the Save View option from the context menu. Name your view (preferably something specific), and click OK. Now the newly saved view appears with the new name in the Project Browser under 3D Views.

9. This will save the angle but not the zoom level. If you want to maintain a certain zoom level, use the Crop View and Show Crop Region

commands covered in steps 6 and 7 of the previous exercise to limit the view to what is most relevant.

This concludes Exercise 1.4. You can compare your results with the sample file c01-ex-01.4end.rvt.

Creating a Simple Layout

In this section, you'll use the Revit Architecture interface to complete basic modeling workflows. You can apply the basic concepts in these exercises to a variety of tools throughout the program.

Exercise 1.5: Create a Floor

To begin, open the file c01-ex-01.5start.rvt from the files you downloaded at the beginning of this chapter.

1. The project opens in a floor plan view. There are a series of dashed green lines for you to use as guides for this exercise. Click the Architecture tab of the ribbon, and find the Floor tool in the Build panel; click the Floor tool to enter Floor sketch mode.

2. Note that the ribbon adjusts to indicate that you are in a sketch mode. The most obvious indication is the Mode panel with the red X and green check mark icons. These allow you to cancel out of sketch mode or commit your changes. You need to draw your floor shape before you click the green check mark.

3. The Draw gallery to the right of the Mode panel has many different drawing tools. You'll use the Pick Lines tool since there are reference lines already in place. Click the second-to-last icon in the lower-right corner of the Draw gallery.

4. Hover your mouse over one of the reference lines, and notice that it highlights to show a preview of the line that will be created. Click each of the reference lines *only once*. A pink sketch line appears after each click. When you're finished, you should see an image similar to Figure 1.6.

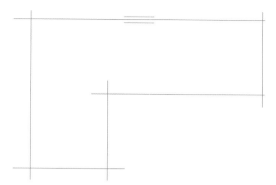

FIGURE 1.6 Floor sketch lines before trimming

The status bar in the lower-left corner of the UI provides feedback when you're using commands like Trim/Extend To Corner. It also displays keyboard shortcuts as you type, and it reports what object your mouse is hovering over.

5. Try clicking the green check mark in the ribbon to commit your sketch lines. You will get an error message about intersecting lines! Revit requires that sketches be closed loops, and you have overlapping intersections at each of the corners. Click Continue, and you will resolve this error in the next step.

6. Find the Trim/Extend To Corner tool in the Modify panel of the Modify | Create Floor Boundary tab in the ribbon. Click the tool and hover your mouse over a portion of one of the sketch lines that you want to keep; it's highlighted blue. Then click the line. Next, click the portion of the intersecting line that you wish to keep. This will trim the unwanted segments from the corner.

7. After the first corner is cleaned up, Revit remains in the Trim/Extend To Corner tool; click the next two intersecting lines to clean up their corner. Repeat these steps until each corner is trimmed, as in Figure 1.7.

8. Finally, click the green check mark; this time you should be successful. Revit has the floor selected when you exit sketch mode. You should see the blue selection color, and you can review your floor's properties in the Properties palette. The floor is on Level 1, and its area is 2500 SF (232 m2).

FIGURE 1.7 Floor sketch lines after the corners are trimmed

This concludes Exercise 1.5. You can compare your results with the sample file `c01-ex-01.5end.rvt`.

Exercise 1.6: Create Walls

Open the file `c01-ex-01.6start.rvt` to start this exercise.

Wall

1. Find the Wall tool in the Architecture tab of the ribbon. Click the Wall tool and choose the Pick Lines tool from the Draw gallery.

2. Turn your attention to the Properties palette. You will set a few parameters *before* you draw your walls. Change the Location Line parameter by clicking in the cell and choosing Finish Face: Exterior from the drop-down list.

3. Also in the Properties palette, change the Top Constraint parameter to Up To Level: Level 2.

4. Now hover your mouse over one of the edges of the floor. Do not click your mouse yet. Notice the light-blue dotted line that appears. This line indicates whether the wall will be placed inward or outward from the reference line. Note that you may need to zoom in to see the blue dotted line.

5. You want your walls to be inward from the green reference line, so move your mouse slightly inward from the floor edges—until the blue dotted line is on the inside—then click your mouse. Repeat for each edge until your drawing looks similar to Figure 1.8.

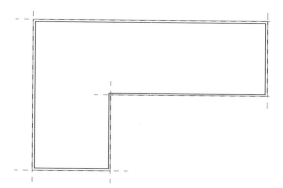

FIGURE 1.8 Walls placed inward from the floor edge

This concludes Exercise 1.6. You can compare your results with the sample file c01-ex-01.6end.rvt.

Exercise 1.7: Create Levels

In Revit Architecture, project datums are very important. Reference planes, grids, and levels are considered datums. These elements are usually visible only in a 2D view. They can be used to move any model element that references them.

To begin, open the file c01-ex-01.7start.rvt.

1. In the Project Browser, under the Views (All) node, locate the Elevations (Building Elevation) node, and double-click the North view. You may need to click the + symbol to expand the tree.

2. Zoom in to the right side of the view, and note the graphic representation of Level 1 and Level 2. Select the level line for Level 2, and notice that both the name of the level and the elevation value turn blue.

3. Click the elevation value for Level 2, and change it from **10'-0"** (~3000 mm) to **15'-0"** (~4500 mm). Zoom out so you can see the walls. Notice that the walls automatically adjust to the new height of Level 2! This happens because the Level datum drives the Top Constraint parameter that was set in step 3 of the previous exercise.

Remember that you can zoom and pan with the mouse while in the middle of commands like Trim/Extend To Corner and Offset.

Level 2
10' - 0" 15' 0"

4. Go to the Architecture tab in the ribbon and find the Datum panel. Click the Level command. Next, choose the Pick Lines tool from the Draw gallery.

5. Turn your attention to the Options Bar just below the ribbon. Verify that the Make Plan View check box is checked. Then change the Offset value to **15'-0"** (**4.500** mm).

6. Move your mouse into the drawing area and hover over the elevation line of Level 2. Wait until you see the light-blue dotted line appear above Level 2. If you don't see the preview line, then move your mouse slightly up. Click to place your new level.

7. Revit automatically names the new level for you based on the last level created. So in this case, Level 3 is the correct sequence and you don't need to rename it. Press Esc to exit the Level tool. If you did want to rename the new level, you'd select the level line and click the level name after it turns blue.

You can double-click the blue level markers to open the plan view associated with that level. You can also double-click any blue view symbol such as a section marker, elevation tag, or a callout head.

8. Select Level 3, and click the Copy tool on the Modify tab in the ribbon. Click anywhere in the canvas to specify a start point for the Copy command; then move the mouse in an upward direction. Type **12'-0"** (**3.658** m), and then press Enter to complete the command. Press Esc to exit the Copy tool. Note that you can press and hold the Shift key to force Copy or Move commands to operate in 6" (100 mm) increments.

9. Select the newest level line, click the level name, and change the name to **Roof**. Click Esc to clear the selection. Note that the level symbol is black, not blue like the others. This is a side effect of using the Copy command. This means there is not a corresponding plan view for this level.

10. Go to the View tab in the ribbon, find the Create panel, click Plan Views, and then click Floor Plan. The New Floor Plan dialog appears. Only levels that don't have views are listed. In this case, you should see only the Roof level. Click OK to create a new view associated with this level.

11. The new floor plan for the Roof level opens, the view is blank. Go to the View tab of the ribbon, locate the Windows panel, and click Switch Windows. This drop-down list shows all of the views you currently have open. You can click any view to switch to it. You can also hold down Ctrl and tap the Tab key to cycle between open Revit views.

Switch Windows

The Switch Windows tool is also located in the Quick Access toolbar (QAT). The keyboard shortcut to cycle through open views is to hold down Ctrl and press the Tab key.

CLOSING UNNEEDED VIEWS

If you have many views open at once, the performance of your Revit session slows down. Be sure to close views when you're not working in them any longer. The Close Hidden Windows command in the View tab of the ribbon will close all views but the currently active one—if your view is maximized. If your view isn't maximized, then Revit will hide only the views that are covered. If you have more than one project open, this command leaves open only one view from each project. This tool is most effective if your view windows are full screen.

This concludes Exercise 1.7. You can compare your results with the sample file c01-ex-01.7end.rvt.

Exercise 1.8: Change Wall Type

In the previous exercise, you created an additional level, thus increasing the overall height of your building. In the following steps, you'll adjust the top constraint of the walls and use the Type Selector to swap generic walls for a more specific wall type.

To begin, open the file c01-ex-01.8start.rvt.

Close Hidden

1. Go to the View tab of the ribbon, find the Create panel, and click the 3D view icon. Or you can click Default 3D View in the QAT or double-click the {3D} view in the Project Browser.

3D View

2. Click the Close Hidden Windows button so that the 3D view is the only view open, Then activate the South view under Elevations (Building Elevation) from the Project Browser.

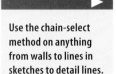

▶

Use the chain-select method on anything from walls to lines in sketches to detail lines.

3. From the View tab in the ribbon, locate the Windows panel, and then click the Tile Windows button. You can also use the keyboard short-cut **WT**. You should see the two active views (default 3D view and South elevation) side by side.

4. In either view, find the Navigation bar, click the drop-down arrow under the Zoom icon, and then click Zoom All To Fit. You can also use the keyboard shortcut **ZA**.

5. Find the Modify button at the far left side of the ribbon. Click the Select button under the Modify button and a drop-down appears. Make sure that the Select Elements By Face option is checked. This will enable easier selection of walls.

6. Click inside the 3D View window to activate the view. Hover the mouse pointer over any of the walls. Press the Tab key once, and all of the walls should highlight, as in Figure 1.9. The status bar should indicate "Chain of walls or lines." Click the mouse once to select the chain of walls.

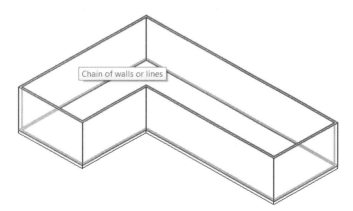

F I G U R E   1 . 9   **Highlighted walls of a chain selection**

7. With all of the walls still selected, turn your attention to the Properties palette. Find the parameter Top Constraint. Change the value to Up To Level: Roof, and then click Apply, or move your mouse into the canvas to automatically apply it. Click Esc, or click in a blank space in the can-vas to deselect the walls. Notice how the walls change height in both the 3D view and the elevation view (Figure 1.10).

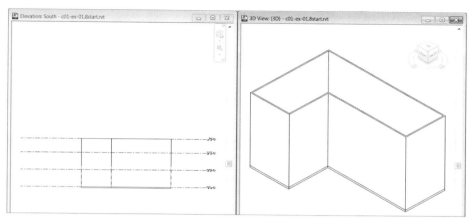

FIGURE 1.10 Tiled windows show the result of modifying the top constraints of the walls.

Changing wall segments from one wall type to another is similar to changing a font in Microsoft Word. You select the sentence and then choose a different font from the font selector—the words stay the same, but the style changes.

8. Look ahead to Figure 1.11 to see the intended result of this step. In the 3D view, select the wall that corresponds to the Front face of the ViewCube. Press and hold the Ctrl key, and select the wall segments adjacent to it, as in Figure 1.11.

FIGURE 1.11 Use the Ctrl key to select multiple elements.

9. With the walls selected, look to the top of the Properties palette to find the Type Selector. Note that it is reporting that the wall type of the current selection set is Basic Wall Generic - 8″ (200 mm). Click the Type Selector to open a list of wall types in the project. Choose the Exterior - Brick On CMU wall type near the top of the list. Click Esc to clear your selection.

10. Zoom into the walls for which you just swapped types. The thickness of these three walls should update to inherit the properties of the type you chose. Also, if you zoom in close enough, you should see a brick pattern on the walls, which the Generic walls do not have.

This concludes Exercise 1.8. You can compare your results with the sample file c01-ex-01.8end.rvt.

Exercise 1.9: Place Interior Walls

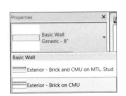

Open the file c01-ex-01.9start.rvt to begin this exercise.

1. From the Architecture tab in the ribbon, click the Wall tool. Use the Type Selector to change the wall type—*before placing the walls* — to Interior - 4 7/8″ (123 mm) Partition (1-hr).

2. In the Draw gallery in the ribbon, choose the Pick Lines icon; then click each of the green reference planes that have been provided as guides for interior walls. Your results should resemble Figure 1.12.

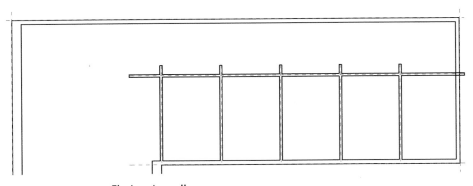

FIGURE 1.12 The interior walls

3. Choose the Trim/Extend Multiple Elements tool from the Modify tab of the ribbon. Select the long horizontal interior wall first. Then move your mouse inside the room on the lower-right side of the plan. Hold your mouse button down and drag a crossing selection window up and to the left to include each of the smaller segments of wall. Release the mouse and Revit should trim off the walls neatly, as in Figure 1.13. Click Esc to clear your selection.

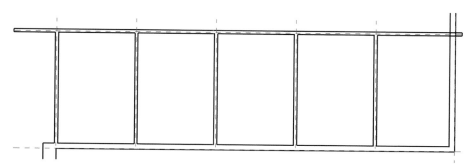

FIGURE 1.13 Results of using Trim/Extend Multiple Elements

The Function parameter of a wall, found in the wall's type properties, helps define its default height. For example, an interior wall defaults to the nearest level, whereas an exterior wall is set to Unconnected Height.

4. Select the Trim/Extend Single Element tool from the Modify tab of the ribbon. First, click the exterior wall to the far right of the plan. Then click the intersecting interior wall. Remember, Revit's Trim tool wants you to click the segments you want to keep.

5. Now select the Trim/Extend To Corner tool from the Modify tab. Click the remaining overlapping corners to clean up the wall construction.

6. Note that the leftmost interior wall is not aligned with the thicker Brick On CMU wall. Click the Align tool from the Modify tab of the ribbon. First, click the inside edge of the thicker wall because that is what you want to align to. The second click should be on the outside edge of the leftmost interior wall. This is what you want to move. The results should resemble Figure 1.14.

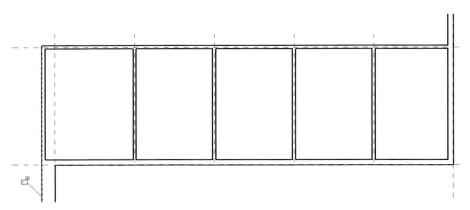

FIGURE 1.14 Results of using the Align tool

This concludes Exercise 1.9. You can compare your results with the sample file c01-ex-01.9end.rvt.

Exercise 1.10: Place Doors and Windows

In this exercise, you'll place doors and windows in the walls. Doors and windows require a wall to host them. You'll use the generic Door and Window families that are loaded in the project, but bear in mind that building components of any size, material, and configuration can be used in Revit.

To begin, open the file c01-ex-01.10start.rvt.

Door

1. Go to the Architecture tab and locate the Door tool. Click the tool and notice that the Type Selector reports that the Door type is Single-Flush 36″ (914 mm) × 84″ (2133 mm).

2. Hover the mouse over one of the interior walls and you'll see a preview of the door being placed in the wall. Press the spacebar and notice that the preview of the door flips the direction in which it is swinging.

3. Move the mouse more toward the inside of the room, and press the spacebar until your door preview swings into the room and is swinging in the correct direction (look ahead to Figure 1.15). Click to place the door.

4. Repeat the same steps to place doors into the other rooms along the interior wall. When you finish, the results should appear similar to Figure 1.15. Note that you may have door tags appear when you place doors. You can turn these off on placement from a button in the ribbon, Tag On Placement, otherwise you can just delete these tags.

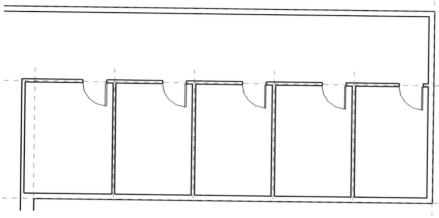

FIGURE 1.15 The doors swing into the rooms

5. Go back to the Architecture tab of the ribbon and locate the Window tool. Click the tool and notice that the Type Selector reports that the Window type is Fixed 36″ (914 mm) × 48″ (1219 mm).

6. Hover the mouse over one of the exterior walls between the interior walls and you'll see a preview of the window being placed in the wall. Move the mouse inside the wall to make the window pane closer to the inside of the room as well. Click to place the window.

7. Repeat the same steps to place windows along the exterior wall for each of the interior rooms. When you finish, the results should appear similar to Figure 1.16.

Window

If you happen to place a door or window and you want to change the door swing or the glass placement, just select the element and press the spacebar. Revit will flip the orientation of the family.

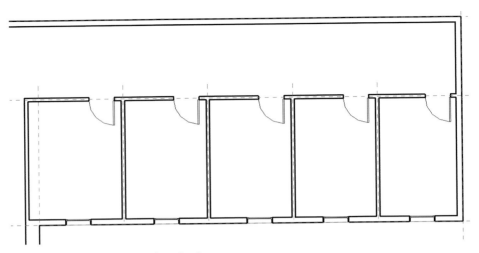

FIGURE 1.16 The windows for the rooms

This concludes Exercise 1.10. You can compare your results with the sample file c01-ex-01.10end.rvt.

Exercise 1.11: Space Elements Equally

In this exercise, you'll use dimensions and temporary dimensions to create an equally spaced relationship between the interior walls, then the doors, and then the windows. This will illustrate the idea of using constraints to create design intent. This is a fundamental concept of Revit's parametric modeling.

Open the file c01-ex-01.11start.rvt to begin this exercise.

Aligned

1. From the Annotate tab in the ribbon, locate the Dimension panel and click the Aligned Dimension tool. In the Options Bar, notice that the Placement drop-down is set for Wall Centerlines. Click in this drop-down and change the placement to Wall Faces.

2. Look ahead to Figure 1.17 for the intended result of this step. Hover your mouse over the leftmost interior wall and you should see the outside edge highlight. Click to start a dimension string.

3. Return your attention to the Options Bar and change the placement from Wall Faces to Wall Centerlines.

4. Move your mouse back into the canvas and hover over the center of the first interior wall until you see a blue highlight in the center of

the interior walls. Click to continue your dimension string. Repeat for each interior wall.

5. Return to the Options Bar and change the placement from Wall Centerlines to Wall Faces. Click the inside face of the exterior wall to finish adding dimensions to your dimension string.

6. Move your mouse above the interior wall and click to place the dimension string in the view. The results should resemble Figure 1.17.

If you want to see the actual dimension values instead of EQ in your dimension strings, right-click the dimension string (after you have placed the dimension string) and select EQ Display to toggle between the two settings. You should see the EQ icon appear anytime you select a dimension string.

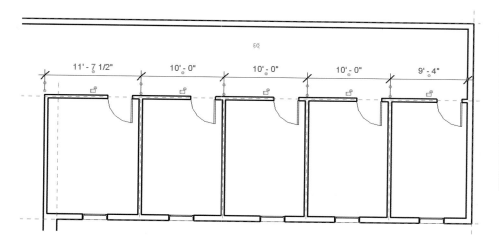

FIGURE 1.17 The dimensions of the interior walls

7. After placing the dimension string, notice the blue EQ icon that appears. This is a valuable shortcut for spacing your elements equally. Click this icon and your walls will automatically space themselves apart evenly.

8. You will most likely get an error because of a door overlapping with a wall. Disregard this warning by closing the small dialog that opens in the lower-right corner. We will use temporary dimensions to help space the doors in the next step. Click the Esc key twice to exit the Dimension tool.

9. Select the rightmost door, and notice the light-blue dimensions that appear. These are called temp dims and are very helpful for locating doors and windows relative to walls. Notice that this door is 2'-6" (.762 mm) from the exterior wall. This is perfect; leave it as is.

10. Select the next door to the left and hover your mouse over the temp dim that appears. The tooltip lets you know you can edit this dimension. Click the blue text and type 2'-6" (.762 mm) into the text box. The door moves to the correct location. Follow these steps for the other doors. The results should resemble Figure 1.18.

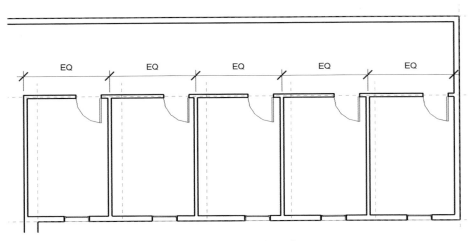

FIGURE 1.18 Doors equally spaced relative to the walls

11. Now you will combine the techniques of using dimensions and temp dims to space the windows equally. Select the rightmost window.

12. The temp dim reference line spans from the center of the window to the center of the exterior wall — turn your attention to the blue circle icon at the center of the exterior wall. Click the blue circle icon once and the circle jumps to the inside face of the wall. Click the same circle again and the temp dim appears along the outside face of the exterior wall.

13. Click the temp dim value to the right and change it to 4'-8" (1422 mm).

14. Follow the same steps to make the center of the leftmost window 4'-8" (1422 mm) from the exterior face of the exterior wall.

15. Click the Annotate tab of the ribbon, and choose the Aligned Dimension tool.

16. Hover your mouse over the middle of the leftmost window. You should see a small vertical blue highlight appear, indicating the center of the window. Click to place a dimension reference there.

17. Hover over the middle of the next window and click to continue your dimension string. Repeat until you have a dimension string between the centers of each of the windows.

18. Move your mouse down below the wall, and click to place the dimension string in the view. Click the EQ button that appears. Press Esc to exit the Dimension tool. Your result should resemble Figure 1.19.

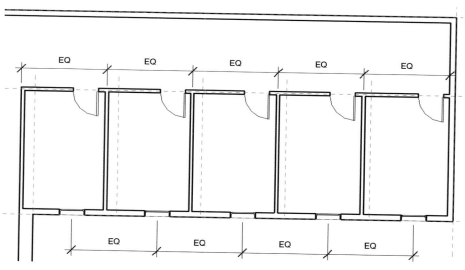

FIGURE 1.19 Windows equally spaced

This concludes Exercise 1.11. You can compare your results with the sample file c01-ex-01.11end.rvt.

Now You Know

The Revit Architecture interface is organized in a logical manner that enforces repetition and therefore increases predictability. Almost every command can be executed by selecting a view from the Project Browser, choosing a tool from the ribbon, specifying settings in the Properties palette, and then placing an element in the drawing window. From there you'll use the View Control Bar and the ViewCube to view your elements as you'd like. In the exercises in this chapter, we covered the basic modeling workflows like walls, doors, and windows and the basic model editing tools, such as Trim, Align, temp dims, and Aligned Dimensions. With this experience you'll be able to apply what you've learned in this chapter to the many exercises exploring other tools in subsequent chapters.

CHAPTER 2

Walls and Curtain Walls

Walls in the Autodesk® Revit® Architecture software can range from simple to complex. Early in the design process, walls and curtain walls can be more generic, essentially serving as vertical containers for space and function. They can also be associated to masses in order to create incredibly complex shapes. As the design progresses, these generic walls and curtain walls can be swapped out for more specific vertical compound walls that indicate a range of materials as well as geometric sweeps and reveals.

In this chapter, you'll learn to:

▶ **Create walls using several different methods**

▶ **Host elements in walls**

▶ **Modify wall parameters**

▶ **Modify and reset wall profiles**

▶ **Create and customize a curtain wall**

▶ **Embed a curtain wall in a basic wall**

▶ **Add/remove grids and add a curtain wall door**

Understanding Wall Types and Parameters

Revit Architecture has three fundamental types of walls: basic, stacked, and curtain walls. In the following sections, we will cover some of the important aspects of each. This is not intended to be an exhaustive guide to creating and editing each wall type but rather an overview to provide some background knowledge before we continue with the exercises throughout this chapter.

Basic Walls

The Revit Architecture default template includes several wall types. Wall types are defined from the exterior to the interior by elements called layers. Each layer is assigned a function, material, and thickness. The function of a wall layer determines how it will join when multiple wall types intersect or when a wall intersects another element such as a floor. The simpler wall types have one layer and are typically named with the prefix *Generic* for easy identification. The more complex wall types use multiple layers to generate the overall structure.

1. On the Architecture tab in the ribbon, click the Wall tool.

2. In the Type Selector at the top of the Properties palette, select the Generic - 8″ (200 mm) Masonry wall type.

3. Click Edit Type just below the Type Selector.

4. Click the Preview button at the lower left in the Type Properties dialog to see a graphic sample of the wall type.

In Figure 2.1, the structural region of this wall is defined by a diagonal crosshatch pattern. This is a basic wall with only one layer pattern defining the wall's structure.

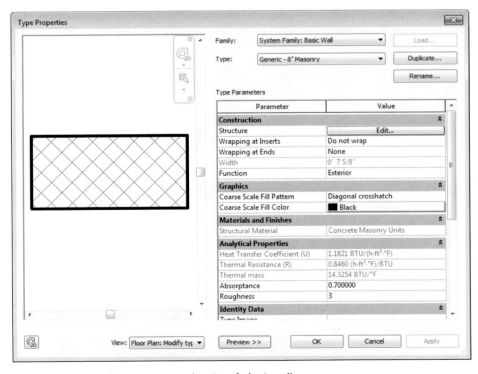

FIGURE 2.1   Masonry structural region of a basic wall

Basic walls can be modified to contain far more structural detail:

1. With the Type Properties dialog still open, go to the Type drop-down.

2. Select the wall type Exterior - Brick On Mtl. Stud, and you'll see the difference (Figure 2.2).

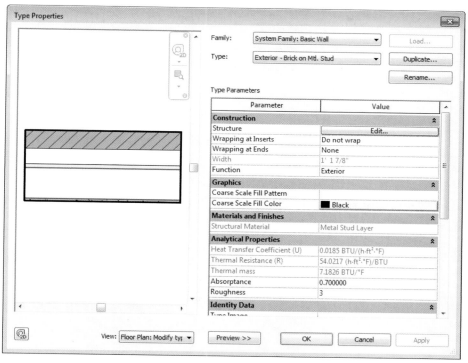

FIGURE 2.2   Compound walls consist of several layers of functional materials.

3. Click the Edit button in the Structure parameter.

You can add or remove geometry in your walls by using profiles that you apply to them. If you're still examining the structure of the previous wall, do the following:

1. Click the Cancel button, and select the wall type Exterior - Brick and CMU on Mtl. Stud. Click the Edit button again in the Structure parameter.

2. In the Preview pane, switch the view to Section.

3. Zoom into the top of the wall sample shown in the preview.

Notice the numerous values that control the function, material, and thickness for this wall type. These values help you coordinate your project information across views and schedules.

You'll see a parapet cap at the top of the wall (Figure 2.3). This is a profile associated to the basic wall type.

Although you can manually add profiles to walls in your project on a case-by-case basis, we think you'll find that adding them to the wall definition makes creating and updating wall types easy and quick.

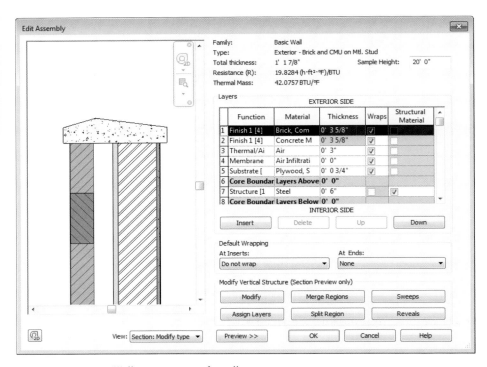

FIGURE 2.3   Wall sweep as part of a wall

Stacked Walls

Stacked walls consist of basic wall types but are combined vertically in a single defined type. Any basic walls can be used to create a stacked wall.

To find the stacked wall types, follow these steps:

1. Start the Wall tool, access the Type Selector, and scroll to the bottom of the list under the Stacked Wall type.

2. Select the wall type Exterior - Brick Over CMU w Metal Stud.

3. Click the Edit Type button, and then click the Edit button in the Structure parameter.

As shown in Figure 2.4, this wall type is defined by two different basic walls, but you can add more if necessary.

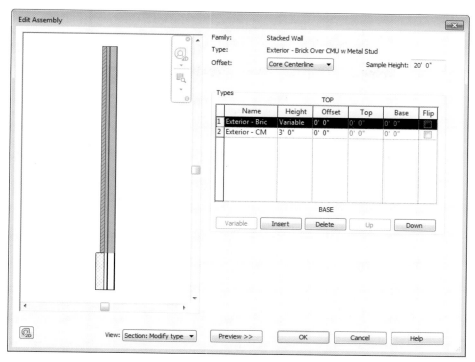

FIGURE 2.4 Type properties of a stacked wall

One of the stacked wall segments must be of variable height to accommodate the vertical constraints of the wall instances you place in a project. If all the segments were a fixed height, it would conflict with varying datum geometry in your project. In addition to specifying the height of the segments, you can adjust the horizontal offset or set a segment to flip its orientation (inside or outside).

Stacked walls have a unique option available (select and then right-click) called Break Up. When a stacked wall is broken up, the segments are reduced to individual basic walls. The basic walls represent the same dimensions specified in the stacked wall.

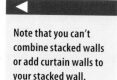

Note that you can't combine stacked walls or add curtain walls to your stacked wall.

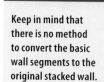

Keep in mind that there is no method to convert the basic wall segments to the original stacked wall.

Curtain Wall Types

Curtain walls are more complex than basic walls or stacked walls. They consist of four elements: a simple wall-segment definition, curtain grids, panels, and mullions. Curtain wall types can be completely instance based (allowing each to vary) or driven entirely by the wall type properties that set grid spacing, panels, and mullion types for interior and border conditions (Figure 2.5).

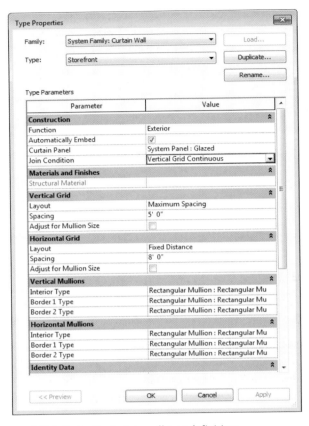

FIGURE 2.5 Curtain wall type definitions

Hosting Elements in Walls

Walls can host other types of elements that are meant to create openings. As long as the walls exist, the elements they are hosting exist as well. Doors and windows are examples of commonly used hosted elements.

Placing a door in a wall is very easy and can be done in plan, elevation, or 3D view. You may notice that you can place doors only in walls. This is because door families are hosted elements and cannot exist without a host. Because of this relationship, hosted elements are automatically deleted if you delete a host element such as a wall.

Creating Wall Configurations

The objective of the following exercise is to create several different wall configurations through drawing and picking existing geometry. The first method you will explore is manually drawing walls using some of the Draw shapes (Figure 2.6).

FIGURE 2.6 Generic configurations for walls

Then you will use additional wall tools to create arc shapes using Tangent End Arc and Fillet Arc configurations to append wall segments to existing wall elements.

Once the exterior walls are created, the last portion of the exercise will focus on creating walls by picking existing geometry to create walls.

Exercise 2.1: Create Wall Configurations

To begin, go to the book's web page at www.sybex.com/go/revit2016essentials, download the files for Chapter 2, and open the file c02-ex-2.1start.rvt.

1. In the Project Browser, under Floor Plans, activate the floor plan named Drawing Walls by double-clicking it. Start the Wall tool, and practice creating segments of walls using various tools in the Draw panel (such as Line or Center-Ends Arc). Don't worry about where you create these walls; it's just practice. Also take note of the settings available in the Options Bar prior to wall placement because they will vary for each tool.

2. Activate the floor plan named Tangent-Fillet Walls. Your goal is to complete the layout of the walls according to the dashed lines shown in the floor plan.

3. In the upper-right corner of the layout, the two perpendicular walls must be joined with a radius wall segment. Select either one of the wall segments, right-click, and select Create Similar from the context menu.

4. On the Draw panel in the ribbon, select the Fillet Arc option. Click one wall segment and then the other perpendicular segment. After you click the second wall segment, a curved segment appears.

5. Place the curved segment near the layout line. Before you continue, click the radial temporary dimension value and change it to 6′ (2000 mm).

6. The Wall command should still be active, so select the two perpendicular walls in the lower-right corner of the layout, and repeat steps 4 and 5.

7. With the Wall command remaining active, return to the Draw panel in the ribbon, and select the Tangent End Arc option. Click the left end of the wall segment at the bottom of the layout, and then click the left end of the wall segment at the top to complete the tangent arc wall. Your results should look like the plan shown in Figure 2.7.

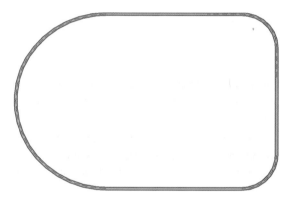

FIGURE 2.7 Results of the Tangent-Fillet Walls steps

8. Activate the Picking Walls floor plan, and then start the Wall tool. Choose the Pick Lines option in the Draw panel in the ribbon. On the Options Bar, set the Location Line to position the wall in relation to the picked path.

9. In the first set of lines in the sample file, pick each individual line segment to place walls.

10. On the second set of lines, use the chain-select method to place all the wall segments at once. Hover your mouse pointer over one of the line segments, and press the Tab key once. When the chain of lines is highlighted, click the mouse button to place the complete chain of walls. Your results should look like the plan shown in Figure 2.8.

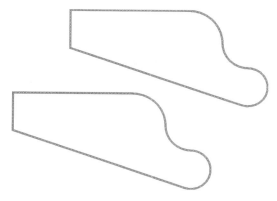

FIGURE 2.8   Result of Pick Lines

CREATING ELLIPTICAL WALLS

Because the need for elliptical walls may occur in your designs, we'll address them now. You should know two things. First, elliptical walls can't be sketched using the Draw tools. Second (and more important), they can be created via workarounds (such as creating an elliptical mass and then picking the face of the mass from which to create an elliptical wall).

So, what's a better way? Create elliptical wall layouts from a series of tangent arcs. Doing so will give you an approximation that is indistinguishable from an actual ellipse, and you'll be able to guide the walls' construction more accurately in the field.

Exercise 2.2: Host a Door in a Wall

To begin, go to the book's web page at www.sybex.com/go/revit2016essentials, download the files for Chapter 2, and open the file c02-ex-2.2start.rvt.

1. Activate the floor plan named Existing Walls.

2. Start the Door tool, and add three doors to the main horizontal wall to the left of the vertical walls.

3. After placing the doors, select any door and notice the temporary dimensions that appear.

4. With the door still selected, adjust the temporary dimension so they are 9″ off the center of the perpendicular walls (left-click the

temporary dimension grip to select Move Witness Line) to toggle the dimension reference.

5. Click the temporary dimension text, which allows you to enter **9″** (**230** mm) (Figure 2.9).

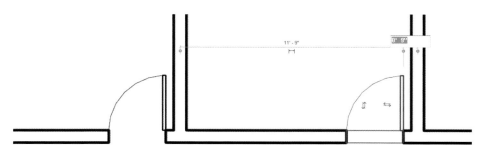

FIGURE 2.9   Hosting doors in a wall

Modifying Wall Parameters

Remember that you can disable the Tag On Placement setting in the Modify | Place Door contextual tab in the ribbon if you don't want a tag to be created when you place a door.

Now that you've created a few wall configurations, it's important to understand how you can modify them. Sometimes this is done simply by selecting the wall and dragging the end or a shape handle to a new position. In other cases, you want to be more exact and assign a specific value.

Your approach depends on where you are in the design process. Just remember that you can update design decisions and all your views, schedules, tagging, and so forth will update—don't get concerned with being too exact early in your design.

The objective of the following exercise is to modify existing wall type and instance parameters. You will start by modifying some type parameters of the wall. Then for the second part, you will modify some instance parameters.

Exercise 2.3: Modify Wall Parameters

To begin, go to the book's web page at www.sybex.com/go/revit2016essentials, download the files for Chapter 2, and open the file c02-ex-2.3start.rvt.

1. Activate the floor plan named Level 1. Sketch a straight segment of a wall, but this time as you draw the wall, type **40** (or **12000** mm). Depending on the default units, typing 40 creates a 40′ segment.

Notice that you didn't have to indicate the units as feet. If you wanted to indicate inches, you'd only have to put a space between the first and second values. Thus, 40′-6″ can easily be entered as 40[space]6.

2. Press the Esc key twice, or click the Modify button in the ribbon. Select the segment of wall you just created.

3. There are two options to modify the length, as shown in Figure 2.10. You can type in a new value by selecting the temporary dimension and entering the value, or you can simply drag either wall end to a new location.

FIGURE 2.10 Modifying the wall length

4. Open to the default 3D view by navigating to the View tab and clicking 3D View, and look at some other modification options. The two blue arrows at the top and bottom of the wall are called *shape handles* (Figure 2.11). You can click and drag them to adjust the top and bottom locations of a wall. As you drag the shape handle, you will see a temporary location line. When you release the shape handle, the temporary line disappears.

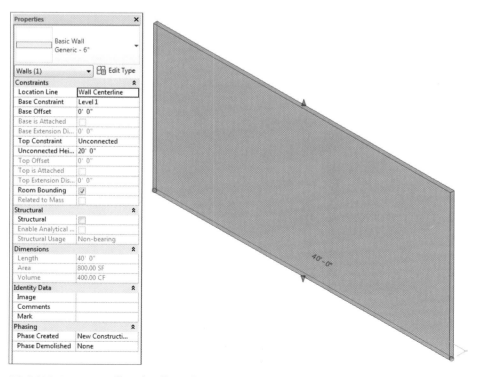

FIGURE 2.11 Shape handles and instance parameters displayed in the Properties palette

5. Dragging either shape handle updates the associated instance parameter (in this example Unconnected Height and Base Offset). Let's look at some additional instance parameters. Changes to these parameters will update only the selected instance(s). First, select the wall and review the Properties palette. These are the specific instance parameters for this wall type.

6. Update the Location Line parameter value to be Finish Face: Exterior. The location line is the origin of the wall. If you swap one wall for another, the location line will be maintained. In other words, if you create an exterior wall and the location line is the inside face, then when you change the properties or select a thicker wall, it will grow to the outside—away from the location line.

7. Next, locate the Base Constraint parameter. Change the value to Level 2. The base constraint is the bottom of the wall. The base constraint can be changed at any time and the wall will move to reflect the change.

8. Locate the Base Offset parameter. Change the value to 1′-0″ (300 mm). The Base Offset or Top Offset is the value above or below the respective constraint (negative dimensions can also be used). For example, if you wanted the bottom of a wall associated to Level 1 but 3′-0″ (1 m) below, the value for Base Offset would be -3′-0″.

9. Locate the Unconnected Height parameter. Change the value to 12′-0″ (3655 mm). The Unconnected Height value is the height of the wall when you do not use a specific datum for Top Constraint. If you change the Base Constraint parameter back to Level 1 and then change the Top Constraint value to Up To Level: Level 2, the Unconnected Height parameter becomes inactive.

Editing and Resetting Wall Profiles

Not all walls are rectilinear in elevation, and for these situations you can edit the profile of a wall. Note that you'll be able to edit the profile of a straight wall only, not a curved wall.

When you edit a wall's profile, the wall is temporarily converted to an outline sketch in elevation. Because the sketch is not plan based, you can edit a profile only in a section, an elevation, or an orthogonal 3D view. You can draw as many closed-loop sketches as you like within the wall's profile, but each loop must be closed.

If you need to remove the edited condition of a wall, don't reenter Edit Profile mode and manually remove the sketches. Select the wall, and click Reset Profile in the Mode panel on the Modify | Walls tab. Doing so will reset the extents of the wall and remove any interior sketches.

Another scenario for using Reset Profile would be when you're attempting to use Attach Top/Base. Depending on how the wall profile was originally edited, Revit could display a join error when attempting to attach the wall. This is most likely to occur if the top of the wall profile was edited previously. Reset the profile first, and then attempt to attach the wall to the roof as needed.

The objective of the following exercise is to edit the profile of a wall from the default rectangle shape to a custom shape in order to create a stepped foundation wall. Then with a second exercise, you will continue using the Attach Top/Base tool to attach the brick wall to the foundation wall.

Exercise 2.4: Edit and Reset the Wall Profile

To begin, go to the book's web page at www.sybex.com/go/revit2016essentials, download the files for Chapter 2, and open the file c02-ex-2.4start.rvt.

1. The starting file should open to the default 3D view. Select the 40′ (12000 mm) Generic - 4″ Brick wall, and click Edit Profile on the Modify | Walls tab.

2. Select the South Elevation view from the Project Browser and add the additional sketch lines as shown in the top illustration in Figure 2.12.

3. Use the Trim tools in the Modify panel as necessary to clean up the sketch lines so they match what is shown in the bottom illustration in Figure 2.12.

4. If you have crossing lines or open segments, you will receive an error when you attempt to finish the sketch in the next step.

5. When you have finished, click Finish Edit Mode. You can disregard the message "The best way to control top and base of the Wall is to modify the Constraints and Offset Parameters in Properties dialog" should it occur.

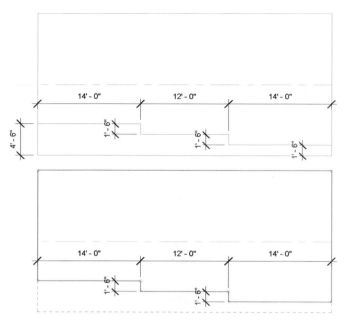

FIGURE 2.12 Adding new sketch lines

Should the design change later and you need to remove the custom wall profile, you can select the wall and use the Reset Profile tool on the ribbon, which
will be available for any wall with a modified profile.

Exercise 2.5: Attach and Detach the Top/Base

To begin, go to the book's web page at www.sybex.com/go/revit2016essen-
tials, download the files for Chapter 2, and open the file c02-ex-2.5start.rvt.

1. The starting file should open to the default 3D view. Select the
   wall and click Copy To Clipboard on the Modify | Walls contextual
   tab. Then click Paste Aligned To Selected Levels and highlight the
   Basement level. Click OK to complete the paste.

2. Because the pasted wall is taller than the distance between Basement
   and Level 1, you will get a "Highlighted walls overlap" warning.
   Ignore the warning for now; you will be adjusting the wall so it no
   longer overlaps.

3. From the Type Selector, change the pasted wall type from Generic
   - 4″ Brick to Foundation - 12″ Concrete. The wall should update in
   appearance to reflect the new wall type (Figure 2.13).

> You can also use
> Windows Clipboard
> commands to copy ele-
> ments. Just remember
> to use the custom Revit
> paste tools for greater
> flexibility.

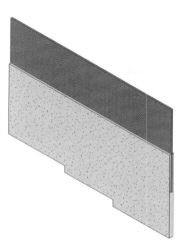

FIGURE 2.13   Pasted updated wall type

4. Select the Foundation - 12″ Concrete wall and click the Reset Profile tool on the ribbon. This will remove the profile edits you made to the wall before you copied and pasted it.

5. Select the Foundation - 12″ Concrete wall again and click the Attach Top/Base tool on the ribbon. Confirm that the Options Bar is set to Top. Then click on the Generic - 4″ Brick wall. Notice that the foundation wall has attached and the profile has been updated to match the brick wall above (Figure 2.14).

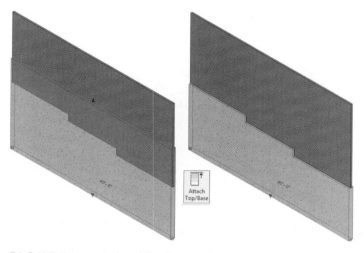

FIGURE 2.14   Attach Top/Base result

The great thing about this technique is that the relationships between the two walls are maintained if you edit the elevation profile of the upper wall. Performing these steps is a lot faster than having to edit the elevation profile of both walls! Let's make a change to the brick wall next to see the result on the attached foundation wall.

6. From the South Elevation view, select the Generic - 4″ Brick wall and click Edit Profile. Adjust the last of the three stepped profiles from 1′-6″ to 4′-0″. Click Finish Edit Mode.

7. Notice that both the brick wall profile and the foundation wall profile have been updated.

A common use of the Attach Top/Base tool is to attach walls to sloped elements, such as the underside of roofs.

Cutting Openings

Openings can be cut in both straight and curved walls. The Wall Opening command tends to be used in curved walls because you already have the option to edit the elevation profile in straight walls. And when you cut an opening, you cannot sketch beyond the extents of the wall boundary or create shapes that are not rectilinear.

The objective of the following exercise is to add and modify wall openings in a curved wall.

Exercise 2.6: Cut Openings in a Curved Wall

To begin, go to the book's web page at www.sybex.com/go/revit2016essentials, download the files for Chapter 2, and open the file c02-ex-2.6start.rvt.

1. The starting file should open to the default 3D view. Select the curved wall. The Wall Opening option will appear on the Modify | Wall tab.

2. Select Wall Opening, and then hover over the wall. You are prompted to create a rectilinear opening with two clicks.

3. Create two wall openings anywhere in the arc wall, similar to Figure 2.15.

    When the wall opening is selected, the Properties palette will display constraints such as Top Offset and Base Offset. This allows input for exact dimensions to modify the opening size and location.

4. Set Base Offset to 1′-0″ for one of the wall openings.

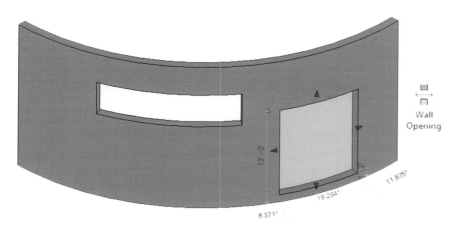

FIGURE 2.15 Creating wall openings

5. If you need to delete an opening, hover over the opening edge and select it (or use the Tab key to toggle the selection) and then press the Delete key.

Splitting Walls

Sometimes, after you've created walls, you realize that you don't need an inner segment—or you need to change a segment to another wall type. The process of deleting and re-creating walls would be tedious work. However, Revit Architecture offers a Split Element tool on the Modify tab of the ribbon that allows you to divide walls, effectively breaking them into smaller pieces. This can be done along both horizontal and vertical edges of either curved or straight walls (Figure 2.16).

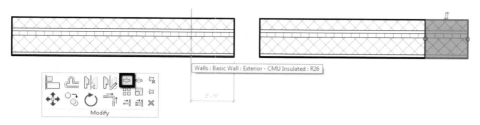

FIGURE 2.16 Splitting walls, before and after

Swapping Walls

By swapping walls for different types, you can avoid the extra work of deleting them and creating new ones. Doing so is as easy as selecting a wall and then selecting the new type from the Properties palette (Figure 2.17). This is especially useful early in the design process, when the exact wall type is likely to be unknown. Generic or placeholder wall types can be used and then swapped later on when the design progresses.

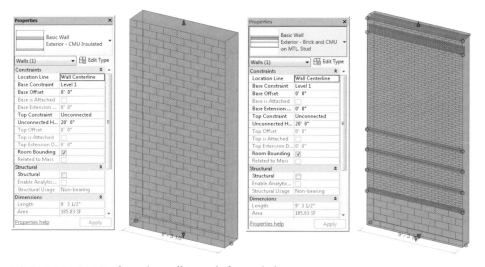

FIGURE 2.17   Swapping wall types, before and after

Creating Curtain Walls

Curtain walls are created in much the same way as regular walls: by selecting the type of curtain wall and then sketching the desired shape. However, the available parameters for curtain walls are different than those for basic or stacked walls.

The objective of the following exercise is to customize a curtain wall that is instance based (meaning you will not define any type parameters yet). You will manually add curtain grids that will subdivide the wall into smaller panels. The last part of the exercise will be to add curtain mullions, which are hosted to the curtain grids, and manually space the grids to the desired width.

Exercise 2.7: Create and Customize a Curtain Wall

To begin, open the book's web page at www.sybex.com/go/revit2016essentials, download the files for Chapter 2, and open the file c02-ex-2.7.start.rvt.

1. The starting file should open to the default 3D view. Select the Curtain Grid tool from the Build panel on the Architecture tab of the ribbon.

2. As you hover over the edge of the curtain wall, you are prompted with a dashed line that indicates where the grid will be placed. Also notice that the dashed line should snap at the midpoint and at one-third of the length of the curtain wall at either end.

3. Using the default All Segments placement option on the ribbon, add three grid lines along the horizontal and vertical directions. At this point the curtain wall should look like Figure 2.18.

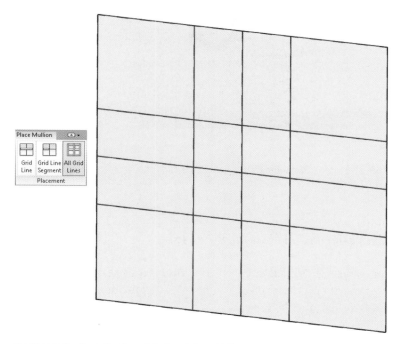

FIGURE 2.18 Completed curtain grid lines

4. Now that you've added curtain grids, you can add mullions to the curtain panel. Select the Mullion tool from the Build panel, and choose the All Grid Lines placement option on the ribbon (Figure 2.18).

5. Hover the cursor over any of the curtain grid lines and they should all be highlighted, indicating where the mullions will be placed. Left-click and mullions will be assigned to all empty grid lines (in this example they should be added everywhere). Press the Esc key once to exit the command.

6. Move the cursor over one of the vertical mullions and press the Tab key until the curtain grid line is highlighted. The Tab key is important when working with curtain walls. Because there are several elements that potentially share a common edge (walls, panels, grids, and mullions), it is necessary to press and release the Tab key to toggle what will be selected (Figure 2.19).

FIGURE 2.19   Mullions and selecting the grid line

Alternatively, you can left-click+drag the curtain grid line to move it in a less precise manner.

7. Once the grid line is highlighted, left-click to select it.
   Once it is selected, two temporary dimensions should be visible.

8. Left-click the temporary dimension text; you can enter exact values to indicate the new location for the grid line.

9. Set the vertical first and last grid lines to be 2′-0″ from the curtain wall edge. Leave the center grid line where it is. Set the horizontal first and last grid lines to be 3′-0″ from the curtain wall edge.

When complete, the curtain wall should look like the one shown in Figure 2.20.

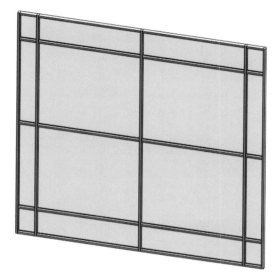

FIGURE 2.20 Final instance-based curtain wall

CURVED CURTAIN PANELS

Curved curtain-wall segments that you create will appear flat until you add the vertical grid lines. But specifying exact grid locations during the design process is often tedious—and difficult to correct. To help, you can create a design panel from a specially created wall that is very thin and transparent. Use this wall to figure out the design, and then swap it out for a curtain wall later. The wall can even have a pattern file associated to it that visually helps it to read as a curtain panel. You can find an example of this type of wall in c02-Curtain Walls.rvt (c02-Curtain Walls Metric.rvt), which is available with this chapter's exercise files.

In the previous exercise you were able to modify the curtain grids and hosted mullion locations using temporary dimensions because the curtain type properties did not have any set spacing parameters. In the next exercise the objective is to set some type property values for spacing and mullion types.

Exercise 2.8: Modify Curtain Wall Type Properties

To begin, go to the book's web page at www.sybex.com/go/revit2016essentials, download the files for Chapter 2, and open the file c02-ex-2.8start.rvt.

1. The starting file should open to the default 3D view. Select one of the two curtain walls and click Edit Type in the Properties palette.

2. Locate the Vertical Grid and Horizontal Grid settings for Layout (currently set to None). Set Vertical Grid Layout to Fixed Distance, Spacing 5'-0". Set Horizontal Grid Layout to Maximum Spacing, Spacing 4'-0". Click OK to close the Type Properties dialog.

3. Both curtain walls should update to show grid lines at the spacing you configured (Figure 2.21).

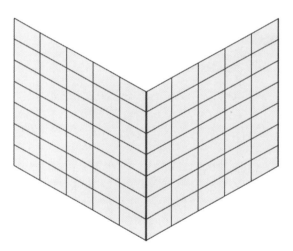

FIGURE 2.21   Curtain wall grids added

4. Select one of the curtain walls and click Edit Type again. Under Construction, set the Curtain Panel parameter to System Panel : Solid. Then set the Join Condition parameter to Border and Vertical Grid Continuous.

5. Scroll down further in the Type Properties dialog to locate the Vertical Mullions and Horizontal Mullions parameters. Set Interior

Type for both Vertical and Horizontal Mullions to Rectangular Mullion : 2.5″ × 5″ rectangular. Do the same for Border 1 Type and Border 2 Type, so all settings are using the same rectangular mullion. Click OK to close the Type Properties dialog and both curtain walls should update (Figure 2.22).

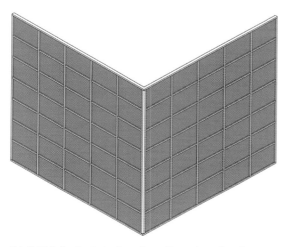

FIGURE 2.22 Curtain wall panels and mullions specified

One condition you may notice is at the corner, where the two curtain walls meet. By default no corner mullion is specified, so the standard Rectangular Mullion : 2.5″ × 5″ is used there for both overlapping ends. Corner mullions can be specified in the type properties under Border 1 or Border 2 Type.

You can also override the mullions already placed in the model, which is more applicable at this condition since you do not want to update every border condition at every curtain wall instance for the entire model. When a curtain wall type contains defined spacing and mullions, you can still modify an individual segment by first using Unpin.

6. From the 3D view, hover the cursor over one of the border curtain mullions (it doesn't matter which you choose). Press the Tab key until the mullion is highlighted; then left-click to select it. While the mullion is selected, right-click and choose Select Mullions ➤ On Gridline. This will select every mullion on this last grid line (Figure 2.23).

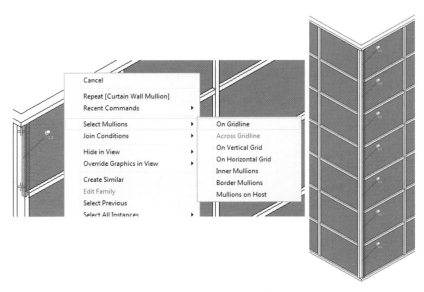

FIGURE 2.23 Mullions selected on grid line

7. Notice that the Properties palette shows the rectangular mullion type as grayed out. You can't simply swap it by default, because the type properties of the curtain wall define this type. To override the type, you need to first unpin the mullions. On the ribbon, in the Modify panel, click the Unpin tool.

8. Every curtain wall mullion on this grid line is now unpinned (and still selected). You don't need curtain mullions at both borders, so you can delete these. Since you unpinned them in the last step, you can simply press the Delete key.

9. Repeat step 6 to select the remaining border mullions along the grid line. Then use the Unpin tool again. For these you want to change the curtain mullion type from the Type Selector. Change the curtain wall mullions to L Corner Mullion : 5″ x 5″ Corner. Now the corner condition should look similar to the one in Figure 2.24.

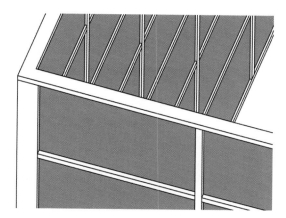

FIGURE 2.24 Curtain wall corner condition

Editing Wall Profiles

Basic, stacked, and curtain walls can have the standard rectangular shape modified to a custom shape using the Edit Profile tool. This tool is available on the ribbon after one wall is selected (it will be disabled if more than one wall is selected). When Edit Profile is activated (Figure 2.25), you can modify the rectangular profile of the wall by adding or modifying the existing sketch lines. Additionally, any closed-loop sketch lines you add in the interior will be considered openings when you click Finish Edit Mode.

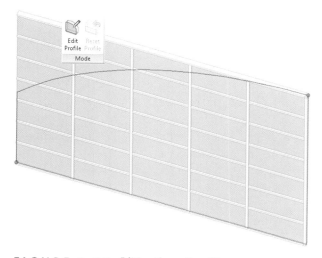

FIGURE 2.25 Editing the wall profile

Embedding Curtain Walls

Curtain walls can also be embedded in walls. This may be useful for a custom storefront or similar conditions where you want the curtain wall to be hosted in a basic or stacked wall and the wall opening to be cut out automatically.

The objective of the following exercise is to add a curtain wall embedded in a basic wall. For the second portion of the exercise you will edit the embedded curtain wall profile to customize the shape.

Exercise 2.9: Embed and Edit Curtain Wall Profile

To begin, open the book's web page at www.sybex.com/go/revit2016essentials, download the files for Chapter 2, and open the file c02-ex-2.9.start.rvt.

1. The starting file should open to the Level 1 view. In this view there is a single basic brick wall.

2. From the Level 1 view, start the Wall tool and change the wall type to Curtain Wall : Storefront using the Type Selector.

3. Click Edit Type, and locate the Automatically Embed parameter. Confirm that it is checked (it should be by default). This parameter controls whether the curtain wall will automatically embed itself into a host wall.

> **For the curtain wall to be embedded into another wall it must be within 6 inches of the wall. The curtain wall and the host wall must also be parallel.**

4. Click OK to close the Type Properties dialog. Click anywhere over the brick wall in the Level 1 view. Click the second point 20′-0″ from the first to add the curtain wall. Because Automatically Embed is checked, the curtain wall will be associated with the brick wall and the opening will be cut out of the wall.

5. Open the South Elevation view. Select the curtain wall, and from the Properties palette, change the Base Offset parameter to 2′-0″ (610 mm). Next, change the Unconnected Height parameter to 10′-0″ (3050 mm) (Figure 2.26).

6. While still in the South Elevation view, select the embedded curtain wall. Click Edit Profile on the ribbon to enter sketch mode.

7. Select the top sketch line and press the Delete key to remove it. Then add a new sketch line, using the Start-End-Radius Arc draw tool. Click Finish Edit Mode to complete the sketch and update the curtain wall.

Revit Architecture may warn you that some of the mullions in the original system can't be created. This is fine, because some of the mullions are outside the sketch area. Click Delete Element(s) to continue.

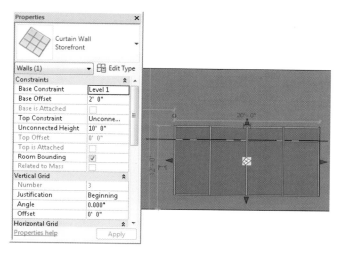

FIGURE 2.26   Curtain wall selected in wall

The host wall will update around the embedded curtain wall to match the new profile defining the boundary condition (Figure 2.27).

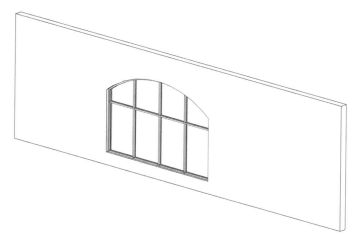

FIGURE 2.27   Curtain wall elevation view complete

Curtain Panels

Curtain panels are defined as part of the curtain wall type properties. Like the other curtain wall components, they can also be assigned on a per-instance basis or unpinned and changed to another infill type. A curtain panel can be a curtain panel family, a basic or stacked wall type, or another curtain wall.

Adding and Removing Grids and Mullions

So far in this chapter you have manually added curtain grids and curtain wall mullions as well as defined the location for grid lines in the type properties. A typical curtain wall type in your project may have the majority of the grid spacing predefined by the type properties. However, you can still add or remove grid lines.

The objective of the following exercise is to manually add additional grid lines and curtain mullions to a curtain wall driven by type properties. In addition, you will remove some of the existing curtain grids to create a larger panel infill.

Then you will continue with a second exercise to modify some of the existing curtain panel instances in the curtain wall. As part of this exercise you will focus on adding a curtain panel door to the area where you removed grids and mullions.

Exercise 2.10: Add and Remove Curtain Grids and Mullions

To begin, open the book's web page at www.sybex.com/go/revit2016essentials, download the files for Chapter 2, and open the file c02-ex-2.10.start.rvt. This file will be used for this and the following exercise.

1. The starting file should open to the default 3D view. The curtain wall type Storefront - Door contains type properties for grid distances and mullion types.

2. Move the cursor over one of the vertical red mullions (colored for exercise identification), and press the Tab key until the curtain grid is highlighted; then left-click to select it.

3. On the ribbon, notice that the Add/Remove Segments tool is now available. This tool appears only when curtain grids are selected. Click Add/Remove Segments and click the cursor over one of the red mullions. It should remove the curtain grid as well as the curtain mullion since it is hosted on the grid.

4. The tool stays active so you can click the other vertical red curtain mullion to remove it. Repeat the steps to remove the remaining red horizontal curtain mullion and you will end up with one panel, as highlighted in Figure 2.28.

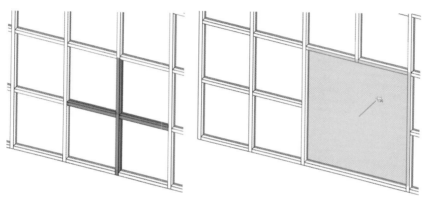

FIGURE 2.28 Removed curtain wall grids and mullions

5. You can also add curtain grids and mullions in addition to those defined in the type properties. Select the Curtain Grid tool from the Build panel on the Architecture tab of the ribbon. Change the Placement option to One Segment.

6. Add four vertical grid lines centered on the remaining lower curtain panels at 1'-8" on each side. Notice that the rectangular mullions are automatically added, because the curtain wall type properties have this type specified for the Interior Type.

7. Select the four new vertical mullions (use the Ctrl key to add them to the same selection set) and use the Unpin tool. While they're still selected, change the curtain wall mullion to the 1" Square type from the Type Selector (Figure 2.29).

8. Next, select the perpendicular curtain mullions above and below the new 1" Square mullions (use the Ctrl key to add multiple items to the same selection set), and on the Mullion panel on the ribbon, click Make Continuous (or click the Toggle Mullion Join symbol shown in Figure 2.30). This will toggle the mullion join at each location. The final model should look similar to Figure 2.30.

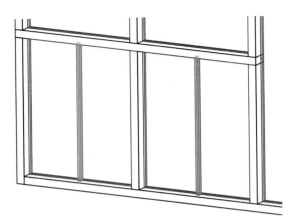

FIGURE 2.29 New grids and mullions

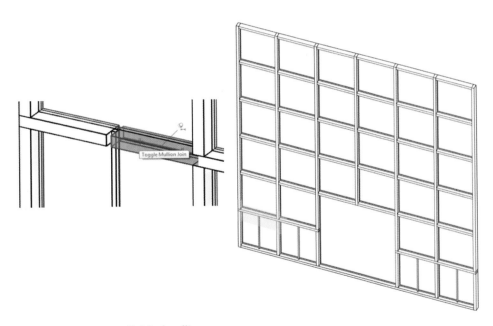

FIGURE 2.30 Finished mullions

Exercise 2.11: Customize Curtain Panels

To begin, open the book's web page at www.sybex.com/go/revit2016essentials, download the files for Chapter 2, and open the file c02-ex-2.11 .start.rvt.

1. The starting file should open to the default 3D view. Select the lower eight curtain panels and click the Unpin tool. Change the curtain panel from System Panel Glazed to System Panel Solid.

2. Next, you want to add a door to the curtain wall in the largest panel. Select the large System Panel Glazed panel in the center and click Unpin. Change the panel to the Curtain Wall Dbl Glass panel from the Type Selector (Figure 2.31).

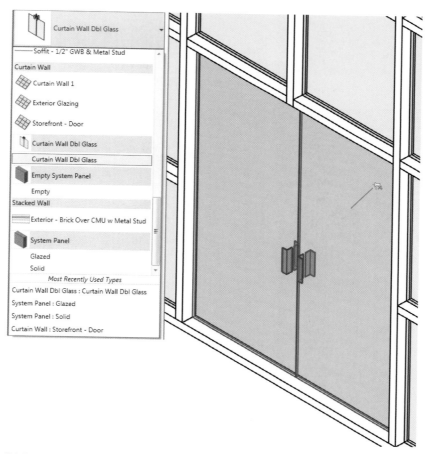

F I G U R E   2 . 3 1   Curtain wall door condition

3. After adding the door, select the lower vertical curtain wall mullions on either side of the door (there are two mullions on each side) and toggle the mullion join to Make Continuous. This will extend the curtain mullions to the base of the curtain wall (first image in Figure 2.32).

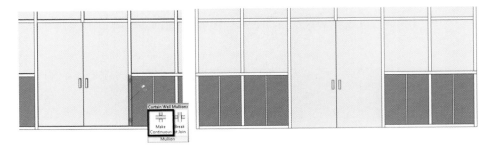

FIGURE 2.32 Final curtain wall

4. Next, remove the rectangular curtain wall mullions directly under the Curtain Wall Dbl Glass panel. Select both pinned curtain wall mullions (in the same selection set) and use the Unpin tool. Once they're unpinned, you can press the Delete key to remove the curtain mullions (second image in Figure 2.32).

5. Notice that the curtain panel door adjusts to fill in the additional space after the mullions are deleted. If at any point you need to revert panel or mullion overrides, using the Pin tool will switch them back to the type defined in the curtain wall type properties.

Now You Know

Walls in Revit Architecture are flexible enough to support the initial conceptual design process all the way through the final iteration of a specific wall type. This flexibility is evident through the numerous techniques we have discussed to edit, manipulate, and build various wall configurations.

In this chapter, you learned about the different wall types and the relevant parameters. You created walls using a variety of different tools and methods. You further modified walls by hosting other objects such as doors, and you adjusted the profile and shape of the walls. In this chapter you also worked through a variety of exercises specific to curtain walls and covering parameters, grids, mullions, and panels.

CHAPTER 3

Floors, Roofs, and Ceilings

This chapter will walk you through the most common horizontal host objects that make up your building. Although the process of creating a floor, roof, or ceiling is somewhat different for each, the tools used to edit each initial design element are similar and have overlapping methodology.

In this chapter, you'll learn to:

▶ **Create floors by sketching, editing, and picking**

▶ **Create sloped floors**

▶ **Create and modify a roof by footprint**

▶ **Create and modify a roof by extrusion**

▶ **Adjust the slope of a roof**

▶ **Create ceilings**

▶ **Create custom ceilings by sketching**

▶ **Add lights to a ceiling**

▶ **Slope and modify the ceiling type**

Creating Floors

There are several methods to create floors in the Autodesk® Revit® Architecture software. The main objective for this chapter is to understand both the various approaches to create floors and what kind of relationships they will create.

The objective of the following exercise is to first create floors by sketching a specific shape. Then, for the second part of the exercise you will use the Pick Wall tool to define the floor boundary.

Exercise 3.1: Create a Floor by Sketch and Pick Walls

To begin, go to the book's web page at www.sybex.com/go/revit2016essentials, download the files for Chapter 3, and open the file c03-ex-3.1start.rvt.

1. Open the Level 1 floor plan view. Select the Floor tool on the Build panel of the Architecture tab.

2. Revit will automatically enter sketch mode, which will allow you to create a sketch to define the boundary of your floor.

3. Use one of the drawing tools to create a simple sketch for the floor, 15′ × 30′ (4500 mm × 9000 mm).

   The dimensions are for reference only; even though this is a simple shape, what's more important is how you can manipulate it.

4. Confirm that the floor type is Generic - 12″ (Generic - 300 mm) in the Type Selector. Finish the sketch, and open your default 3D view. Your floor should resemble the one shown in Figure 3.1.

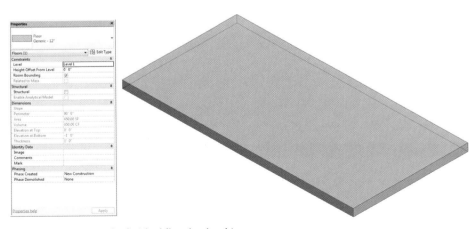

F I G U R E   3 . 1   The finished floor by sketching

5. Next, you will create a floor by picking walls. Open the Level 1 view and select the Floor tool on the Build panel of the Architecture tab to enter sketch mode. Select the Pick Walls tool from the Draw palette. Doing so allows you to select an individual wall or an entire chain of walls.

6. Move the cursor over one of the wall edges to the right and then press and release the Tab key. Your selection cycles from one wall to the series of walls. Once all of the walls are highlighted, select them with one pick.

7. In the Properties palette, set the Height Offset From Level parameter to 0″ (0 mm). Click Finish Edit Mode to exit the sketch. Select and move some of the walls that were used to determine the floor sketch. Notice that the boundary of the floor automatically updates (Figure 3.2). This is incredibly powerful for a multistory building, where updating one floor at a time would be nearly impossible.

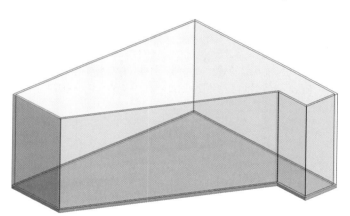

FIGURE 3.2 The finished floor created by picking walls

Note that the edge of the new floor is constructed where you click your mouse when you pick the wall in reference to the interior or exterior of the wall. The floor goes to the outside of the wall; you have to pick the outside edge of the wall—otherwise, the floor aligns with the interior. The entire chain of sketch lines is created and corresponds to all the walls.

EXTEND INTO WALL (TO CORE)

When using the Pick Walls tool, there is a setting on the Options Bar called Extend Into Wall (To Core). By default, when you pick a compound wall with multiple layers, the floor sketch will extend to the core boundary of the wall. If desired, you can specify an offset using a positive or negative value. If this option is unchecked, the floor sketch will use the outer interior or exterior face of the wall.

Exercise 3.2: Edit the Floor Boundary

The objective of the following exercise is to edit and modify an existing floor boundary. To begin, open the file c03-ex-3.2start.rvt.

1. Open the Level 1 floor plan view, select the floor, and click Edit Boundary from the Modify Floors contextual tab.

2. Add additional sketch lines to generate the lines and arc shape at the lower right in Figure 3.3. Don't forget to trim back any intersecting lines.

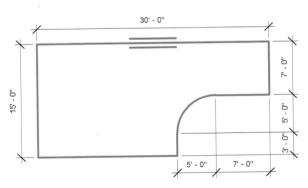

FIGURE 3.3   Modifying the floor sketch

3. Finish the sketch by clicking Finish Edit Mode. Select the floor, and notice that the options and dimension properties have already updated, as shown in Figure 3.4.

FIGURE 3.4 The modified floor

4. Create another floor of the same type and same initial dimensions, 15′ × 30′ (4500 mm × 9000 mm), near the first floor (reference Figure 3.5 for the location). Leave some space between the two floors.

5. Offset the floor 1′-0″ (300 mm) above Level 1 by entering this value into Height Offset From Level in the Properties palette.

6. Finish the sketch to complete the floor (Figure 3.5).

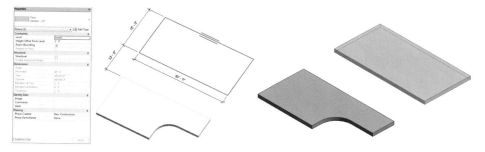

FIGURE 3.5 New floor 1′-0″ (300 mm) above Level 1

Not all floors are flat, and Revit Architecture has several tools to create sloped conditions. In the following exercise you will investigate both options by creating and modifying sloped floors using two tools: Slope Arrow and Shape Editing.

Exercise 3.3: Create Sloped Floors

To begin, open the file c03-ex-3.3start.rvt.

1. Begin by sketching another floor between the two previous floors, filling the gap between the two (Figure 3.6). Set Height Offset From Level to 0″ (0 mm) prior to finishing edit mode.

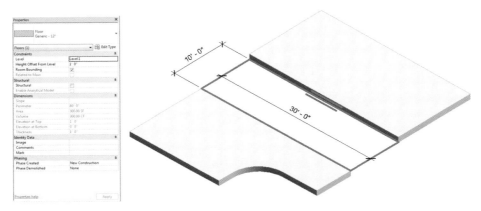

FIGURE 3.6 New floor at Level 1

2. If you were to finish the sketch like this, the floor wouldn't connect the upper and lower sections. You need to add a slope arrow. Do so by selecting the Slope Arrow tool on the Draw panel. Sketch the arrow as shown in Figure 3.7. The first location that you pick is the tail of the arrow; the second location is the head.

3. Select the slope arrow, and modify the parameters as shown in Figure 3.7 so they match the location of the upper and lower floors. Be sure to specify the height offset for the tail and head.

4. Finish the sketch, and return to your default 3D view (Figure 3.8), which shows the finished condition. Now the sloped floor connects the lower and upper floors.

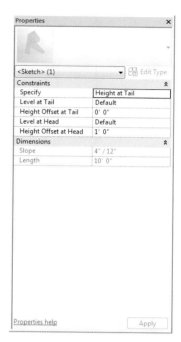
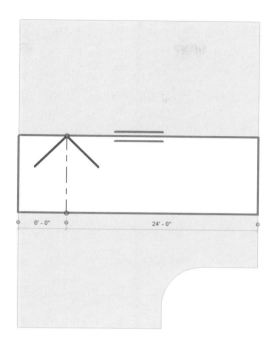

FIGURE 3.7 Slope arrow parameters

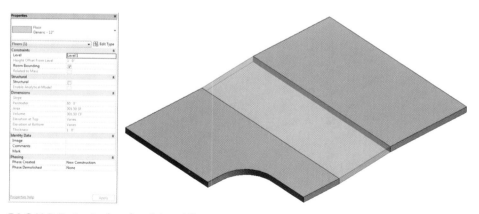

FIGURE 3.8 Completed sloped floor

You could create slightly sloped floors and depressions with slope arrows and separate floors, but this approach would probably be too complex because you'd have to create a lot of separate pieces of geometry. For these kinds of conditions, you have the Shape Editing tools.

5. Select the upper floor. Now you can see the Shape Editing tools in the Shape Editing panel on the Modify Floors tab.

6. Let's suppose that this entire floor is at the correct level, except for one small portion that needs to be slightly depressed in order to accommodate a loading area. Define the upper and lower boundaries of this depressed area by selecting the Add Split Line option on the Shape Editing panel. Add the lines as shown in Figure 3.9. Dimensions are shown for reference.

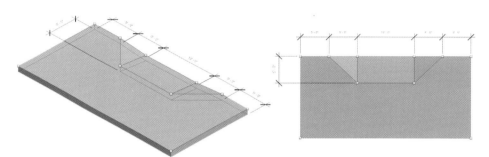

FIGURE 3.9 **Adding split lines**

7. Now that you've added the proper locations to break the slope, you need to modify the points at the ends of the lines to change the slope of the floor. Start by returning to your default 3D view. As you hover over the endpoint of the line, Revit Architecture highlights the shape handles. Press the Tab key to highlight a specific handle, and then select it (Figure 3.10).

8. Adjust the elevation of the shape handle as shown in Figure 3.10. In this case, you're depressing the floor, so the value must be negative. But you could also increase the elevation in a small area by using a positive value.

9. Do the same for the shape handle to the right. When you've finished, the depressed area resembles Figure 3.11.

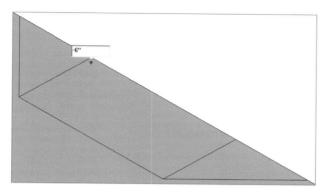

FIGURE 3.10 Editing the shape handle

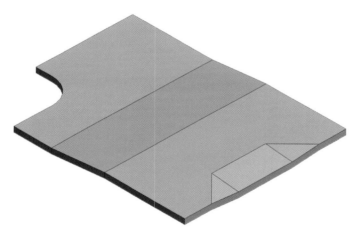

FIGURE 3.11 The finished depression

For the occasional or irregular opening in a floor, it's easy to add an opening using the Opening tools. For openings that occur from level to level and are vertically repetitive (such as a shaft or an elevator core), you can use the Shaft tool. This tool allows you to create openings in numerous floors, roofs, and ceilings quickly and easily.

The objective of the following two exercises is to create openings in your floor objects. The first exercise will focus on the Opening By Face tool. The second exercise will focus on the Shaft Opening tool.

Exercise 3.4: Create an Opening with the Opening by Face Tool

To begin, open the file c03-ex-3.4start.rvt.

1. From the Architecture tab on the ribbon, select the Opening By Face tool on the Opening panel.

2. Select any edge of the sloped floor you created to initiate sketch mode.

3. Sketch an opening 10′ × 3′ (3000 mm × 1000 mm) in the center floor panel. There's no limit to the number of interior sketches you can create.

4. Click Finish Edit Mode to complete the sketch. The result resembles Figure 3.12.

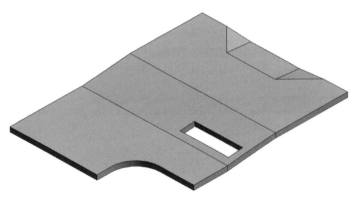

FIGURE 3.12   The finished opening

You can also edit previously created sketches by selecting the opening and clicking Edit Boundary from the ribbon. An opening of this type remains perpendicular to the slope of the floor, roof, or ceiling. On the other hand, a vertical opening remains perpendicular to the level on which it was created.

> If you have a number of openings that are predictably shaped (circular, rectilinear, and so on), *highly* repetitive, and scattered throughout your project, create a host- or face-based opening (with parameters for options) as a family component and load it for use in your project. ▶

5. Select the Vertical tool from the Opening panel, and sketch a new opening of the same size and dimensions above the first one. The result resembles Figure 3.13.

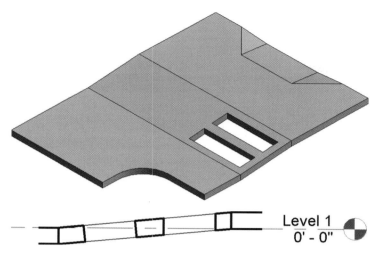

FIGURE 3.13 Completed openings of the same size and dimensions

The differences are subtle but very important. By creating a section through both openings, you can see the difference in an opening that remains perpendicular to the floor compared to one that remains perpendicular to the level (Figure 3.13).

Exercise 3.5: Create an Opening with the Shaft Opening Tool

To begin, open the file c03-ex-3.5start.rvt.

This example file has 10 total levels, which are evenly spaced.

1. Select all three floors on Level 1, and copy them to the Clipboard. Now the geometry is ready to be pasted to each of the levels.

2. The best way to do this is by using the Paste tool, which allows you to select all the levels to which you intend to paste the floors.

3. Click the Paste drop-down from the Clipboard panel of the Modify | Floors tab, and then select Aligned To Selected Levels.

4. You're given the option to select all the levels: Select Levels 2–10 (Figure 3.14). The resulting floors are shown in the figure.

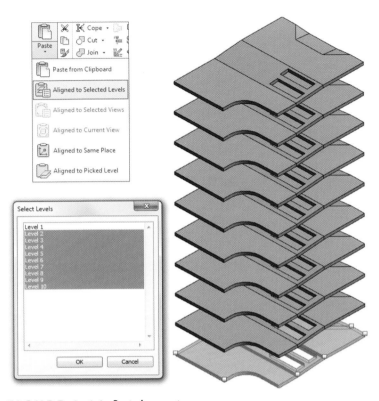

FIGURE 3.14 Pasted geometry

5. Return to the Level 1 view, and select the Shaft Opening tool from the Opening panel.

6. Create a new 20′ × 3′ (6100 mm × 1000 mm) rectangle perpendicular to the last two you drew.

7. Confirm that the top constraint is set to Level 10 so the shaft goes up to the top floor. Then set the top offset to a minimum of 1′ (300 mm) to ensure that it fully cuts the floor. A higher value can be specified as needed.

8. Be certain to assign a Base Offset value of –1′ (-300 mm), because the upper floor is slightly above the level (Figure 3.15).

   Figure 3.16 shows the resulting shaft in 3D. All the floors were cut automatically. Any ceilings, roofs, and additional floors created later that are between the same levels will be cut automatically as well.

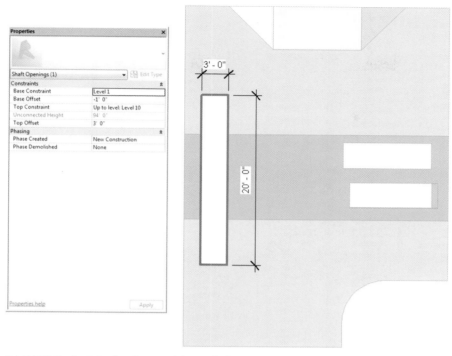

FIGURE 3.15 Creating a multistory shaft

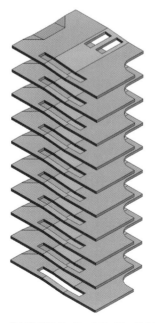

FIGURE 3.16 The finished multistory shaft

Creating Roofs

There are two primary methods for creating roofs, which you will explore in this chapter: by footprint and by extrusion. You create a roof by footprint much as you would create floors: from a sketch resulting from either drawn lines or picked walls. And as with floors, if you pick the exterior walls as a reference, moving the walls will move the corresponding edges of the roof. Roofs can be created in elevation using the Roof By Extrusion tool, which we will cover in Exercise 3.7.

The objective of the following exercise is to create a roof by picking the outline of existing walls.

Exercise 3.6: Create a Roof by Footprint

To begin, open the file c03-ex-3.6start.rvt.

1. Open the Level 1 plan view. Select the Roof By Footprint command from the Roof drop-down menu on the Architecture tab. At this point, Revit Architecture automatically asks you to select the level with which this roof is associated.

2. Select the Roof level. The associated level can be easily modified later should the roof need to be hosted on a different level.

   Again, you don't have to pick all the walls individually or sketch all the roof boundary lines.

3. The Pick Walls option on the Draw panel of the Modify | Create Roof Footprint tab should be set by default. Uncheck the Defines Slope setting on the Options Bar.

4. Enter 1'-6" (257 mm) for the Overhang parameter on the Options Bar.

5. Move the cursor over one of the exterior walls and press the Tab key until the entire chain is highlighted; then left-click. All the roof boundary lines will be created.

6. We want this to be a sloped roof, so you need to individually specify which roof edges will feature a slope. Select the sketch lines specified in Figure 3.17 and check Defines Slope on the Options Bar.

Note the icon with double arrows on the sketch lines for the roof: clicking it flips the boundary lines to the inside or outside of the wall face. Click this icon to move all the boundary lines to the inside of the wall's faces.

Then from the Properties palette, enter **6″/12″** (**150** mm × **300** mm) for the Slope parameter.

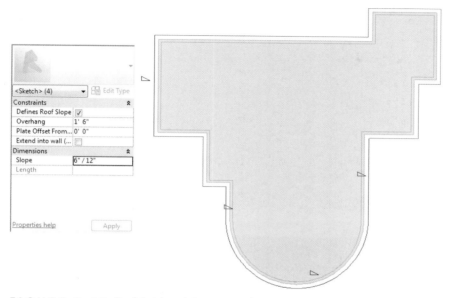

FIGURE 3.17 Roof sketch and slope properties

7. Click Finish Edit Mode to finish the sketch, and open the default 3D view.

8. Select the roof and set the Base Offset From Level parameter in the Properties palette to **6′-0″** (**1830** mm).

9. Next you need to revise the walls so they are attached to the roof slope, using the Attach Top/Base tool we utilized in Chapter 2. Move the cursor over one of the exterior walls and press the Tab key until the entire chain is highlighted.

10. Click to select the chain of walls. Use the Attach Top/Base tool from the ribbon and click on the roof to both attach the walls and revise the geometry to reflect the roof slope (Figure 3.18).

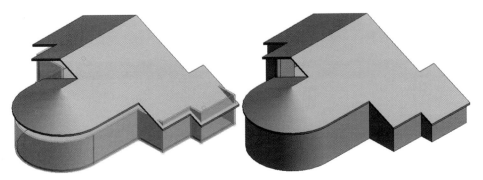

FIGURE 3.18   Adjusting the wall height

11. Notice that most of the walls appear correctly except for the one area where there is a gap in the exterior wall (Figure 3.19).

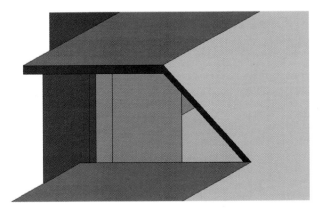

FIGURE 3.19   Exterior wall to revise

12. Select the roof and click Edit Footprint to reenter sketch mode.

13. Let's adjust three of the roof edges to be sloped in order to better accommodate the wall geometry. Individually select the roof edges as shown in Figure 3.20 and check Defines Slope on the Options Bar.

14. Click Finish Edit Mode to generate the new roof geometry (Figure 3.20).

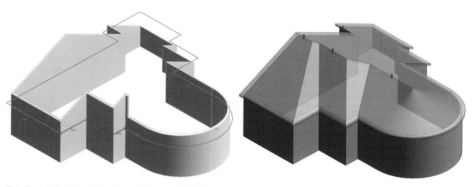

FIGURE 3.20 Completed roof by footprint

The objective of the following exercise is to create an extruded roof and join it to an existing roof.

Exercise 3.7: Create a Roof by Extrusion

To begin, open the file c03-ex-3.7start.rvt.

1. Select the Roof By Extrusion command from the Roof drop-down menu on the Architecture tab. The Work Plane dialog will prompt you to specify a new work plane. Choose the Pick A Plane option and click OK to switch back to the 3D view.

2. Pick the roof face highlighted in Figure 3.21.

3. After you pick the roof face, the Roof Reference Level And Offset dialog will open. You need to associate the extrusion roof to a level. This step is important for scheduling purposes; however, you can easily modify the value later to move the roof if needed. Select the Roof level, leave Offset at 0'-0" (0 mm), and click OK to start creating the sketch.

4. For a roof by extrusion, the sketch line isn't a closed loop. It's just a line (or series of connected lines) that defines the top of the extruded roof. The overall thickness will be determined by the roof type and can be modified later. For this example, you'll create an arc. Select any of the Arc tools from the Draw panel.

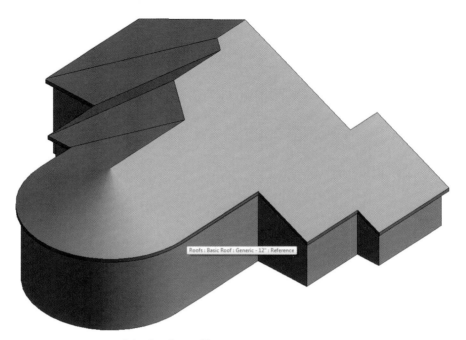

Roofs : Basic Roof : Generic - 12" : Reference

FIGURE 3.21 Selecting the roof face

5. Create the arc approximately as shown in Figure 3.22. When you've finished drawing the arc, set Extrusion End in the Properties palette to -20'-0" (-6100 mm). Click Finish Edit Mode to return to the model.

6. The roof is generated from the arc you created, but it's not completely reaching the existing roof and not connected to the face. This issue is easy to resolve.

7. Select the roof extrusion, and then select the Join/Unjoin Roof tool on the Modify | Roofs tab of the Geometry panel.

8. Hover over the rear edge of the extruded roof, as shown in the image on the left in Figure 3.23, and select the edge. Then select the face of the previously created roof that you want to connect to the extruded roof, as shown in the image on the right in Figure 3.23.

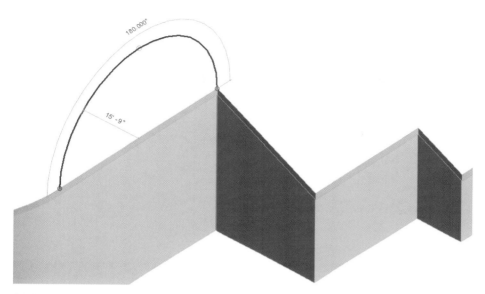

F I G U R E 3 . 2 2 Creating the arc

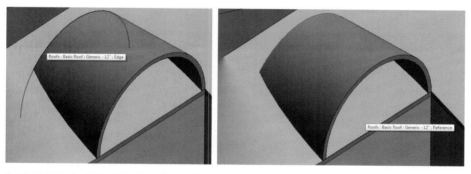

F I G U R E 3 . 2 3 Attaching the roof

9. The extruded roof now extends back to meet the face of the other roof. However, notice that the original arc shape is too high and the join is not able to maintain the shape because of the existing roof height (Figure 3.24).

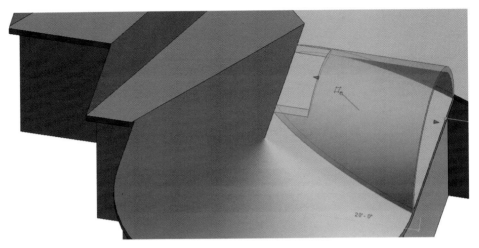

FIGURE 3.24 Extrusion roof too high

10. Let's adjust the original sketch so it is lower than the roof it is joining to. Select the extrusion roof and click Edit Profile.

11. Select the arc sketch and you should see the radius temporary dimension. Left-click the temporary dimension and enter **12'-0″** (**3657** mm). The arc sketch will update to be smaller.

12. Click Finish Edit Mode to return to the model, and notice that the roof by extrusion geometry has updated, maintaining the previous join condition (Figure 3.25).

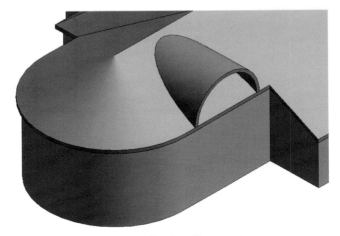

FIGURE 3.25 Completed roof by extrusion

Another approach to control the slope of a roof is to use a slope arrow. Slope arrows allow you to specify two references and specify both the level and height offset at each (the head and the tail).

The objective of the following exercise is to modify an existing flat roof condition using slope arrows to create a specific sloped roof shape.

Exercise 3.8: Create Slope Arrows

To begin, open the file c03-ex-3.8start.rvt.

1. Select the roof, and click Edit Footprint on the ribbon to enter sketch mode.

2. Select the Slope Arrow tool on the Draw panel, and add a slope arrow as shown in Figure 3.26. Note that the Height Offset At Head value is set to 6′ (2000 mm). The tail of the slope arrow must reside on the boundary of the sketch, but the head of the slope arrow may point in practically any direction.

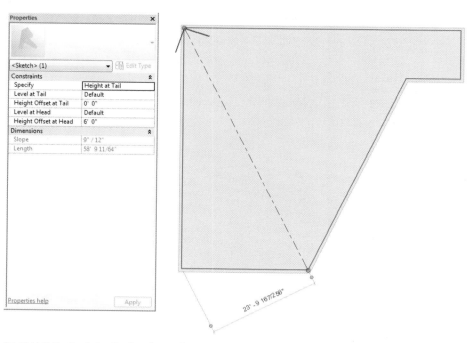

FIGURE 3.26 Sloping the roof

3. Finish the sketch. Notice that a single slope proceeds across the roof. A single slope in this direction would be nearly impossible to specify without slope arrows.

   You can also create roof slopes using multiple slope arrows. This technique is incredibly helpful when you want to create sloped conditions where two perpendicular slopes must meet at exactly the same location. Again, this is something that's difficult to do without slope arrows.

4. Select the roof and click Edit Footprint to reenter sketch mode. Delete the existing slope arrow.

5. Sketch two new slope arrows along the north\south and east\west roof boundary edges so that the heads of the arrows meet at the upper-left corner. The slope arrows should have the following properties:

   Set Height Offset At Tail to 0″ (0 mm).

   Set Height Offset At Head to 6′-0″ (2000 mm).

6. Make sure Height Offset is the same for both tails and both heads. Finish the sketch. The results resemble the roof in Figure 3.27.

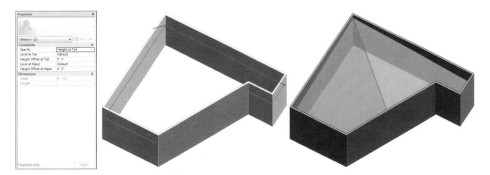

F I G U R E 3 . 2 7 **Roof created from two slope arrows**

The objective of the following exercise is to create multiple slopes that are perpendicular to the edges using the Defines Slope option.

Exercise 3.9: Create Multiple Roof Slopes

To begin, open the file c03-ex-3.9start.rvt.

1. Select the roof and click Edit Footprint to enter sketch mode for the roof. Delete both existing slope arrows.

2. Select all the lines that represent the roof sketch. You can do this by holding down Ctrl and selecting the lines individually or by clicking one line, pressing Tab, and clicking again to select the rest of the lines.

3. With the lines selected, in the Options Bar enter -3'-0" (-1000 mm) for the overhang. The overhang direction will move positive in relation to the side of the wall picked (exterior or interior). Positive or negative dimensions can be entered if the sketch moves in the opposite direction.

Note that the Overhang option is available only for roof sketch lines created using the Pick Walls option.

4. Select the Defines Roof Slope option for all the boundary edges from the Properties palette. Modify the Slope property for each sketch line to be 9"/12" (750 mm/1000 mm). (Entering 9 for the Slope property will get you 9"/12".) Finish the sketch. At this point the roof should look like Figure 3.28.

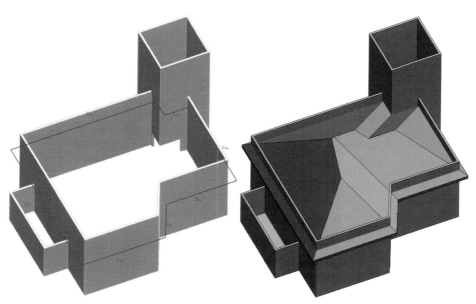

FIGURE 3.28 Offsetting the roof sketch and defining slopes

Attach
Top/Base

5. Initially, the edges of the wall extend beyond the overhang of the roof. Select the exterior walls specified in Figure 3.29 (use the Tab key), and then select the Attach Top/Base option on the Modify | Walls tab. Click the roof to attach the walls (Figure 3.29).

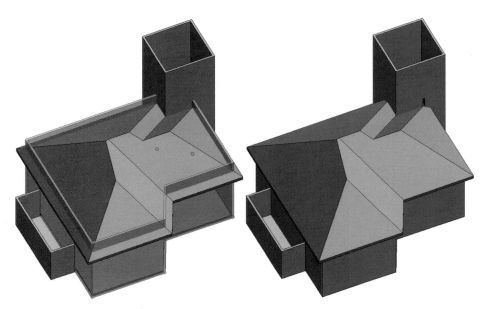

FIGURE 3.29   Attaching the walls to the roof

6. The two overlapping roof edges at the tower wall condition need to be corrected. Select the roof and click Edit Footprint to reenter sketch mode. Set Overhang to 0'-0″ (0 mm), uncheck Defines Slope, and move the sketch lines to the other side of the wall, as shown in Figure 3.30.

7. Next let's create a roof at the tower walls. Start the Roof By Footprint tool and specify Level 6 when prompted with the Lowest Level Notice dialog.

8. Using the Pick Walls tool, click on the tower walls. Set the Slope parameter to 3″/12″ (76/305 mm). Set the Overhang to 2'-0″ (610 mm). The completed tower roof should resemble the image on the right in Figure 3.31.

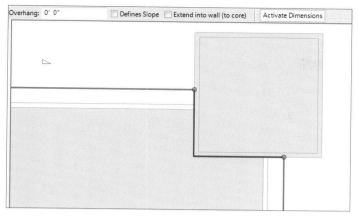

FIGURE 3.30   Adjusting roof edges at tower

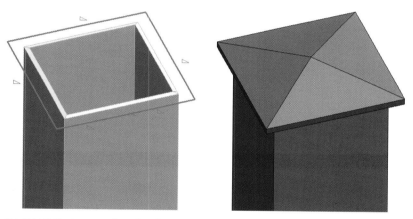

FIGURE 3.31   Completed tower roof

9. There is one remaining roof to be created for the lower walls. Start the Roof By Footprint tool and specify Level 2 when prompted with the Lowest Level Notice dialog.

10. Use the Pick Walls tool to pick the three walls. Draw the connecting sketch line along the face of the exterior wall.

11. For the three lower walls, set the Slope parameter to 2″/12″ (50/305 mm). Set Overhang to 1′-0″ (305 mm). Click Finish Edit Mode, and when prompted, attach the walls to the roof (Figure 3.32).

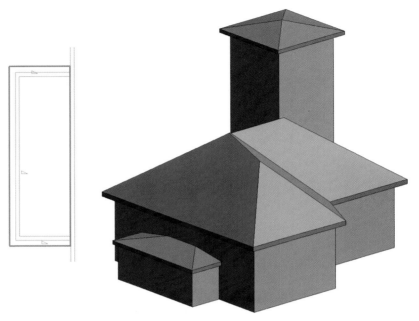

FIGURE 3.32   **Completed roof**

Adding Ceilings

Ceilings in Revit Architecture are easy to place as well as modify. As you move the walls, the ceiling associated to those walls will stretch to fit the new conditions. There are two different tools used to create ceilings in Revit Architecture:

Automatic Ceiling Tool   The Ceiling tool is on the Build palette of the Architecture tab. When you select the tool, the default condition is Automatic Ceiling. This means that as you hover over a space, Revit Architecture will attempt to find the boundary of walls.

Sketch Ceiling Tool   The Sketch Ceiling tool is useful for customized conditions, such as a ceiling soffit or bulkhead where it is necessary to draw the boundary, or simply for boundaries where the ceiling objects do not span the entire space.

The objective of the following exercise is to first create ceilings automatically. Then you will create a more custom, sketch-based ceiling.

Exercise 3.10: Add Automatic and Sketch Ceilings

To begin, open the file c03-ex-3.10start.rvt.

1. Using the Automatic Ceiling option, add a ceiling toward the bottom of the image (Figure 3.33). As you hover over the space, Revit Architecture indicates the boundary.

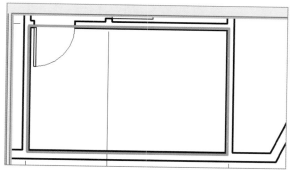

FIGURE 3.33 Revit Architecture outlines the boundary

2. As you can see from the Properties dialog, Revit Architecture offers four default ceiling types: one basic type and three compound types. Select the 2′ × 2′ (600 mm × 600 mm) ACT System type.

3. When you click to place the first ceiling in the floor plan view, you get a warning. This can happen frequently: you've placed the ceiling, but you can't see it. As a rule, you shouldn't ignore warnings because you could place multiple ceilings in the same place. Open Ceiling Plans - Level 1 under Views in the Project Browser, which has ceiling objects visible.

4. Select the Ceiling tool on the Architecture tab, and pick inside the rooms shown in Figure 3.34 to automatically place the ceilings. Notice that Revit Architecture centers the grid based on the space you've selected.

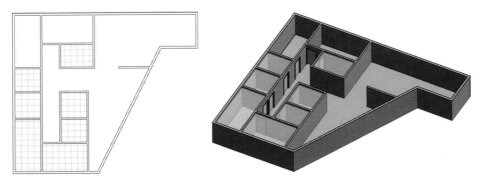

FIGURE 3.34   Resulting automatic placed ceilings

5. Next, you'll place ceilings in the upper-left corner of the ceiling plan for Level 1, but this time you'll share the ceiling between the two spaces. This practice is common in interior projects. The partitions extend only to the underside of the ceiling (rather than connect to the structure above). Select Sketch Ceiling on the Ceiling panel of the Modify | Place Ceiling tab. Add sketch lines as shown in the first image in Figure 3.35. The result is shown in the second image.

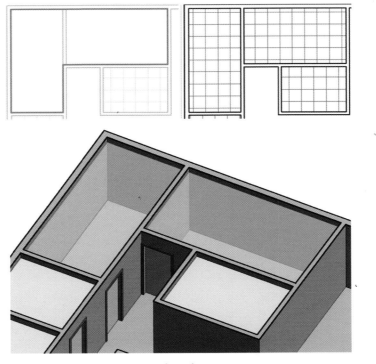

FIGURE 3.35   Sketching the ceiling

6. Create another ceiling using Sketch Ceiling in the upper-right area of the plan (Figure 3.36). Choose the 2′ × 4′ (600 mm × 1200 mm) ACT System type from the Type Selector before you finish the sketch of the ceiling.

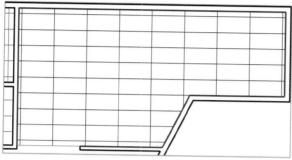

FIGURE 3.36   A 2′ × 4′ (600 mm × 1200 mm) ceiling

7. Create a GWB On Mtl. Stud ceiling for the area shown in Figure 3.37.

For a more detailed overview of materials, feel free to look ahead to Chapter 9, "Materials, Visualization, Rendering."

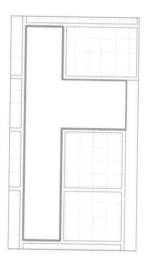

FIGURE 3.37   Creating a GWB On Mtl. Stud ceiling

By default, the GWB material doesn't have a surface pattern. Although this material would be too graphically busy for walls, it's fine for ceilings. So, let's create a new material for GWB associated to ceilings and give it a pattern.

8. Select the ceiling, and click Edit Type from the Properties palette. Click the Structure Edit button from the Type Properties dialog to open the Edit Assembly window.

9. Locate the Finish layer, and then under the Material column, click in the cell for Gypsum Wall Board. Click the ellipsis (…) button that appears in the cell to open the Material Browser. Right-click and duplicate the existing material. Rename the new material **Gypsum Ceiling Board**.

10. On the Graphics tab, locate Surface Pattern and associate the surface pattern called Sand to the material.

11. Click OK until you close all the dialog boxes and return to the ceiling plan view.

The result is shown in Figure 3.38. You can now distinguish the ceiling from the open areas that have no ceiling.

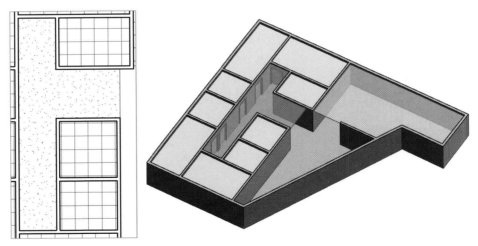

FIGURE 3.38 Assigning materials to a ceiling

The objective of the following exercise is to create a bulkhead condition to separate two ceilings.

Exercise 3.11: Create a Bulkhead

To begin, open the file c03-ex-3.11start.rvt.

1. Place the walls that will act as the bulkhead, as shown in Figure 3.39. Be sure to set the Base Offset value in the Properties palette of the

If the ceiling type does not contain grid lines, you can hover over the edge of the ceiling and use the Tab key to cycle through options until the edge of the ceiling is highlighted.

walls to 7'-9" (2400 mm) and the Unconnected Height value to 2'-3" (700 mm). This creates two walls above head height.

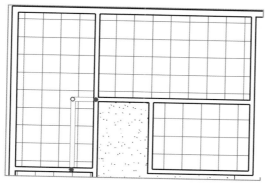

FIGURE 3.39 Creating a bulkhead

2. The easiest method for editing a ceiling is to select a grid line and choose Edit Boundary from the Mode panel on the Modify | Ceilings tab. Modify the ceiling as shown in the first image in Figure 3.40.

3. Sketch a new GWB ceiling that is 9'-0" (2700 mm). The second image in Figure 3.40 shows the final ceiling shape before you click Finish Edit Mode.

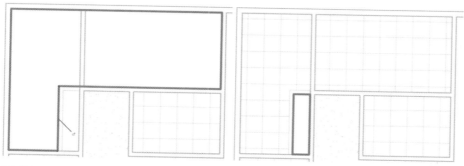

FIGURE 3.40 Editing the boundary

4. Click Finish Edit Mode.

5. To get a better idea of the finished configuration in 3D, go to a 3D view and orient a section box of the Level 1 plan view.

6. Right-click the ViewCube, and from the Floor Plans flyout of the context menu, select Level 1.

7. Orbit the view or use the ViewCube to choose the desired angle.

8. Use the grip arrows to pull the boundaries of the section box to resemble Figure 3.41. You'll find that working this way is helpful because having both 2D and 3D views aids in communicating any design issues.

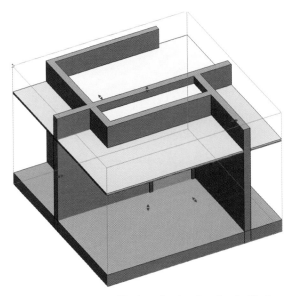

FIGURE 3.41 Final section box location in 3D view

The objective of the following exercise is to add light fixtures hosted to the ceiling. Then, for the second part of the exercise, you will rotate the ceiling grid.

Exercise 3.12: Add Lights and Rotate the Grid

To begin, open the file c03-ex-3.12start.rvt.

1. On the Insert tab, select Load Family on the Load From Library panel.

2. Browse to and open the Lighting\Architectural\Internal folder, and double-click the family Ceiling Light - Linear Box.rfa.

3. Click the Place A Component button on the Systems tab, and the ceiling light family should be the default.

4. Select the 2′ × 4′ (2 Lamp) - 120V (0600 mm × 1200 mm) type from the Type Selector. You'll place lighting fixtures into the 2′ × 4′ (0600 mm × 1200 mm) ceiling in the upper-right ceiling plan.

5. The insertion point for the light is the center of the light. Place the first light, and then use the Align tool to move it into the right spot.

6. Use the Copy tool on the Modify panel to copy the first light based on the intersection of the ceiling grid. All the lights are shown in Figure 3.42.

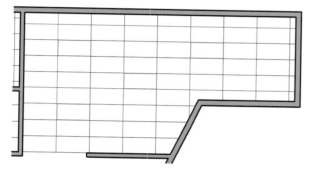

FIGURE 3.42 Placing lights

7. To rotate the grid, select any grid line, and use the Rotate tool on the Modify panel to rotate it. In this case, specify a 10-degree angle. Notice that the lights rotate as well.

8. Click and drag the ceiling grid lines to better center the lights in the overall space. Again, the lights move with the grid. The Move, Align, and Rotate tools are all available to modify ceilings when a grid line is selected.

This technique is incredibly helpful for maintaining design coordination. The finished condition is shown in Figure 3.43.

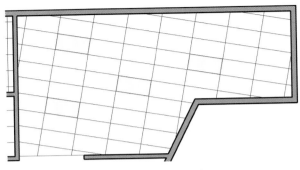

FIGURE 3.43   Rotated ceiling grid

The objective of the following exercise is to slope the ceiling by placing a slope arrow while editing the boundary of the ceiling. You will also change the ceiling type during this exercise.

Exercise 3.13: Slope the Ceiling

To begin, open the file c03-ex-3.13start.rvt.

1. First, select the ceiling, and using the Type Selector in the Properties palette, change the ceiling type to GWB On Mtl. Stud. Notice that the ceiling updates to reflect the new ceiling type.

2. Select the edge of the ceiling, and choose Edit Boundary on the Mode panel on the Modify | Ceilings tab.

3. Place a slope arrow as shown in the top image in Figure 3.44. Set the Height Offset values for the tail and head to 0'-0" (0 mm) and 3'-0" (1000 mm), respectively.

4. Finish the sketch. The result (bottom image in Figure 3.44) is shown in 3D using a section box. The lights should follow the revised ceiling slope.

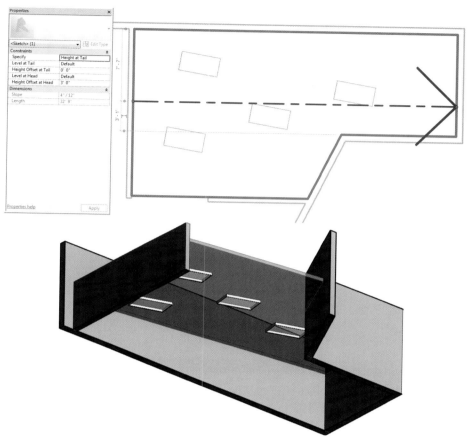

F I G U R E 3 . 4 4 Adding a slope arrow to the ceiling

Now You Know

Floors, roofs, and ceilings in Revit Architecture are very different object types that share a relatively common set of modification tools. You have the flexibility to create a set of objects and come back to them when additional information is known or the design intent changes. Revit makes it easy to swap types, edit the boundary, or revert to the original condition with a consistent set of modification tools.

In this chapter, you learned about creating floors and later about modifying the floor to add openings, change the boundary, or add slope. You learned about the different methods for creating roofs and later about modifying the roof slope to create varying conditions. And last, you learned about creating ceilings and then modifying the ceiling boundary, type, and hosting light fixtures.

CHAPTER 4

Stairs, Ramps, and Railings

Autodesk® Revit® Architecture software contains powerful tools for creating stairs, railings, and ramps. These elements are created and controlled with separate tools, which we will discuss and utilize in this chapter. In addition, these separate elements can interact with each other to form more complex systems, which we will also cover during some of the exercises in this chapter.

In this chapter, you'll learn to:

▶ **Create and modify railings**

▶ **Create stairs by component**

▶ **Create stairs by sketch**

▶ **Customize stair landings**

▶ **Create multistory stairs**

▶ **Create and customize ramps**

Creating a Generic Railing

Stairs contain numerous parameters, but not all of the parameter controls are equally important during the design process. Design is often about the intent of what something is as well as where it is meant to go. Once the intent is identified, it's necessary to go back and revise the specifics of how something will be carefully assembled or to add additional detail when known.

Because the tools for railings, stairs, and ramps are somewhat separate, you'll begin the exercises by first creating a simplified railing. This way, when you create a series of stair configurations, you'll have a new, default railing to apply to each of them.

In the following exercise you will create a railing and edit the various properties and components that make up the railing tool.

Exercise 4.1: Create a Generic Railing

To begin, go to the book's web page at www.sybex.com/go/revit2016essentials, download the files for Chapter 4, and open the file c04-ex-4.1start.rvt.

1. Open the default 3D view by selecting the small house icon on the Quick Access toolbar (QAT) . Select the Architecture tab, and choose the Railing drop-down menu from the Circulation panel. Select the Sketch Path option to enter sketch mode.

   Before you draw a railing, you'll create a new type.

2. Select Edit Type from the Properties palette, and with the type Handrail - Rectangular current, click Duplicate in the Type Properties dialog box. Name the new railing **Handrail - Design**, and click OK twice to exit all the dialog boxes.

3. Draw a path line 30′ (10000 mm) long.

   This line will define your railing path. In Revit Architecture, each railing must be a single connected sketch (you cannot have multiple disconnected sketch lines in the same railing).

4. Click Finish Edit Mode to exit the sketch, which will create the railing. This will be the default rail in the exercise file (Figure 4.1).

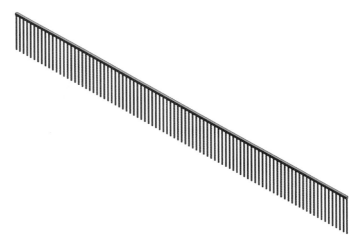

FIGURE 4.1   The default railing: Handrail - Design

Next, you will edit some of the newly created railing properties.

5. Select the railing, and choose Edit Type from the Properties palette to open the Type Properties dialog, as shown in Figure 4.2.

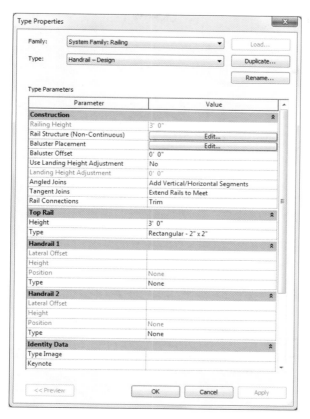

FIGURE 4.2 Railing type properties

6. Click Edit for the Rail Structure (Non-Continuous) parameter. In the resulting dialog box, click Insert. This will add another rail to your railing type. In the Name field, enter **Low Rail**. Set Height to 1′-0″ (**300** mm) and change the Profile parameter to Rectangular Handrail : 2″ × 2″ (Rectangular - 50 × 50 mm) (Figure 4.3). Close the dialog box by clicking OK to return to the Type Properties dialog.

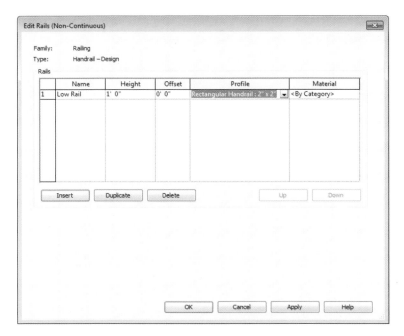

FIGURE 4.3   Edit Rails dialog box

7. Locate the Top Rail section. Set the height to 3′-6″ (**1060** mm). Leave the type as Rectangular - 2″ × 2″ (Rectangular - 50 × 50 mm). The Top Rail parameter controls the top rail used in the railing. Each railing type requires a minimum of one railing; otherwise, Revit will be unable to create the type.

   Next, you will modify the balusters.

8. In the Type Properties dialog box, click the Edit button for the Baluster Placement parameter.

9. In the resulting dialog box, find the Main Pattern panel, select the second line (Regular Baluster), and set its Baluster Family value to Baluster - Square : 1″ (Baluster - Square : 25 mm). Set the Dist. From Previous parameter to 5″ (**125** mm).

10. In the Posts area, set the Baluster Family value for the Start Post, Corner Post, and End Post parameters to None (as shown in Figure 4.4). This will prevent additional posts from being created at the start and end.

11. Click OK to close the Edit Baluster Placement dialog box, and click OK again to close the Type Properties dialog box.

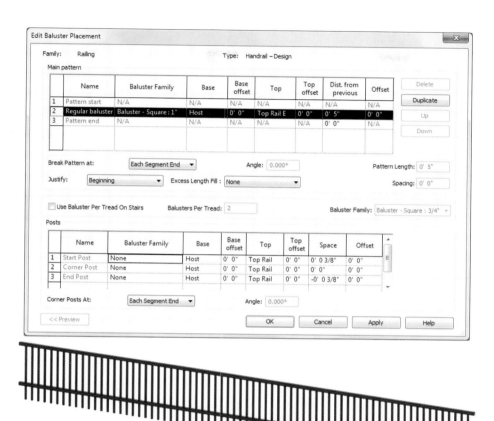

FIGURE 4.4 Baluster settings and completed railing

Creating Stair Configurations

Revit Architecture has two stair tools: Stair By Component and Stair By Sketch. The tools are located on the Architecture tab on the Circulation panel. The Stair By Component tool was added in Revit Architecture 2013. As the name suggests, this tool will help you create stairs that can be broken down into their individual components for easier manipulation. This is the default stair tool on the ribbon in Revit Architecture. The original stair tool, Stair By Sketch, is located in the Stair drop-down menu. The majority of our exercises in this chapter will focus on the Stair By Component tool.

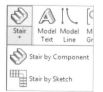

In the following exercise you will create a straight run stair by component to familiarize yourself with the options and components of the stair.

> ### SWAPPING OUT FAMILY TYPES IS EASY
>
> Note that stairs, railings, and ramps, like other system families, can be changed dynamically using the Type Selector. This process works the same for Revit Architecture component families. Suppose your design changed or you haven't yet determined the exact stair type you will be using. At any point during the design process, you can swap out one family type for another and your stair as well as all your views will update accordingly. This is useful early on when you might know the location and dimensions of a stair but not necessarily the final specifications.

Exercise 4.2: Create a Stair by Component

To begin, go to the book's web page at www.sybex.com/go/revit2016essentials, download the files for Chapter 4, and open the file c04-ex-4.2start.rvt.

1. From the Level 1 plan view, start the Stair By Component tool. The Run component should be the active tool. Click anywhere in the view to the left, and then slowly move your cursor to the right.

   As you move the cursor, notice that Revit Architecture displays how many risers remain to complete a stair that starts on Level 1 and goes through Level 2 (Figure 4.5).

FIGURE 4.5   Risers remaining to finish stair

2. Click when you see the message "9 Risers Created, 9 Risers Remaining." This will complete the first run of the stair. Since you have not created

A landing is automatically created between the two runs because the Automatic Landing setting on the Options Bar is checked by default. If needed, you could uncheck this parameter to avoid automatically creating a landing. You can always add one later with the Landing component.

enough risers to reach Level 2, you need to start another run. Move the cursor over to the right until the temporary dimension displays 5′-0″ (1525 mm). Click again to start the second run and move the cursor to the right. Click when you see "9 Risers Created, 0 Risers Remaining." This will complete the second run (Figure 4.6).

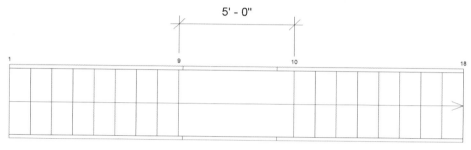

FIGURE 4.6 Component stair run with landing

3. While still in edit mode, click the Railing tool in the Tools panel of the ribbon. Specify the Handrail - Rectangular type (Figure 4.7), and click OK to close the dialog.

FIGURE 4.7 Specifying the railing type

Revit Architecture will use this default handrail whenever you create this stair, until you specify another type. The railing can be edited, modified, or deleted from the stair at any later time.

4. Click Finish Edit Mode to complete the component stair.
   The resulting stair is shown in the default 3D view in Figure 4.8.
   Now you'll create a second component stair to adjust some additional parameters.

5. Start the Stair By Component tool again, but before you pick a point to start the first run, choose the Location Line option from the Options Bar.

Each stair run component can have its own width, which is set by using the Actual Run Width parameter on the Options Bar or Properties palette. You can enter this value either before or after placement.

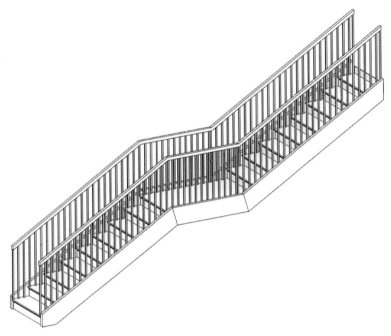

FIGURE 4.8 The resulting stair with railing

6. Set the Location Line option to Exterior Support: Left. This will align the outside edge of the stair with your pick points, making it easier to snap to existing geometry.

7. For the start of the first run, click the end point of reference plane 1 where it meets the wall. Move to the right 6'-5" (955 mm), and click again to complete this run.

8. Start the second stair run using the same Exterior Support: Left Location Line setting, and click at the end point of the reference plane 2 where it meets the wall. Move the cursor down anywhere past 9'-0" (2750 mm), and click the last point to complete the second run (Figure 4.9).

   One of the nice features of component stairs is that you have the ability to dynamically change the stair using shape handles.

9. Select the landing that was automatically created and notice the shape handles. Drag the landing edge shape handle down any distance to enlarge the landing. Notice that the stair run automatically moves down to reflect the new landing size.

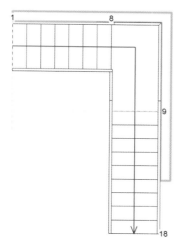

FIGURE 4.9   Second stair along wall

10. Click Finish Edit Mode to complete the component stair (Figure 4.10).

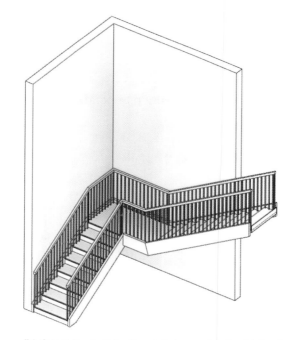

FIGURE 4.10   Completed second stair with landing

In the following exercise you will create a straight run stair using the Stair By Sketch tool to familiarize yourself with the workflow and properties of this stair tool.

Exercise 4.3: Create a Stair by Sketch

For sketch-based stairs, the default green lines represent the stair boundary and the default black lines represent risers.

To begin, go to the book's web page at www.sybex.com/go/revit2016essentials, download the files for Chapter 4, and open the file c04-ex-4.3start.rvt.

1. From the Level 1 plan view, start the Stair By Sketch tool from the Stair drop-down menu. Click any two points from left to right (far enough apart for Revit to display "18 Risers Created"). This will create an 18-riser straight stair between Level 1 and Level 2.

2. Select the top boundary line and drag the end grip back two risers (Figure 4.11).

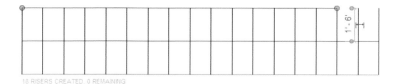

FIGURE 4.11   Sketch-based stair boundary line

3. Using the boundary line, draw a new boundary for these two risers to create a custom condition using the Start-End-Radius Arc drawing tool.

4. Using the Trim/Extend Single Element tool, extend the riser line to meet the new boundary line you added in step 3 (Figure 4.12).

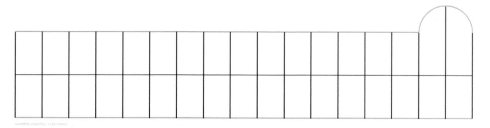

FIGURE 4.12   New boundary and riser sketch lines

5. Select the lower boundary line and notice that the temporary dimension appears, showing 1'-6".

6. Click the temporary dimension text and enter 2'-6" to move the lower boundary line down.

    Notice that the riser sketch lines did not automatically move down with the boundary line.

7. Use the Trim/Extend Multiple Elements tool to extend the riser lines to meet the new boundary line location (Figure 4.13).

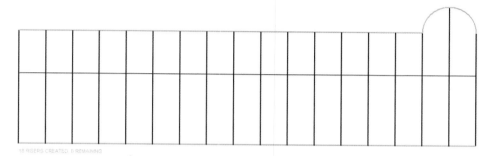

18 RISERS CREATED 0 REMAINING

FIGURE 4.13 Updated boundary line location

8. Click Edit Type to open the stair type properties.

9. Under Risers, uncheck the End With Riser parameter and click OK to close the dialog.

    This will remove the riser that is generated at the end of the stair.

10. While still in edit mode, click the Railing tool in the Tools panel of the ribbon. Set Position to Stringer; this will determine the location the railing is hosted on the stair.

11. Click Finish Edit Mode to complete the stair.

    Ignore any warnings received about the actual number of risers created.

12. Select the two railings that were automatically created, and swap the type in the Type Selector to Glass Panel - Bottom Fill. The completed stair is shown in Figure 4.14.

In the following exercise you will edit an existing Stair by Component landing and make several modifications to the design.

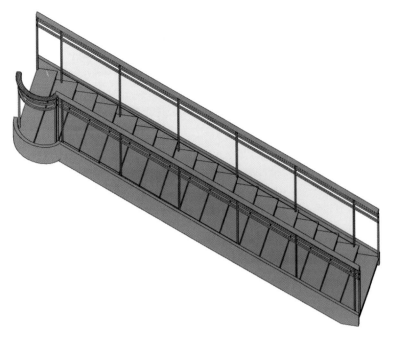

FIGURE 4.14 Completed sketch-based stair

Exercise 4.4: Customize and Create a Component Stair Landing

To begin, go to the book's web page at www.sybex.com/go/revit2016essentials, download the files for Chapter 4, and open the file c04-ex-4.4start.rvt.

1. From the Level 1 plan view, select the existing stair and click Edit Stairs to enter edit mode.

2. Click to select the existing landing object.
   You need to customize the landing shape so you will need to convert the landing to a sketch.

3. Click Convert To Sketch-Based on the Tools panel. Close the dialog confirming that this conversion is irreversible.

4. Notice there is a new option called Edit Sketch on the same Tools panel.

5. Click Edit Sketch to edit the landing boundary. Select and delete the existing landing boundary line (the longest line closest to the wall).

6. Set the type for the lines to Boundary in the Draw panel. Set the draw mode to Pick Lines. Set the Options Bar Offset parameter to 2″ (50 mm) so you can compensate for your support distance along the wall.

7. Pick the faces of the interior wall lines to create the new landing sketch lines. Use the Trim/Extend To Corner tool to clean up the new boundary lines.

8. For the last segment, at the start of the second stair run, you will need to create a small sketch line with the same 2″ (50 mm) offset. This offset will accommodate the stringers that will automatically be created around the landing when you finish edit mode.
   The final sketch is shown in Figure 4.15.

FIGURE 4.15 Revised landing sketch

9. Click Finish Edit Mode.
   Notice that you are still editing the component stair; you simply finished editing the landing sketch.
   While still editing the stair, add a second landing.

10. On the Components panel, click Landing. Choose the Create Sketch option.

11. Confirm that the landing's Relative Height parameter in the Properties palette is set to 15′-0″ (4570 mm). With the Draw option set to Boundary, sketch a second landing at the end of the second run, as shown in Figure 4.16.

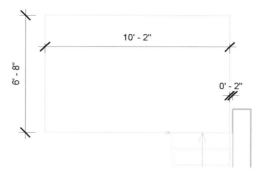

FIGURE 4.16   Revised landing sketch

12. Click Finish Edit Mode to complete the new landing sketch. Click Finish Edit Mode again to complete the stair.

The finished stair is shown in Figure 4.17.

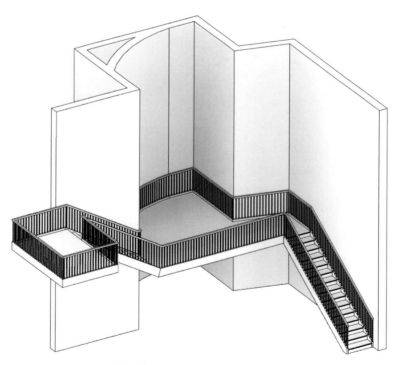

FIGURE 4.17   Complete stair with new landings

In the following exercise you will update an existing stair to span multiple project levels using the Multistory Top Level instance property.

Exercise 4.5: Create a Multistory Stair

To begin, go to the book's web page at www.sybex.com/go/revit2016essentials, download the files for Chapter 4, and open the file c04-ex-4.5start.rvt.

The example file has five project levels, and you want to repeat the existing stair between them since they are consistent level heights.

1. Activate the 3D view saved in the exercise file.

2. Select the stair, and from the Properties palette, locate the Multistory Top Level instance parameter.
   Currently it is set to None.

3. Change the value to Level 5 and notice what happens (Figure 4.18).

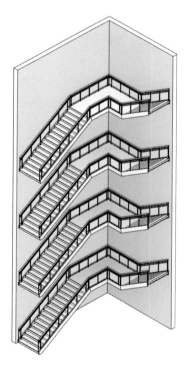

FIGURE 4.18 Multistory stair up to Level 5

Revit will repeat the stair up to the level you specified, including any railings that are currently attached to the stair.

4. Select one of the railings, and notice that all four instances of the railing are selected.

5. Change the railing type to Guardrail - Pipe, and notice that all four railings update to reflect the type change.

6. Select the stair and click Edit Stairs to enter edit mode.

7. Open the Level 1 floor plan view. Select the landing, and using the shape handles, adjust it to be 2′-6″ (760 mm) on each side that meets the run (Figure 4.19).

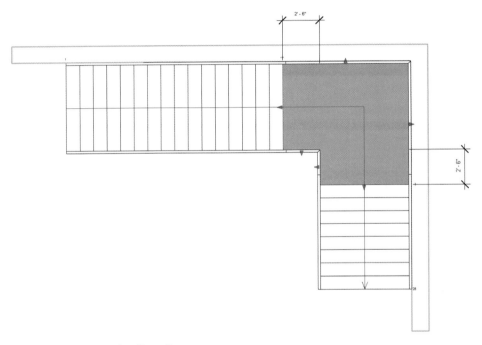

F I G U R E   4 . 1 9 Landing adjustment

8. Click Finish Edit Mode to return to the project.

9. Open the 3D view again, and notice that every stair landing has also been updated.

10. Select the stair and change the Multistory Top Level parameter to Level 4.

    The stair will update to reflect the new top-level assignment (Figure 4.20).

In the following exercise you will modify the height of an existing level and then make changes to the stair geometry to reflect this new floor-to-floor height.

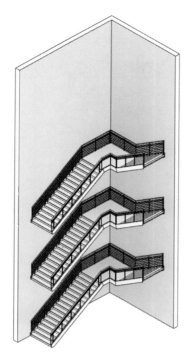

FIGURE 4.20 Complete multistory stair

Exercise 4.6: Modify Level and Stair Height

To begin, go to the book's web page at www.sybex.com/go/revit2016essentials, download the files for Chapter 4, and open the file c04-ex-4.6start.rvt. The example file has two project levels, and one existing stair.

1. From the North Elevation view, select the Level 2 level object. Click the 12'-0" (3657 mm) level text and enter **15'-0"** (4570 mm) instead.

2. After the level height updates, the stair will generate a warning that the stair top end exceeds or cannot reach the top elevation of the stair. Essentially, you need additional risers to reach the new height.

3. Select the stair and click the Edit Stairs button on the ribbon. Open the Level 1 floor plan view.

4. In the Properties palette, notice the Desired Number Of Risers and Actual Number Of Risers parameters. The desired number is 26, but you actually have only 21 risers. You need to add 5 additional risers to the stair to reach Level 2.

5. Select the last run, which is currently risers 15 to 21. Slide the blue drag control labeled Drag The Run End. Notice the halftone outline of the stair as you start dragging. This is the end point you should drag to if you wish to create the desired number of 26 risers (Figure 4.21).

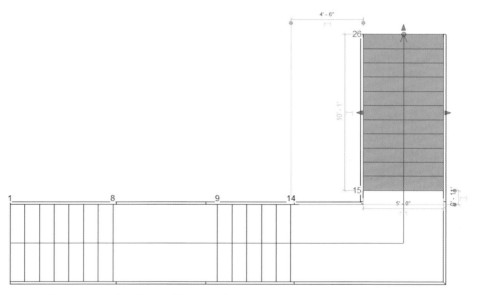

FIGURE 4.21 Complete multistory stair

6. Click Finish Edit Mode to return to the project. Open the North elevation view and notice that the stair now actually reaches Level 2.

7. Let's adjust a few additional properties of the stair. Open the default 3D view, select the stair, and click Edit Stairs to reenter edit mode. Select the last run, and from the Properties palette, uncheck End With Riser. This will remove the last small riser from the stair (Figure 4.22).

8. Click to deselect the run. While still in edit mode, click Edit Type. Under Supports, check the Middle Support option to add an additional stringer to the stair.

9. Under Construction, locate Run Type. Click the ellipsis (...) button to launch the 2" Tread 1" Nosing 1/4" Riser run type properties. Change Tread Thickness to 1.5" (38 mm) and Nosing Length to 1.5" (38 mm).

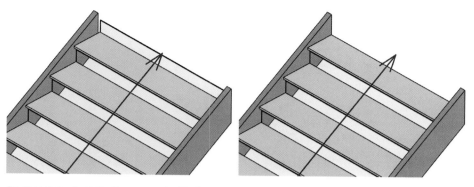

F I G U R E   4 . 2 2   **Remove end with riser**

10. Click OK to return to the main 7″ Max Riser 11″ Tread type properties. Under Supports, locate Right Support Type and click the ellipsis (…) button to open the Stringer - 2″ Width type properties.

11. Under Dimensions, change the section profile to the C-Channel-Profile : C9X15. Check the box for Flip Section Profile. Click OK to return to the main 7″ Max Riser 11″ tread type properties.

12. Click OK to close the stair type properties. Click Finish Edit Mode to return to the project. Ignore any warnings related to the stair unable to reach the top elevation of the stair. The completed stair is displayed in Figure 4.23.

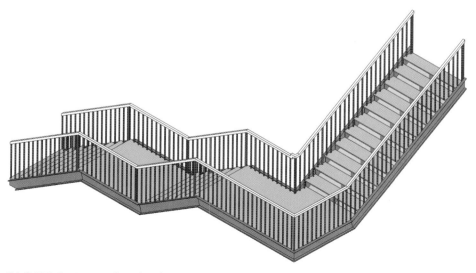

F I G U R E   4 . 2 3   **Completed stair**

In the following exercise you will create a new railing and set the host to use an existing stair.

Exercise 4.7: Host a Railing to a Stair

To begin, go to the book's web page at www.sybex.com/go/revit2016essentials, download the files for Chapter 4, and open the file c04-ex-4.7start.rvt.

1. From the Level 1 plan view, click the Railing drop-down menu and choose Sketch Path.

2. Using the Pick Lines draw tool, select the inner line for each of the three stringers (see the sketch in Figure 4.24).

3. Then, from the Properties palette, set the Tread/Stringer Offset instance parameter to **2″ (50 mm)**.

   This will allow you to pick a specific reference but still assign a set value to move the railing to (Figure 4.24).

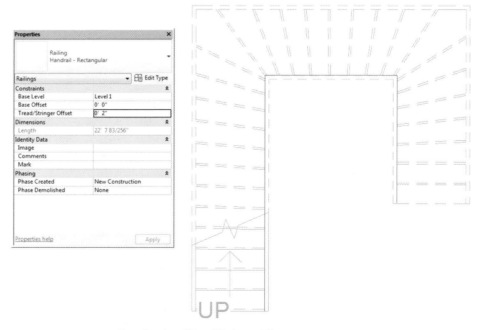

FIGURE 4.24   First sketch and Tread/Stringer Offset

4. Click Finish Edit Mode to complete the railing.

5. Create another railing using the same steps but for the opposite outside three stringers. Instead of using 2″ (50 mm) for the Tread/ Stringer Offset value, use -2″ (-50 mm) (Figure 4.25).

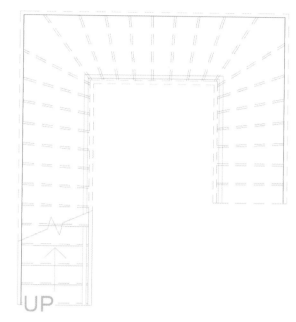

FIGURE 4.25 Second sketch and Tread/Stringer Offset

6. Click Finish Edit Mode to complete the sketch.

7. Open the default 3D view and note that the railings are not yet hosted to the stair but are instead hosted to Level 1.

8. Select one of the railings and click Pick New Host on the Tools panel.

9. Click the stair; this will change the railing host from Level 1 to instead attach and follow the geometry of the stair.

10. Click Pick New Host for the second railing to complete the new railing host (Figure 4.26).

Pick
New Host

In the following exercise you will customize an existing railing top rail to allow for a custom termination condition.

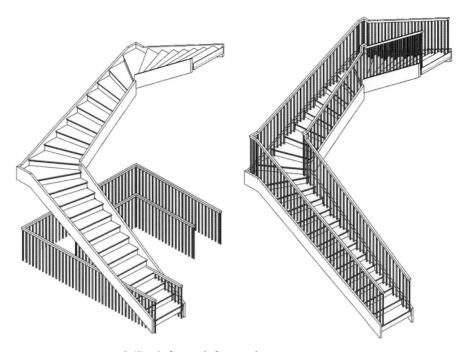

FIGURE 4.26 Railing before and after new host

Exercise 4.8: Edit Railing Top Rail and Slope

To begin, go to the book's web page at www.sybex.com/go/revit2016essentials, download the files for Chapter 4, and open the file c04-ex-4.8start.rvt.

1. The example file should open to the default 3D view.

2. Move the cursor over the top rectangular rail and press the Tab key once. The top rail should be highlighted.

3. Click to select the top rail (Figure 4.27).

4. Once it's selected, click Edit Rail on the Continuous Rail panel.

5. Click Edit Path and choose the Line draw tool.

6. Draw a custom path for the top rail starting at the end point of the existing path, similar to Figure 4.28.

7. Click Finish Edit Mode twice to finish editing the top rail and return to the project.

Next, you'll correct the railing condition at the top of the landing to match the flat slope.

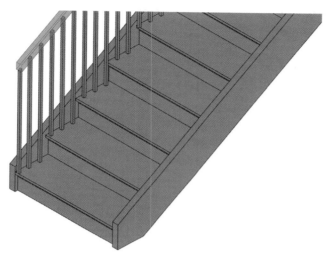

FIGURE 4.27 Select the top rail

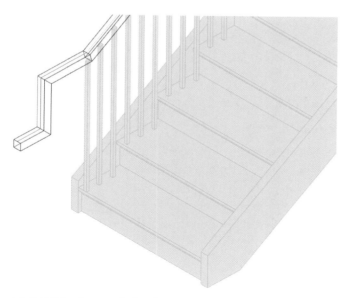

FIGURE 4.28 Updated top rail path

8. Open the Level 1 floor plan view.

Edit
Path

9. Select the railing and click Edit Path to return to sketch mode.

10. Use the Modify panel's Split Element tool 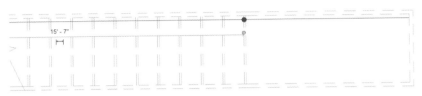 to split the railing path at the edge of the landing (Figure 4.29).

FIGURE 4.29 Split railing path sketch

11. Press the Esc key twice, and select the split railing sketch path over the landing.

12. On the Options Bar, change the Slope to Flat.

13. Click Finish Edit Mode to exit the railing sketch.

14. Open the default 3D view, and notice that the railing condition is now flat over the landing.

    You can use the Slope controls for railing conditions when you need to override how the default slope will be calculated. The completed railing is shown in Figure 4.30.

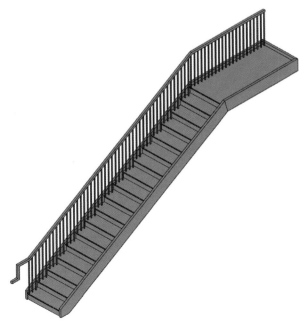

FIGURE 4.30 Completed railing

Designing Ramps

Now that you're familiar with designing and modifying a number of stair configurations, ramps should come easily since they are based on the Stair By Sketch tool. It's the same basic process of sketching a desired shape and then completing the sketch, with two major differences: far more frequent landings and a shallower slope.

You access the Ramp tool on the Circulation panel on the Architecture tab. Keep in mind that ramps have different constraints than stairs, based on slope and length. Understand that the maximum length of a ramp in one section is 30'-0" (9000 mm) with a 1:12 slope (8 percent). These parameters can be changed, but by default they correlate to common code requirements.

In the following exercise you will create a straight run ramp between Level 1 and Level 2. Because you're traversing Level 1 to Level 2 (and they are 10' [3000 mm] apart), this will require a ramp length of 120' (36,600 mm) at a maximum 1:12 slope, not including landings.

Exercise 4.9: Create a Ramp and Edit the Boundary

To begin, go to the book's web page at www.sybex.com/go/revit2016essentials, download the files for Chapter 4, and open the file c04-ex-4.9start.rvt.

1. Open the example file to the Level 1 view.

2. Select the Architecture tab, and choose the Ramp tool from the Circulation panel.

3. In the Properties palette, set Ramp Type to Ramp 1; the base level is Level 1 and the top level is Level 2.

4. Using the Run Draw tool, add straight runs similar to Figure 4.31.

5. To get all the landings and ramps into the right location, select the boundary and riser lines after creation and move them using the Move tool on the Modify panel.

   The ramp should look similar to the image in Figure 4.31.

> The Multistory Top Level parameter is also available for ramps, similar to stairs.
>

6. Click Railing on the Tools panel, and specify the Handrail - Rectangular railing. Click OK to close the dialog.

7. Click Finish Edit Mode to complete the sketch. Open the default 3D view; you should see a ramp that's similar to the one in Figure 4.32.

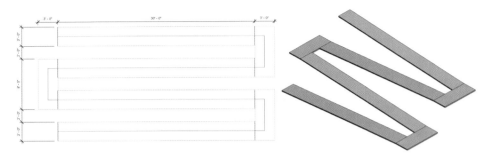

FIGURE 4.31 Straight runs of ramps

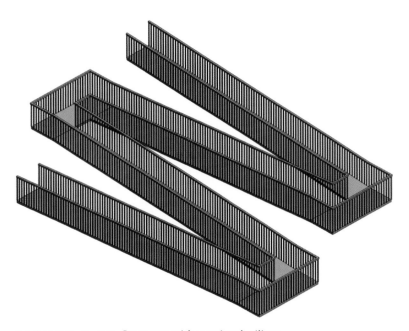

FIGURE 4.32 Ramp runs with associated railings

8. Return to the Level 1 view, select the ramp, and click Edit Sketch.

9. Delete the three green boundary lines that represent the outside edges of the landings, as shown in Figure 4.33.

10. Select the Boundary tool on the Draw palette, and then choose the Tangent End Arc tool on the Draw panel.

11. Create the new boundaries shown in Figure 4.34 by picking one boundary edge and then the other.

FIGURE 4.33 The modified ramp in plan view with removed exterior boundary edges

FIGURE 4.34 Modified ramp with curved boundary

12. Click Edit Type to open the ramp type properties.

13. Under Construction, set Shape to Solid. Click OK to close the dialog. This will create a solid slab ramp instead of maintaining a consistent thickness value.

14. Click Finish Edit Mode to complete the sketch. Revit Architecture has already modified the railings to accommodate the new boundary (Figure 4.35).

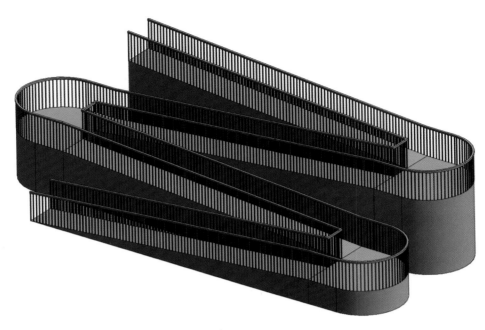

FIGURE 4.35 Completed ramp in 3D

The end exercise file c04-ex-4.9end.rvt has both ramp shapes, included as two separate ramps, for reference.

Now You Know

Stairs, railings, and ramps are separate object types in Revit Architecture that share some underlying parameters. In addition, objects such as railings do not require a stair to exist; they can be created independently or created using a stair as a host for additional complexity.

In this chapter, you learned about the properties that make up railings and balusters. You created railings and hosted them to stairs. You also customized the top railing and overrode the slope for some railing segments. For stairs, you created railings using both the Stair By Component and Stair By Sketch tools. You customized the boundaries and landings and set some to span multiple stories. And finally, you created ramps, edited the boundary, and adjusted various properties.

CHAPTER 5

Adding Families

What is a family in Autodesk® Revit® Architecture? In the simplest terms, a family is a repeatable piece of geometry you can use throughout your project. In this chapter you will review and work with various exercises to develop a better understanding of the different types of families.

In this chapter, you'll learn to:

▶ **View and modify the family category**

▶ **Work with and load system families**

▶ **Work with and load component families**

▶ **Save out and reload component families**

▶ **Work with hosted families**

▶ **Work with face-based families**

▶ **Work with shared nested families**

▶ **Create an in-place family**

▶ **Find and load family content into your project**

Understanding the Model Hierarchy

In Chapter 2 ("Walls and Curtain Walls"), Chapter 3 ("Floors, Roofs, and Ceilings"), and Chapter 4 ("Stairs, Ramps, and Railings"), you learned about some basic model elements such as walls, floors, and roofs. These types of objects are known as *system families* in Revit Architecture. To better explain what a family is and how it relates to your workflow, let's explore how data is organized in the Revit Architecture platform.

One of the unique characteristics of the program is its inherent model hierarchy. In a simple description, this hierarchy can be expressed as (from broad to specific) *project*, *category*, *family*, *type*, and *instance*.

Project   This is the overall container for the model geometry and information.

Category   This is the structure of the content that will be placed in the project. This is how the Revit Architecture software ensures consistency and manages the behavior of elements such as how a door interacts with a wall. You also use categories to manage graphic display and visibility of elements.

Family   Similar to blocks in AutoCAD, families are the basis of geometry you create in a Revit Architecture project.

Type   This is a repeatable variation within a family. For example, the six-panel door family may have multiple types—each type could have size or material variations without duplicating geometry. For example, the door panel extrusion could adjust size based on the door type width.

Instance   This is an actual element you place in the project model. For example, door 607 may be the 25th instance you've placed in the project of the 36" × 80" Wood (0915 × 2032 mm) type of the six-panel door family.

In the following exercise, you will set some display properties for the entire project using Object Styles. Then you will change the settings for one view using the Visibility/Graphic Overrides dialog. Last, you will change the visibility settings of several instances using Override Graphics In View ➤ By Element.

Exercise 5.1: Exploring the Model Hierarchy

To begin, go to the book's web page at www.sybex.com/go/revit2016essentials, download the files for Chapter 5, and open the file c05-ex-5.1start.rvt.

1. Open the Level 1 view and click the Manage tab; then choose Object Styles from the Settings panel.

   The categories you see in the Object Styles dialog box (Figure 5.1) are those that are established by the software and cannot be changed. You can use these categories to modify the default display characteristics of element categories in your project.

2. On the Model Objects tab, find the Walls category, and click in the Line Color field to open the Color dialog box. Set the line color to Red, and click OK.

3. Click OK to close the Object Styles dialog box. All walls in every project view are now displayed with red lines instead of black.

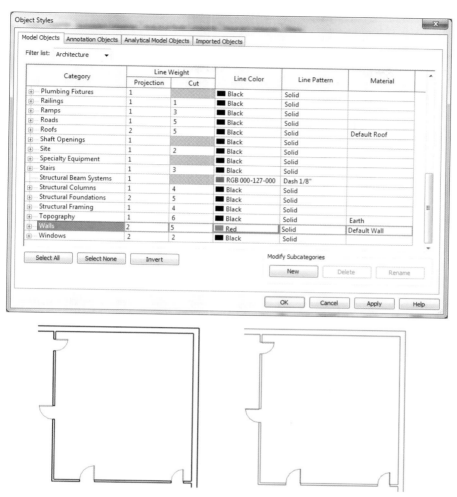

FIGURE 5.1 Object Styles Walls Line Color

4. Type **VG** on your keyboard (this is the keyboard shortcut for the Visibility/Graphic Overrides command, located on the View tab of the ribbon).

   You can also access this dialog from the Properties palette for each view using the Visibility/Graphic Overrides Edit button.

5. In the Visibility/Graphic Overrides dialog box on the Model Categories tab, find the Doors category, and place a check in the Halftone column.

6. While still on the Model Categories tab in the Visibility/Graphic Overrides dialog, uncheck Visibility for the Furniture category. This will turn off the display of all furniture category elements in this view only.

7. Click OK to close the dialog box. Doors are now displayed in the Level 1 floor plan as halftone, and furniture is no longer visible.

8. Select several of the doors in the Level 1 view, right-click, and select Override Graphics In View ➤ By Element.

9. Uncheck the box for Visible, and click OK to close the dialog box.
   The door instances are no longer visible in the Level 1 floor plan, yet other door instances are still visible in this and other views (Figure 5.2).

Use Reveal Hidden Elements to view the doors and set them to be visible again using the Unhide Element tool on the ribbon.

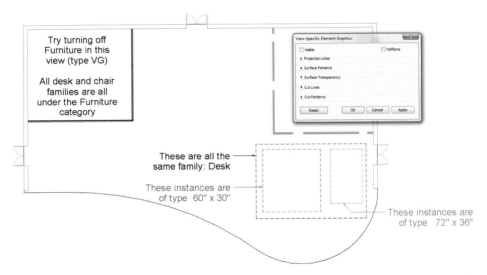

FIGURE 5.2 Completed project, view, and element overrides

In the preceding exercise, you made changes to objects on three levels. Object Styles is a project-wide change for the selected category. The Visibility/Graphic Overrides dialog is a view-specific override for the selected category. Override Graphics In View ➤ By Element is a view-specific override for an instance of the selected category.

Revit Architecture uses three types of families: *system*, *component*, and *in-place* families. System and in-place families exist only in the project file, whereas component families are created and stored as RFA files outside the project environment. In-place families should be used only for unique, one-of-a-kind objects for which you require nearby geometry as a reference when you are designing them. You cannot have multiple instances of the same in-place family.

We will start by exploring system families because they reside directly in the project. Then we will further explore component and in-place families later in this chapter.

Working with System Families

The first type of family you need to understand is the *system* family. The best way to characterize system families is to consider them the *hosts* for other types of geometry. 3D elements such as walls, floors, ceilings, and roofs allow other elements such as doors and windows to exist on them or in them. Other 3D elements, such as stairs and railings, are also system families.

System families are unique in that they create geometry by using a set of rules applied to guiding geometry. If you think about a simple wall, for example, its thickness is defined by a series of structural layers (framing, sheathing, and finishes), its length is expressed by a linear path, and its height is established by some set of horizontal boundaries (either a datum or another element like a roof). As another example, a floor's thickness is defined by a series of layers, its vertical location is determined by a datum (level), and its boundary extents are defined by a series of lines. In the project, these rules are the instance and type properties.

Some system families are 2D. These types of system families include text, dimensions, and filled regions. Although the 2D variety of families are still considered system families, we think they are better referred to as *project settings* to avoid confusing them with the more common understanding of families.

Loading System Families

Because system families exist only in the project environment, there are only a few ways you can load them between projects. The first method is to use the Transfer Project Standards command. This method transfers all the families and types in a selected category between projects.

A more informal method of transferring system families is to use the Windows Clipboard functions and copy/paste content between projects. This method is useful if you want to load a limited number of specific families into your active project.

Although it isn't an active loading method, the final technique to manage system families is to include them in your project templates. After you establish a level of comfort with working in Revit Architecture, you will begin to customize your own templates, thus minimizing the amount of loading required throughout the design and production process.

In the following exercise, you will explore copying wall families between two projects using the Transfer Project Standards tool.

Exercise 5.2: Transfer Project Standards

To begin, open the file c05-ex-5.2start.rvt.

1. In the exercise project file there are some custom wall types you want to copy into a new project (TypeA.1, TypeB.3, and TypeC.4). Keep the c05-ex-5.2start.rvt project file open.

2. Create a new project file using the default template.

3. In the new project, go to the Manage tab's Settings panel, and click Transfer Project Standards.

4. In the Select Items To Copy dialog box, click the Check None button, and then select Wall Types from the list, as shown in Figure 5.3.

5. Confirm that Copy From lists c05-ex-5.2start.rvt.

   This is especially important to verify if you have more than two project files open to ensure that you copy from the expected file (Figure 5.3).

FIGURE 5.3 Selecting Wall Types to transfer between projects

6. Click OK. Choose New Only, if prompted, to close the dialog box and complete the transfer. New Only will copy only walls that are not

currently in the new project (and avoid overwriting types with the same name).

7. Start the Wall tool from the Architecture tab in the new project, and locate the transferred wall types TypeA.1, TypeB.3, and TypeC.4.

8. Create some wall segments with these new types.

In the following exercise, you will place wall families through various methods.

Exercise 5.3: Place System Families

To begin, open the file c05-ex-5.3start.rvt.

1. Open the Level 1 view. In the Project Browser, toward the bottom of the list, click the + to expand the Families heading.

2. Expand the Walls category and you see three values (Basic Wall, Curtain Wall, and Stacked Wall). These are the three families of walls contained within a project.

3. Expand the Basic Wall list and you see all the wall types in the Basic Wall family.

4. Using the cursor, left-click+drag the wall type named TypeB.3 from the Project Browser into the Level 1 view.
   Notice how it automatically starts the Wall tool using the type you dragged in.

5. Draw some wall segments in the view and press the Esc key twice to exit the command.

6. Next, in the Project Browser right-click the same wall type and select Create Instance. Notice that this is another method to add a new instance of the wall type.

7. Select one of the walls you added in the Level 1 view and right-click Create Similar (Figure 5.4). This is yet another way to create a new instance of the same wall type you selected in the view.

There is another method to create a wall. Since you just used the Wall tool in step 7, you can access it by right-clicking Recent Commands. You can do this with nothing selected in the view to start creating another wall. And it should default to the last wall type you created.

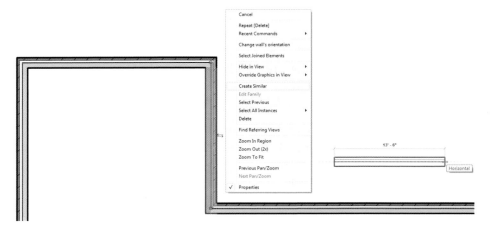

FIGURE 5.4   Using Create Similar to place walls

Working with Component Families

The second type of family you need to understand is the *component* family. These types of families live outside the project environment in RFA files and consist of everything from doors and windows to furniture and equipment. You might think of component families as anything that would be manufactured away from the job site and delivered for installation. This is in contrast to the aforementioned system families, which can be thought of as anything that is assembled at the job site.

Similar to system families, there are also 2D view–specific versions of component families, including tags, symbols, detail components, and profiles:

Tags   These component families are scale-dependent annotations that contain what are known as *labels* (the equivalent of block attributes in Autodesk® AutoCAD® software). Labels are special text elements that report information from model elements. Remember, the information (number, name, keynote, and so on) is stored in the component—not in the tag. Tags are attached to system or component families in the project.

Symbols (Generic Annotations)   These component families are scale-dependent annotations that can also contain labels (similar to a tag). The main differentiator between symbols and tags is that symbols can be placed freely and do not need a host in the project. Symbols can also be loaded and used in other families such as tags.

Detail Components These component families are most commonly used in drafting views or in model views to add additional detail. Detail components can be used as a more intelligent alternative to simple detail lines. These components can be tagged or keynoted as if they were model components. You will find much more information on detailing in Chapter 11, "Details and Annotations."

Profiles Profile families are a special type of 2D family used to generate model geometry—the specific profile you draw will be used to create the extrusion. They are used in conjunction with other system families such as railings, wall sweeps, and curtain-wall mullions. After you create a profile family, it must be loaded into a project and then associated with a respective system family type. A profile's function must be defined in the family parameters (Figure 5.5).

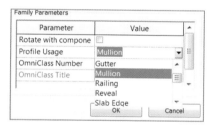

F I G U R E 5 . 5 Defining a profile's function

In the following exercise you will examine the family's category. Then you will explore various methods to load families into your project.

Exercise 5.4: Create a New Family and Load It into a Project

A family's initial category is determined by the template used when the family is created. For this exercise you will be creating a new family using one of the default templates, so no exercise file is required.

1. From the Application button, click New ➤ Family. The New Family – Select Template File dialog box opens (Figure 5.6).

   The list of family templates is consistent with the list of categories you saw in the project environment (Object Styles, Visibility/Graphic Overrides). Each of the available family templates is preconfigured for a specific category in terms of properties, basic materials, and reference planes.

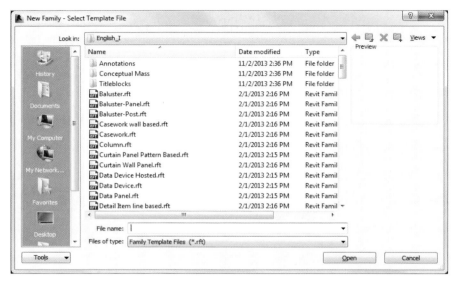

FIGURE 5.6 Selecting a family template

2. Select Plumbing Fixture.rft (Metric Plumbing Fixture.rft), and click Open.

   The Revit Architecture user interface changes slightly to what is known as the Family Editor (keep in mind that you are still within the main Revit Architecture application).

3. Go to the Create tab's Properties panel, and click the Family Category And Parameters button.

   The Family Category And Parameters dialog box opens (Figure 5.7); it shows the category to which the family is assigned (Plumbing Fixtures).

4. Click OK to close the dialog.

   Next, you want to practice saving this family and loading it into a project (let's pretend for now that you added geometry in the Plumbing Fixtures family).

5. From the Application button, click Save As ➤ Family. Call the family **Plumbing Test** (notice that the filename extension is now .rfa).

   When the save completes, you'll load this family into a new project.

You can change the category of a family in the Family Category And Parameters dialog before loading it into a project; however, frequent manipulation is not recommended because graphics and parameters vary greatly across family categories.

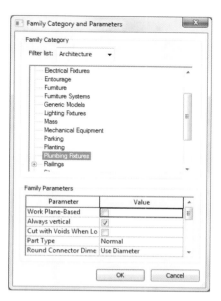

FIGURE 5.7 Viewing the family category and parameters

6. Create a new project with the default template. Then navigate back to the Plumbing Test.rfa family. From any tab in the ribbon, under the Family Editor panel, click Load Into Project And Close. Unlike the Load Into Project command, Load Into Project And Close will not leave the family file open.

If you have more than one project file open, Revit will prompt you for which one to load. If you have one project open, Revit will switch you to the project and immediately start placing the family you just loaded. Notice how Place Component is now active and the Plumbing Test family is current.

7. Press the Esc key to cancel placing the family.

Another method to load families is to use the Load Family tool located on the Insert tab's Load From Library panel.

8. Click the Load Family tool to open the Load Family dialog box, which should open to the family library location.

9. Open the Doors folder. Notice that you can select multiple families to load at the same time by holding down the Shift or Ctrl key.

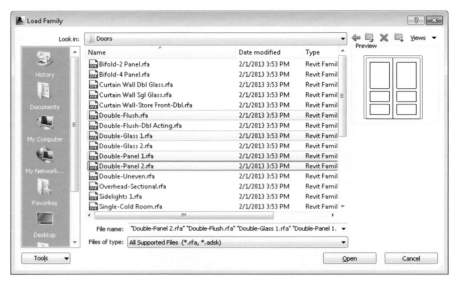

FIGURE 5.8 Selecting multiple files when loading families

Another method to load families is by dragging and dropping them from any folder on your computer into the Revit Architecture window. This works much the same way as in steps 8 through 10.

10. Select several families and click Open.

In the following exercise, you will save a family from the project out as an RFA and then later reload it over a different family in another project.

Exercise 5.5: Save Out and Reload Families from Project

To begin, open the file c05-ex-5.5start.rvt.

At certain milestones in your project work you may need to save specific families out of your project to use in other projects or to a content library. Or you may need to replace one family with another family (and subsequently update all instances).

1. From the default 3D view, you should see four double glass doors; these are instances of the family Double-Door_TypeA. You want to save these out of the project (let's pretend the original family file you loaded in can no longer be found).

2. From the Project Browser, expand Families ➤ Doors and select Double-Door_TypeA. Right-click on the family and click Save to open the Save Family dialog. Browse to your Chapter 5 file location and click Save to save the family. This saves the door family out as an RFA file (Figure 5.9).

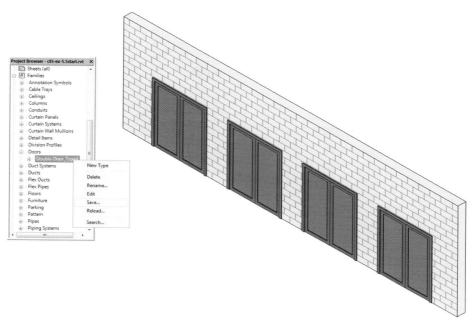

FIGURE 5.9 Saving a specific family out

3. Next, create a new project using the Architectural template. Draw four walls to create a rectangle shape and place several instances of the Single-Flush door family in each wall.

4. In the new project, from the Project Browser expand Families ➢ Doors and select Single-Flush. Right-click on the door family and click Reload.

5. This will launch the Open dialog. Browse to the location where you previously saved out the Double-Door_TypeA.rfa family. Select the door family and click Open.

6. Revit will not remove the existing family types from the Single-Flush door family. When prompted that the family already exists, choose Overwrite The Existing Version.

7. Notice that the family name changed in the Project Browser to reflect the family from which you reloaded. Any family types from the reloaded family are now present in the project as well. All instances of the old Single-Flush door are still using the original family type. We want to swap those to the new Exterior type.

8. Right-click one of the door family instances in the default 3D view and choose Select All Instances ➤ Visible In View. This will select all of the door families; then from the Type Selector, change the type to Exterior (Figure 5.10).

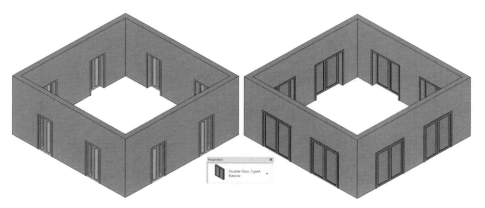

FIGURE 5.10   Swapping to the new family type

Working with Hosted Families

For 3D component families, one key distinction you should understand is whether a family is *hosted*. How do you know whether a family is hosted or unhosted? A simple way to find out is to observe the cursor when a component command is activated and you attempt to place a family. For a hosted family, the cursor will change to this ⊘ to indicate that you cannot place the family unless you are clicking over a suitable host.

The main limitation to a hosted element is that it cannot exist without its host. Certain component families, such as doors and windows, must be hosted because their behavior dictates that they cut their host geometry when placed. For example, you can see this when creating a new door or window family. Notice that when opening the family, there is also a system family wall, which serves as the host. Other components, such as furniture, plumbing, and light fixtures, may not need to be modeled as hosted components. These types of objects are placed in a model and almost always maintain a reference to the level on which they were placed.

A slightly different version of a hosted family is known as a *face-based family*. These types of families can be placed on virtually any surface or work plane, including linked Revit models. They don't suffer the same limitations as hosted families. Face-based families can exist without a host element even after a host is deleted. When the family is initially created, the family template used will determine the category of the family and whether it is hosted, not hosted, or face based.

In the following exercise, you will work with hosted and unhosted families to explore the default behaviors. In Exercise 5.7, you will place and modify face-based families, which are another type of hosted family.

Exercise 5.6: Work with Hosted Families

To begin, open the file c05-ex-5.6start.rvt. The example file should open to the Level 1 view.

1. On the Architecture tab, in the Build panel, select the Place A Component tool, and then click Load Family on the ribbon. Navigate to the location of the downloaded exercise family files, and load the ex-5.6hosted.rfa file.

2. In the room at the upper right in the layout, place five instances of the ex-5.6hosted.rfa family on the horizontal partition wall (Figure 5.11). Space the first and last fixtures roughly 3′-0″ off the wall ends, and set the other three equally spaced. Notice that you can place these components only on a wall.

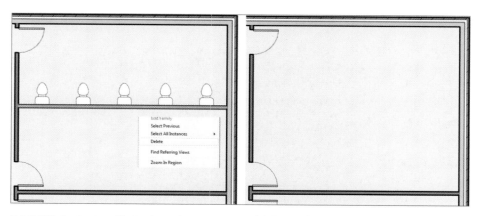

FIGURE 5.11 Placing hosted components and deleting the wall

3. Click the Modify button on the ribbon or press the Esc key to exit the command, and then move the host partition wall up and down. Observe how the components move with the wall.

4. Delete the partition wall where you placed the components in step 2. The hosted plumbing fixtures are automatically deleted when the wall segment is deleted (indicated in Figure 5.11). Use the Undo command to restore the wall and hosted fixtures.

5. Next, you will use the unhosted version of the family. Start the Place A Component command again, and click the Load Family button. Navigate to the c05-ex-5.6unhosted.rfa file, and load it into your project.

6. Place five instances of the c05-ex-5.6unhosted.rfa family along the opposite side of the same partition wall, as shown in Figure 5.12. You can use the Align tool after placement to easily align them to the wall and the opposite side elements.

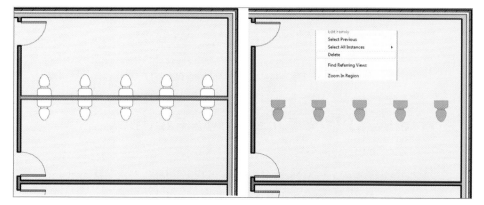

Use the spacebar to rotate components while you're placing them, if needed.

F I G U R E   5 . 1 2   Placing unhosted components in a model

7. Select the five c05-ex-5.6unhosted.rfa families, go to the Options Bar, and select the Moves With Nearby Elements setting.

8. Move the host partition wall up and down, and observe that the fixtures display the same behavior as the hosted versions.

9. Delete the partition wall (as indicated in Figure 5.12). The unhosted fixtures remain (but the hosted fixtures are deleted again). You can easily move selected components from one level to another by changing the Level parameter in the Properties palette (Figure 5.13).

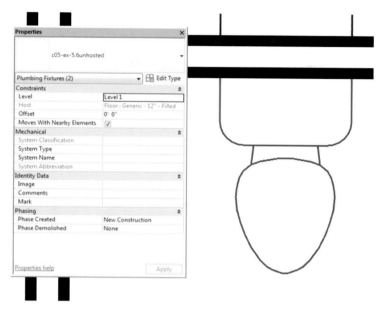

FIGURE 5.13 Adjusting an object's Level property

Exercise 5.7: Place Face-Based Families

To begin, open the file c05-ex-5.7start.rvt.

1. The example project should open to the default 3D view, and you see the extents of the sample project with multiple roofs.

   The c05-ex-7.Facebased.rfa generic model family is already loaded in your c05-ex-5.7start.rvt project. There is one instance placed on the roof (Figure 5.14). If needed, it can be located from the Project Browser under Families ➤ Generic Models ➤ c05-ex-7 .Facebased. This family was originally created with the family template Generic Model face based.rft.

2. On the Architecture tab in the ribbon, select the Place A Component tool.

   The default family should be c05-ex-7.Facebased.

3. Before placing a family instance, take note of the ribbon options for Placement.

   Place On Face and Place On Work Plane are available since this is a face-based family (the default should be Place On Face).

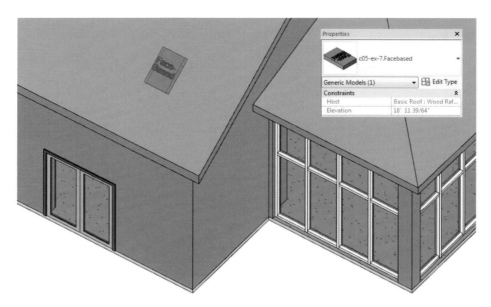

FIGURE 5.14   Face-based family on the roof

4. With the placement method set to Place On Face, add several instances of the family to the roof and walls. Notice as you move the cursor over an object that the face will pre-highlight, indicating what the face-based family will be hosted to.

5. Now select one of the families you added to a wall.

   In the Properties palette, take note of the Host parameter, which is grayed out. This indicates the object the face-based family is attached to.

6. Now delete one of the project walls the c05-ex-7.Facebased family is hosted to.

   Take note of two things. First, the face-based family is not deleted with the host. And second, the Host parameter has updated to <not associated> to indicate that the family is no longer associated with a host (Figure 5.15).

Most families in Revit Architecture have a setting called Shared. This is especially important for Revit families that contain other Revit families—a practice referred to as nesting. When a nested family is set to Shared, three primary changes will occur:

1. The nested family will appear in a schedule.

2. The nested family will also be loaded into the project individually when the host family is loaded into the project.

3. The nested family can be selected in the project by using the Tab key to toggle between the host family and nested family.

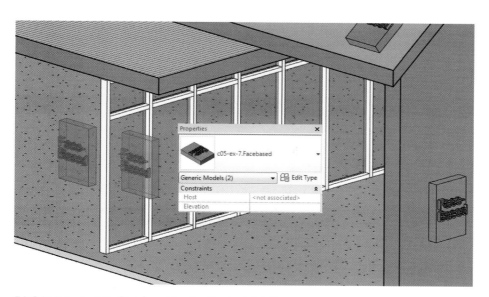

FIGURE 5.15 Face-based family after host deletion

In the following exercise, you will modify the Shared setting for a nested family and explore the behavioral changes that occur in the project environment.

Exercise 5.8: Shared Nested Families

To begin, open the file c05-ex-5.8start.rvt.

1. The exercise file should open to the Level 1 view. There are eight Work Station Desktops furniture system families, which contain two nested families—a chair and storage pedestal. Also, open the default 3D view and the Desk Layout Schedule view (Figure 5.16).

2. Notice that this schedule does not include the chair or storage pedestal. Currently those nested families are not set to Shared, so they are not included in project schedules. You can also confirm that they do not exist in the project on their own; expand the Project Browser ➤ Families ➤ Furniture Systems and you will only see the Cube Panel and Work Station Desktops families.

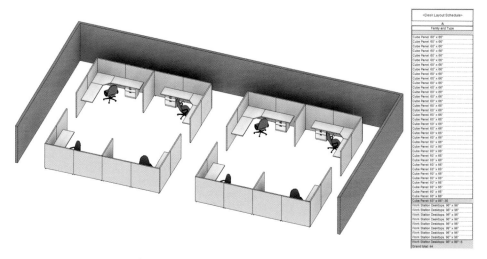

FIGURE 5.16 Work stations and schedule

3. Select one of the Work Station Desktops family instances and click Edit Family. Once the family is open for editing, you can see that it contains extrusions for the desktop as well as nested families for the chair and storage pedestal.

4. Select the Chair-Executive family first and click Edit Family to open this nested family for editing. In the Properties palette, check the Shared property box.

5. Next you will load the nested Chair-Executive family back into the host Work Station Desktops family. Click the Load Into Project And Close button. When prompted, check Work Station Desktops.rfa and click No when prompted to save the file.

6. You now want to do the same thing for the nested Storage Pedestal family. Repeat steps 4 and 5 and load the Storage Pedestal family back into Work Station Desktops.rfa when prompted.

7. At this point you have set both nested families shared in the host Work Station Desktops family. You now want to load the host family back into the exercise project. While in `Work Station Desktops.rfa`, click Load Into Project And Close and click No when prompted to save the file.

8. Because the Work Station Desktops family already exists in the project, you are prompted with the Family Already Exists dialog. Click Overwrite The Existing Version (Figure 5.17).

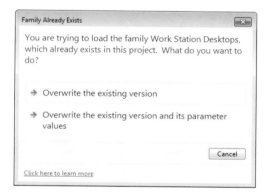

FIGURE 5.17 Family Already Exists dialog

Overwrite The Existing Version simply overwrites the project version with the family version. Overwrite The Existing Version And Its Parameter Values does the same but also overrides any parameter values that may have been updated in the family version.

9. Expand the Project Browser ➢ Families ➢ Furniture Systems and you will now see that the nested Chair-Executive and Storage Pedestal families have been loaded into the project. This is because you set them to Shared.

10. Next, move the cursor over any of the chair family instances and press the Tab key. When the chair is displayed as pre-selected, left-click to select it. You can even click Edit Type in the Properties palette to see the various chair properties in read-only mode. This behavioral change also occurred because you set the family to Shared.

11. The most dramatic change with shared nested families is the inclusion in project schedules. Open the Desk Layout Schedule view you opened in step 1.

12. The Chair-Executive and Storage Pedestal families are now included in the project schedule (Figure 5.18).

For families that need to be included in project schedules, this is important to remember: nested families will not schedule unless they are set to Shared.

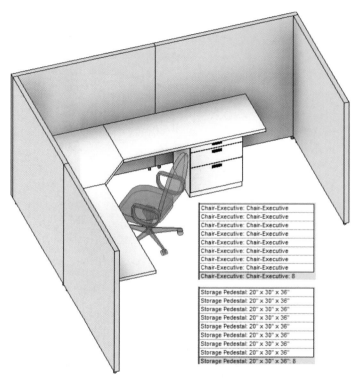

FIGURE 5.18 Updated selection and schedule

Working with In-Place Component Families

In-place component families are a special type of component family unique to the current project. They are created in the project environment vs. the Family Editor, so project geometry can be used as a reference. They do not exist outside of the current project. The command is located on the Architecture tab's Component drop-down menu; it's called Model In-Place.

The major difference between in-place component families and component families is in regard to multiple instances. When component families have multiple instances in the project, updating the family geometry will update all instances. In-place component families do not support multiple instances of the same family. For this reason, they should be used only for unique geometry since a copy of an in-place component has no relationship to the original (and will not update with changes to the original instance).

In the following exercise you will modify an existing in-place family.

Exercise 5.9: Modify an In-Place Family

To begin, open the file c05-ex-5.9start.rvt.

1. Open the project to the default 3D view.

2. Select the countertop extrusion, and choose Edit In-Place on the ribbon to edit the Casework family (Figure 5.19).

   Unlike in the Family Editor environment, take note that you are editing the family in the context of the project. This can be a very useful technique for custom project families where existing conditions or geometry is required to create the family.

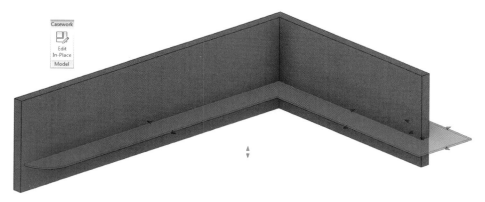

F I G U R E   5 . 1 9   Editing the Casework in-place family

3. Select the counter extrusion and click Edit Extrusion on the ribbon.
   You want to make a slight change to the shape of the countertop to remove the curved edge.

4. Select the curved sketch line and press the Delete key.

5. Add a new sketch line creating a 90-degree corner instead, making sure to close the sketch loop.

6. When the sketch is complete and closed, click the Finish Edit Mode button.

   Notice that you are still editing the family. This is useful if you needed to create additional extrusions or further modify the family.

7. To return to the project and finish editing the in-place family, click Finish Model on the In-Place Editor ribbon panel (Figure 5.20).

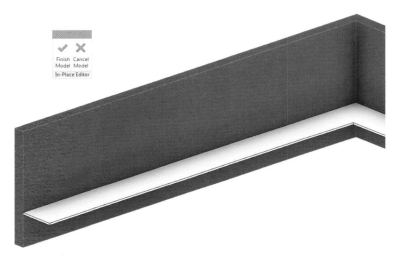

F I G U R E   5 . 2 0   Completing the in-place family

Finding Content

Now that we have reviewed the fundamentals of Revit Architecture families, we'll discuss one of the most important issues you may face as you start designing: the discovery of suitable content. The best place to begin is with the content installed with Revit Architecture. These default families are created with relatively simple geometry and should be sufficient as a basis for the most common building types. If you installed Revit Architecture with the default settings, you will be able to access the default library whenever you use the Insert tab ➤ Load Family command.

Autodesk has created an online resource called Autodesk® Seek to provide content for its design software (http://seek.autodesk.com). You can search for families on Autodesk Seek directly from Revit Architecture. Let's explore this option:

1. Go to the Insert tab's Autodesk Seek panel.

2. In the search bar, type **chairs**, and press the Enter key.

3. Your default web browser opens to the Autodesk Seek website.

    The results displayed match the search criteria of *chairs* and are filtered to show only content that offers Revit Architecture families (Figure 5.21).

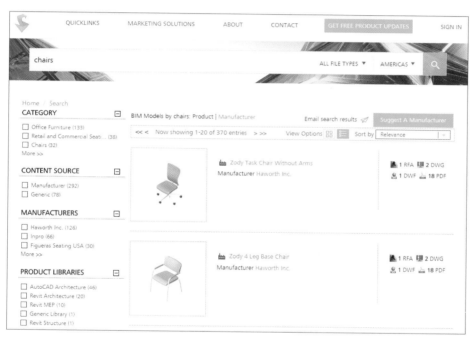

FIGURE 5.21　Content search results in Autodesk Seek

You will note on Autodesk Seek that you can choose from generic or manufacturers' content. The generic content is similar to that found in the installed library. Other content should be used with a level of care. Although an exhaustive review of such criteria is outside the scope of this book, here are some aspects you should understand about component families:

Avoid Imported Geometry　Component families should not be created by simply opening an RFA file and importing 3D geometry from other modeling software. Content with imported geometry may also adversely affect functions such as rendering. For example, a light-fixture family using an imported CAD model might not have the correct material transparency to allow a light source to render properly.

Watch for Overmodeling   Families should contain only the geometry necessary to document the component. That said, this level of modeling will be slightly different depending on whether you want to create a photorealistic rendering or a construction document. Excessive modeling such as fasteners, switches, knobs, dials, and so on should be avoided.

Use Appropriate Repetition   A Revit Architecture family should have a moderate level of repetition built into it. The repetition should not be too complex (all possible variations in one family) or too simple (a separate family for each variation). Reasonable content will offer a family for each set of common geometry (for example, one model line of a light fixture) with types for subtle variations (the various lamping and size options of that light fixture model).

Now You Know

Families in Revit make up the majority of your project geometry, and we have just scratched the surface in terms of this potential. In this chapter, you've learned about the three categories of families: system, component, and in-place families. You have exercised model hierarchy for Object Styles, view visibility, and element overrides. And you have utilized different categories and options for component families. We will expand on this family knowledge in the next chapter.

CHAPTER 6

Modifying Families

Now that you have added a number of families to your project and the design has progressed, you'll often find it necessary to modify the families. Sometimes swapping out a generic family component for one that is more specific is the best solution. In other cases, it's simply a matter of opening the component family that you started with and tweaking the geometry to better fit your design. Either solution is viable—which you choose depends on the result that is better for your design process.

In this chapter, you'll learn to:

▶ **Modify family categories**

▶ **Edit component families**

▶ **Edit the insertion and room calculation points**

▶ **Edit profile families**

▶ **Place and modify detail components**

▶ **Edit a title block family**

▶ **Place and modify nested families**

▶ **Review various family tips and best practices**

Modifying 3D Families

As you learned in Chapter 5, "Adding Families," finding and placing content is pretty straightforward, but learning to modify it will take a bit more time. One of the first things you want to consider when loading a family into your project is the level of detail the family displays at different orientations and scales. It's not likely that every part of a component family needs to be displayed at all scales. It's more likely that too much detail will be confusing (particularly at smaller scales). Back when we used pencils, knowing when to stop drawing detail was pretty easy. But high-resolution computer displays that give you the ability to zoom in and out, as well as modern printing technologies, have allowed us to create far more detail than is necessary or meaningful. So, how do you display just the right level of detail in the Autodesk® Revit® Architecture software? In this chapter, we'll explore some fundamental techniques you can use to modify families to meet your needs.

In the following exercise, you will work with different zoom levels to optimize the view for how information will be displayed. For the second part of the exercise you will change the view detail level and note visibility changes.

Exercise 6.1: View Scale and Detail Level

To begin, go to the book's web page at www.sybex.com/go/revit2016essentials, download the files for Chapter 6, and open the file c06-ex-6.1start.rvt.

1. The exercise file should open to the South elevation view. Zoom to the desk by right-clicking in the view and selecting Zoom In Region. Pick two points to draw a rectangle around the desk. This will zoom the view in around the desk; however it doesn't give you a sense of what will be legibly printed (Figure 6.1).

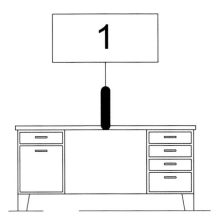

FIGURE 6.1 Using the Zoom In Region option

2. The best method to confirm what will be graphically legible when you print is to click the down arrow under the magnifying glass icon on the Navigation bar (on the right side of the view) and select the Zoom Sheet Size option. Doing so will take the scale of the view into account when you're zooming in (or out). The result is shown in Figure 6.2.

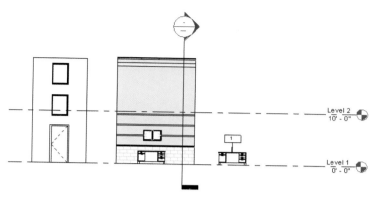

FIGURE 6.2 Using the Zoom Sheet Size option

3. Open the Desk elevation view and change the scale in the View Control Bar to 1/2″ = 1′-0″ (1:20), and then click the Zoom Sheet Size button under the Navigation bar again. You may need to pan the view slightly, depending on where it zoomed.

You will see a more visible difference in what is displayed on the screen relative to the scale of the view. Notice in both the previous figures that the hardware on the desk is completely visible in both views.

4. Next, change the scale to 1″ = 40′-0″ [1:500], then 1″ = 20′-0″ [1:200], and, last, 1″ = 10′-0″ [1:100]. You can see the change in the desk's appearance at different scales (Figure 6.3).

As you can see, all the geometry of the desk—drawers and hardware—is visible at all view scales. But it doesn't have to be this way. A good rule of thumb is that if two lines are overlapping to the point that they'll print like a single line, they probably don't need to be seen.

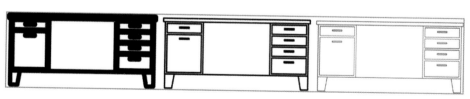

FIGURE 6.3 Elevation at different scales

5. To view the settings for how Revit displays information at different scales, navigate to the Manage tab ➤ Settings ➤ Additional Settings ➤ Detail Level. As shown in Figure 6.4, you can see which view scale is associated with each detail level. Click OK to close the dialog.

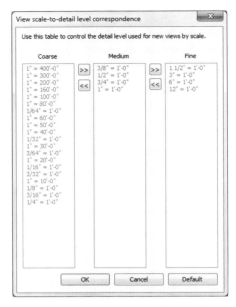

FIGURE 6.4 View Scale-To-Detail Level Correspondence settings

DETAIL LEVEL

In the Detail Level settings, you can choose which view scales use one of three detail levels: Coarse, Medium, or Fine. Based on the scale of the view when it's first created, some elements will automatically be displayed or hidden. But to take advantage of this power, you must make sure the content in your project has the appropriate view scale-to-detail level correspondence. You should also know that the Detail Level and View Scale parameters are separate properties of project views. Thus, if you change the scale of a view, the detail level does not automatically change. The settings shown in Figure 6.4 are automatically applied only when a view is first created.

Now let's interactively look at how Revit utilizes the view scale-to-detail level correspondence to control the visibility of families.

6. Open the elevation view named Cabinet. This view displays a cabinet family with the other objects hidden in the view.

7. The detail level of the view is currently set to Coarse. Change the detail level from Coarse to Medium and notice what happens. You now see the cabinet panels and swing lines in the view (Figure 6.5).

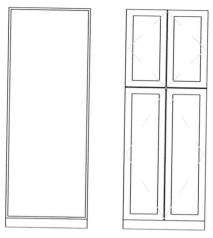

FIGURE 6.5 Coarse and Medium detail levels

8. Change the detail level from Medium to Fine and note what happens again. You now see the cabinet hardware that was not visible in Coarse or Medium detail (Figure 6.6).

FIGURE 6.6 Medium and Fine detail levels

So what controls which elements are displayed in a family at a specific detail level? In the following exercise, you will edit a family and assign geometry visibility to specific detail levels, reproducing the same family from scratch.

Exercise 6.2: Assign Visibility to Detail Levels

To begin, open the file c06-ex-6.2start.rvt.

1. From the Level 1 view, select the cabinet family, and choose Edit Family from the Mode panel of the ribbon (or right-click and choose Edit Family from the context menu).

2. From the 3D view, select the hardware (cabinet face handles) on the front of the cabinet. Click the Visibility Settings button from the Mode panel on the Modify | Extrusion tab of the ribbon to open the Family Element Visibility Settings dialog box (Figure 6.7).

> When you open a family or choose Edit Family from within a project, the user interface changes to offer you various tools and commands for developing families. This mode is called the Family Editor.

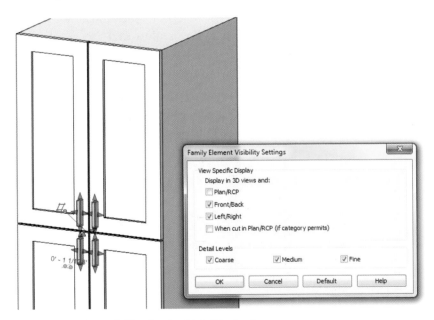

FIGURE 6.7   Editing levels of detail for hardware

This dialog box allows you to determine the visibility for both the orientation and level of detail for the hardware. Currently the hardware shows up at all levels of detail (Coarse, Medium, and Fine).

3. Change the settings so that it shows up only at the Fine level of detail by unchecking Coarse and Medium (Figure 6.8).

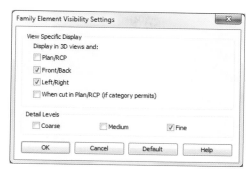

FIGURE 6.8 Set Detail Levels to Fine only.

4. Click OK to close the dialog. Select both cabinet face panel extrusions (there are two separate extrusions that make up the front of the cabinet: the border and the recessed panel). Change the visibility settings so they show up at the Medium *and* Fine levels of detail but not Coarse. Click OK to close the dialog.

5. Next, you want to do the same for the model lines since they are also displayed in 3D views. An easy way to select only the model lines is to use the Filter tool. Select everything in the 3D view and click Filter from the Selection ribbon panel.

6. Click Check None, and then check Lines (Casework). Click OK to return to the model with only the lines selected (Figure 6.9).

7. Click the Visibility Settings button on the Modify tab of the ribbon and uncheck Coarse. Click OK to return to the model. Next, you want to select just the lines around the hardware extrusions. From the same 3D view window, do a selection window around the hardware and use the Filter tool again to select just Lines (Casework). Open the Family Element Visibility Settings dialog again and uncheck Medium so only Fine is checked (Figure 6.10).

8. Open the Front elevation view. Select the dashed elevation swing lines (eight of them) and click Visibility Settings from the ribbon. Uncheck Coarse so you also do not see these lines in the project when the cabinet doors are not visible.

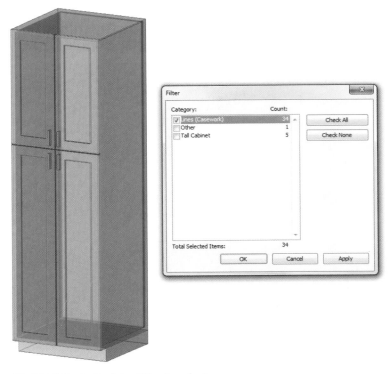

FIGURE 6.9 Using Filter for selection

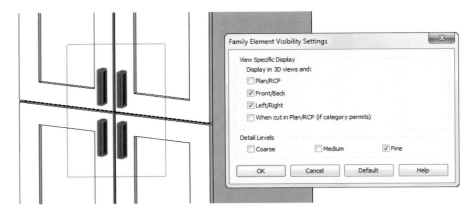

FIGURE 6.10 Window selection and filter

9. On the Modify tab of the ribbon, click the Load Into Project button to reload the cabinet family into the project. Click Overwrite The Existing Version when prompted.

10. Back in the project, the last step is to open the Cabinet elevation view where you can see the front of the cabinet. Change the detail level to Coarse. The cabinet lines, panels, and hardware should not be visible. Change the detail level to Medium and you should see panels plus the dashed lines. Change the detail level to Fine and you should also see the hardware (Figure 6.11).

FIGURE 6.11 Cabinet appearances for detail levels

Family Categories

Family components schedule according to their category, which is determined when you start to model a new family component. When you create a new family component, you must first select the appropriate template.

It is important to differentiate between the category of the family and the template that the family was created with. While the family category can be changed later, the type of host cannot be changed afterward. For example, several generic model family templates are available when you're creating a new family, such as the following examples:

- Generic Model ceiling based.rft
- Generic Model face based.rft
- Generic Model floor based.rft
- Generic Model roof based.rft
- Generic Model wall based.rft

If you start a new family with `Generic Model floor based.rft`, you can always change the category from Generic Model to Furniture. However, it is not possible to change the host from floor to wall-hosted. The Host family parameter is fixed according to the starting template.

In the following exercise, you will change the category of an existing family and load it back into the project.

Exercise 6.3: Edit the Family Category

To begin, open the file `c06-ex-6.3start.rvt`.

1. From the 3D view, select and right-click the face-based box, and choose Edit Family from the context menu.

   When the Family Editor opens, notice the "platform" the box is sitting on. This is the context for the "face" of the face-based family (Figure 6.12). Face-based and hosted families already have geometric context (along with critical parameters and reference planes) in their templates so you can model in context and test parametric behavior.

   When this component was initially created, it needed to be face based. So, the default face-based template was used, `Generic Model face based.rft`. Because the family category has never been modified, it is still configured using the original Generic Models category. Now let's assume the design has progressed and the component needs to schedule as Specialty Equipment.

> Keep in mind that changing to or from the Mass category is not allowed.

> Alternatively you can select the family and take note of the Properties palette—it will display the family category under the Type Selector.

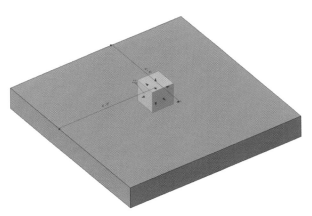

FIGURE 6.12 Editing the face-based family

2. Go to the Create tab's Properties panel, and click Family Category And Parameters.

3. When the Family Category And Parameters dialog box appears, the current category is selected. Select Specialty Equipment from the list (Figure 6.13), and click OK.

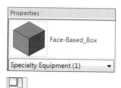

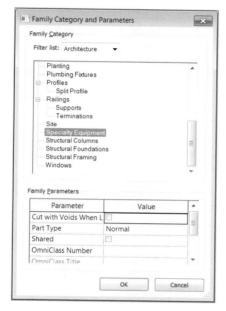

FIGURE 6.13 Changing the family category

4. Click Load Into Project from the Modify tab on the ribbon to reload the family into the project environment.

5. Select the option to override the existing version. The family doesn't appear to have changed, but it now schedules according to its new category.

6. To confirm the updated category move your cursor over the family and the tooltip should display the updated family category.

In the following exercise, you will update the origin of a family for both plan and elevation. Then you will load the updated family back into the project.

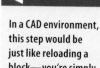

In a CAD environment, this step would be just like reloading a block—you're simply updating the element with the new information.

Exercise 6.4: Update a Family Origin

To begin, open the file c06-ex-6.4start.rvt.

UNDERSTANDING THE ORIGIN

A family will flex around its origin; therefore, the origin is maintained when the family's dimensions change.

The family origin will be positioned on the cursor during placement.

If you replace one family with another of the same category, they should have the same origin. Otherwise, if you have a family with an origin that is at a corner and swap it with another family whose origin is at the center, the family instance will shift.

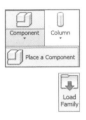

1. Open the Level 1 plan view. Go to the Architecture tab's Component flyout, and click Place A Component.

2. From the Modify | Place Component contextual tab, click the Load Family button; under the Furniture folder, Seating subfolder, choose the Chair-Executive.rfa (M_Chair-Executive.rfa) family. Place it as shown in the left image in Figure 6.14, making sure the chair is centered under the desk's opening. Once the chair is placed hit the Esc key.

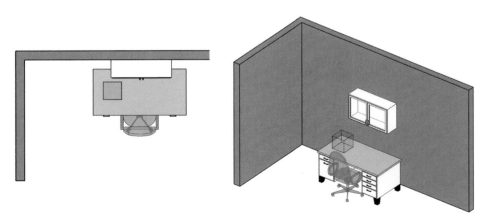

FIGURE 6.14 Chair location in project

3. Select the desk. In the Type Selector, choose the 72″ × 36″ (1830 × 915 mm) type.

The changes in the desk dimensions are applied from the upper-right corner; therefore, the chair is no longer centered and will have to be moved. If there were many chairs and desks in this situation (such as in an office layout), this task would be very tedious! Let's change the origin of the desk to avoid this situation in future design iterations.

4. Select the desk, and click Edit Family in the ribbon to open the desk in the Family Editor. Open the Ground floor, floor plan view.

   The origin of a family is determined by any two reference planes that have the Defines Origin property. In the next step, you will change the reference planes with this parameter.

5. For each of the two reference planes (highlighted in blue with tooltip in Figure 6.15), select the plane and select the check box for the Defines Origin parameter in the Properties palette.

You may need to press the Tab key several times while the cursor is over the horizontal reference plane because of its close proximity to other geometry.

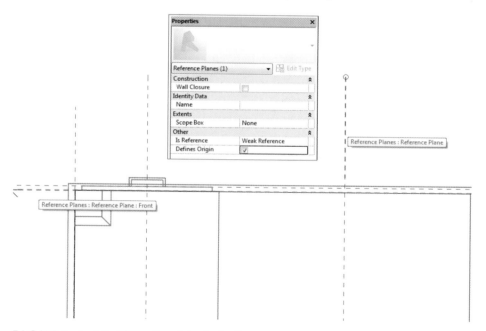

FIGURE 6.15 Editing the origin of a family

6. Click Load Into Project from the ribbon to reload the family into the project, and choose Overwrite The Existing Version from the Family Already Exists dialog. The family initially moves to align the old origin with the new origin, effectively relocating the desk. Select the desk, and move it back relative to the chair. Afterward, if you change the type, it will use the new origin and resize at the current location (Figure 6.16).

FIGURE 6.16 Different-size desks

The Defines Origin parameter can also be set in elevation for specific types of families, such as wall-based families. For example, this may be useful for wall cabinets where specifying an exact elevation for the top of cabinets is required.

7. Open the default 3D view, select the Upper Cabinet family above the desk family, and click Edit Family in the ribbon to open the cabinets in the Family Editor.

8. Open the Placement Side elevation view, and select the reference plane at the top of the cabinets. Select the check box for the Defines Origin parameter in the Properties palette as you did for the reference planes earlier (Figure 6.17). Take note that the reference plane elevation is 6′-0″ (2000 mm) above the floor line.

Only one horizontal reference plane can be checked in an elevation view for the Defines Origin parameter.

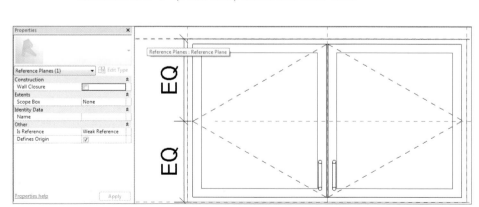

FIGURE 6.17 Reference Planes Defines Origin parameter

9. To reload the family, click Load Into Project And Close from the ribbon, and specify No when prompted to save changes. If you have multiple files open, you will need to specify the start project. Select Overwrite The Existing Version as you did earlier. As with the Desk family, the Upper Cabinet family updates to reflect the new origin.

10. Switch back to the Level 1 floor plan view, and place a new instance of the overhead cabinet family on any of the walls.

    Notice that the default elevation when placing an instance in the floor plan view matches the 6'-0" (2000 mm) elevation of the reference plane. If you select the family, there is an Elevation instance parameter in the Properties palette, which should now be set to 6'-0" (2000 mm), as shown in Figure 6.18.

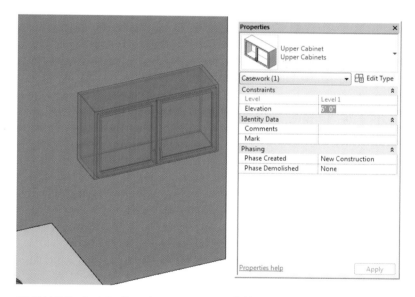

F I G U R E   6 . 1 8   Elevation parameter available in project

Changing this parameter value will move the cabinet family in elevation relative to the reference plane you set in the Placement Side elevation view. In this example, you can enter a precise value for the top of the cabinets (Figure 6.18).

In the following exercise, you will enable the room calculation point in a door family, make a change to the location, and then load it back into the project to review the changes.

Exercise 6.5: Enable and Modify the Room Calculation Point

To begin, open the file c06-ex-6.5start.rvt.

1. Open the exercise file to the Level 1 view. There are numerous storage units, each with a Double-Flush door family. Each unit contains a room (refer to Chapter 8 for additional information on rooms), which is offset from the corridor wall. From the Project Browser, open the Door Schedule and notice that the Double-Flush door family detects the Corridor room (the doors are adjacent to that room) but not the Storage rooms (the doors aren't touching those rooms.

    Most component families in Revit are single-room aware, meaning they will detect a room they are either contained in or adjacent to (left image in Figure 6.19). Some families, such as doors and windows, can detect two rooms—for example, the room you will pass through and the room you will enter through the door (right image in Figure 6.19).

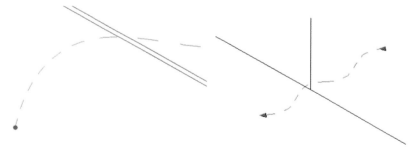

FIGURE 6.19   Single versus two calculation points

2. For conditions where you need to override the default adjacency, you can enable the room calculation point from Figure 6.19, which will give specific control over the point Revit uses to calculate which room it is associated with. Select one of the Double-Flush door family instances and click Edit Family from the ribbon.

3. Once in the Family Editor, open the Floor Line plan view. In the Properties palette, locate and check the Room Calculation Point parameter. You should now see two graphical arrows along with a curved dashed line. This is the room calculation point. The two arrows indicate the direction of passage for the associated From and To room; click on the points to select them (Figure 6.20).

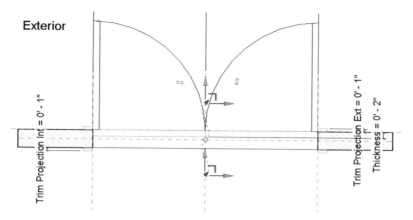

FIGURE 6.20 Room calculation point

4. Next, you'll adjust the To room calculation point to be farther away from the door geometry, so it detects the room. Click on the room calculation point again and drag the point (on the door swing side) past the EQ dimension text, similar to what is shown in Figure 6.21.

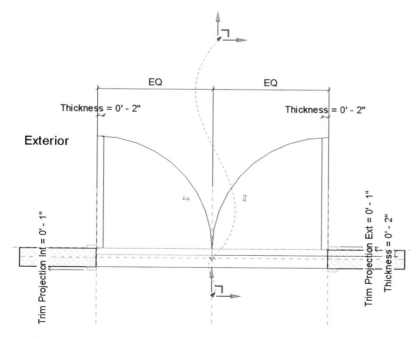

FIGURE 6.21 Updated room calculation point

5. Once the room calculation point has been updated click Load into Project And Close from the ribbon. When prompted, do not save the family, and choose to overwrite the existing version.

6. Click on one of the Double-Flush door family instances to select it. Notice now in the project that when you select any of these door family instances you can see the room calculation point marker. While you cannot modify the point inside the project, it will display exactly where it is.

7. Open the door schedule again and notice that the To Room: Name fields have been populated with the Storage rooms. Enabling the room calculation point allows you to specify the exact location you want Revit Architecture to use for calculating which room to associate for component families.

8. Last, select one of the Double-Flush door family instances. Press the spacebar until the door flips to the opposite side; this also flips the room calculation point geometry. Open the door schedule to confirm the that To Room: Name now reports the Corridor room (Figure 6.22).

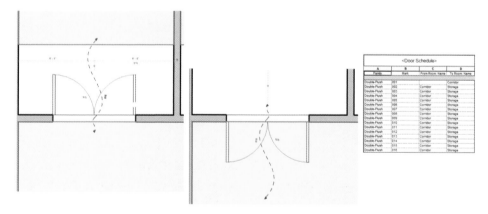

FIGURE 6.22 Flipping the door direction

In the following exercise, you will make various changes to a generic host window that is part of the default library. A hosted family has a required relationship to a specific host category, such as Floors, Walls, Roofs, or Ceilings. Without the host, the hosted family can't be placed.

Exercise 6.6: Modify Hosted Components

To begin, open the file c06-ex-6.6start.rvt.

1. Under Families in the Project Browser, locate and expand the Windows category. Right-click Fixed, and select Edit from the context menu to open the family in the Family Editor (Figure 6.23).

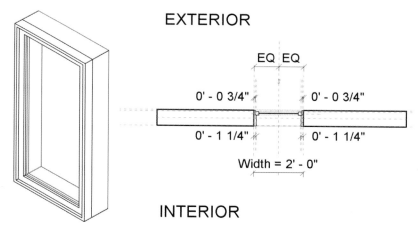

FIGURE 6.23   Window plan and 3D view in the Family Editor

2. Open the 3D view View 1. Press VV on the keyboard to access the Visibility/Graphic Overrides dialog (the left image in Figure 6.24). On the Model Categories tab, make sure the Walls category is checked as shown and click OK. The 3D view now resembles the image on the right in Figure 6.24. Use Zoom To Fit to adjust your view.

3. Activate the Exterior elevation view from the Project Browser window by double-clicking the view (Figure 6.25).

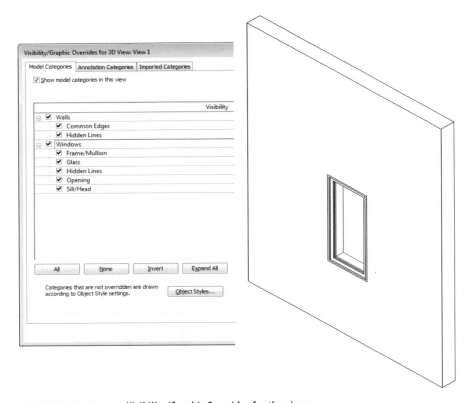

FIGURE 6.24 Visibility/Graphic Overrides for the view

Reference planes (displayed as green dashed lines) serve as a framework that allows the geometry to flex. As you can see, the window geometry has not been directly assigned to dimension parameters. Instead, the parameters are associated to the reference planes. The window geometry is then constrained to the reference planes. This is the recommended method for constructing family geometry.

4. Go to the Create tab's Datum panel, and click the Reference Plane tool. Draw a horizontal plane around the midpoint of the window.

5. Go to the Modify | Place Reference Plane tab's Measure panel, and click the Aligned Dimension tool. Create a continuous dimension between the two outermost horizontal reference planes and the new plane you created in step 4. Click the temporary EQ icon that is active when you select the dimension just created to establish an equality constraint (Figure 6.26).

▶
No matter how the window height changes, the new reference plane will remain centered.

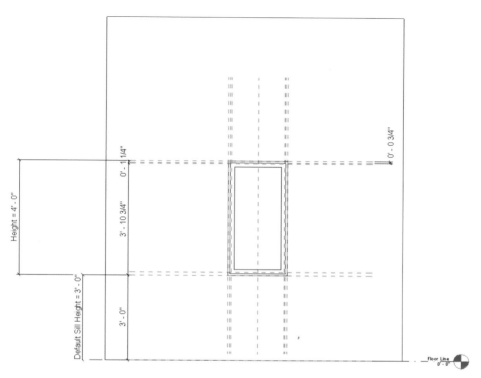

FIGURE 6.25   Reference planes and dimension parameters

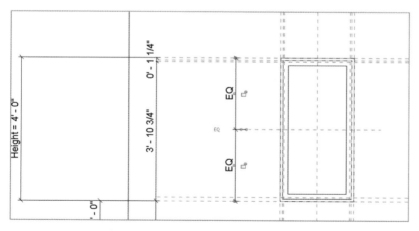

FIGURE 6.26   Adding a new reference plane and keeping it equally spaced

MODIFYING CONTENT IN A FAMILY

Making changes to a hosted component is an important part of modifying existing content. This window family is full of dimension parameters that control different types. You do not need to create new geometry from scratch; you can modify what is already in the family. This approach may seem like cheating, but this is usually how content is modified. In addition to this process being efficient, the geometry that you modify will likely continue to "remember" existing relationships to reference planes and other parameters.

6. Select the frame/mullion extrusion, and click Edit Extrusion from the ribbon (Figure 6.27).

7. Sketch new internal lines, as shown in Figure 6.28, to split the window into three panels. Before you finish the sketch, delete the sketch segments between the new lines (for example, by using the Split tool with the Delete Inner Segment option checked from the Options Bar). When complete, the sketch should look like the area outlined in the blue highlighted area in Figure 6.28.

8. Click the green check mark on the ribbon to finish the sketch. After the sketch is finished, it's important to flex the family to make sure the different sizes will behave before you load the family into the project.

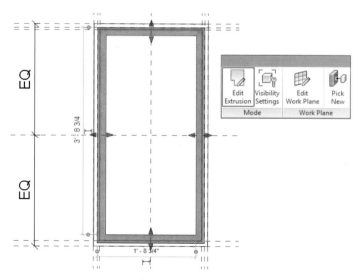

FIGURE 6.27 Completed frame/mullion extrusion

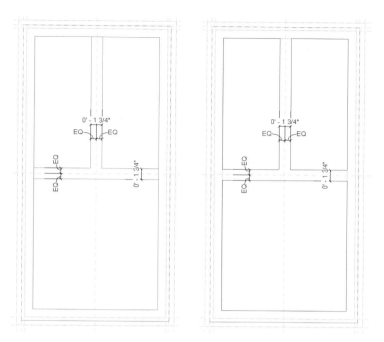

FIGURE 6.28 Editing the existing window frame

9. Click the Family Types button to view all the various family types. Select a few different types from the drop-down at the top of the dialog box and click Apply after each type is specified.

10. Click OK to close the dialog box and look at the window in 3D. The window geometry is flexing but the window pane is still one piece of glazing.

11. Select the glazing, and then click the Edit Extrusion button from the Mode panel on the contextual Modify | Glass tab. Return to the Exterior elevation, and add sketch lines aligned with your previously modified window trim, as shown in Figure 6.29. You can use the Pick Lines option in the Draw panel to make this process even easier. Remember to remove the segments of outer line using the Split tool, as you did in step 7.

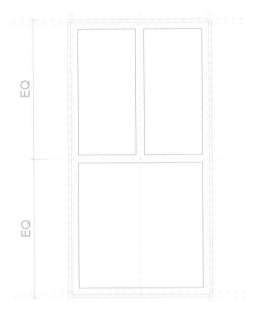

FIGURE 6.29 Modifying the window glazing

12. Click Finish Edit Mode to finish the sketch, and then repeat the previous process of testing a few different family-type parameters to make sure the window glazing will flex with the different sizes.

In the following exercise, you will edit an existing door family and incorporate a nested family for the door handle.

Exercise 6.7: Incorporate Nested Families

To begin, open the file c06-ex-6.7start.rvt.

1. The example file should open to the default 3D view. Select one of the door family instances and click Edit Family from the ribbon.

2. On the Create tab of the Family Editor, click Component to place a nested family. In this example you have not loaded a family yet, so you will be prompted with a dialog to do so. Browse to the Chapter 6 files and select Door_Handle.rfa.

3. This family was created with the face-based template, so it can use most geometry in the project or family as a host. From the ribbon, the active placement method should be Place On Face. From the 3D view, click anywhere on the door panel face to place an instance of the nested handle family (Figure 6.30).

SPACEBAR ROTATION

Don't forget that you can rotate component families before or after placement by using the spacebar.

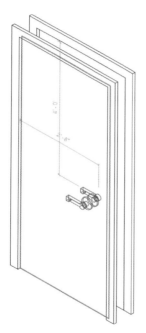

FIGURE 6.30 Initial nested family placement

4. Open the Ground floor plan view. Depending on which side of the door you placed the door handle family, you may need to flip the work plane. If it looks similar to the left image in Figure 6.31 (not aligned to the door panel face), select the door handle family and click the symbol to Flip Work Plane (Figure 6.31).

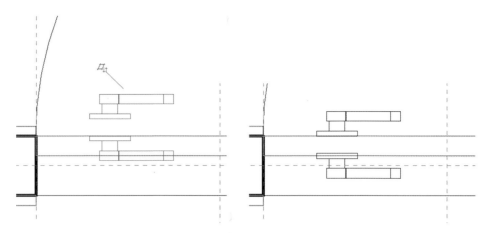

FIGURE 6.31   Flip Work Plane, before and after

Now that the nested family is close to the correct position, you can adjust for the door panel thickness. The nested door handle family contains a parameter for the door thickness. You need to associate that nested family parameter to the host family parameter. That way, the nested family will update automatically if the host family door panel changes thickness.

5. Select the nested door handle family instance and click Edit Type from the Properties palette. Locate the parameter called Door Thk; this is the parameter in the nested family. Click the Associate Family Parameter button in the = column.

6. From the Associate Family Parameter dialog, select the Thickness parameter; this is the parameter in the host family. Notice that the nested door handle family updates to use the 2″ (50 mm) dimension from the host family instead of the nested family dimension for the door thickness. It also grays out so you can't manually enter a dimension, because it is driven by the host parameter now. Click OK to close the Associate Family Parameter dialog and click OK again to close the Type Properties dialog.

7. You also need to make sure the nested door handle family remains at the correct location should the door geometry move or change size. From the Ground floor plan view, add an aligned dimension

between the reference plane on the left and the center of the door handle family.

8. Select the door handle family, and then click on the dimension text and enter 4″ (**101** mm). Click the Esc key to deselect the text. Click on the dimension and then click the padlock icon to create an alignment constraint. This will hold the dimension distance.

9. You'll now do the same in one of the elevation views. Open the Back elevation view and add an aligned dimension between the Ground floor level and the center of the door handle.

10. Select the door handle family, and then click on the dimension text and enter 3′-6″ (**1066** mm). Click the Esc key to deselect the text. Then click on the dimension and then click the padlock icon to create an alignment constraint. This will hold the dimension distance. Both the plan and elevation conditions are displayed in Figure 6.32.

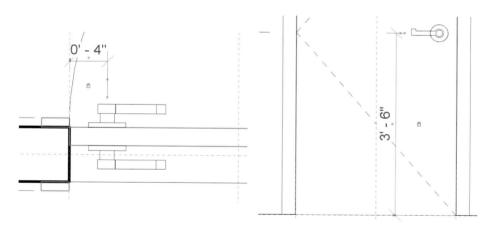

FIGURE 6.32 Lock door handle dimensions

11. Click Load Into Project And Close, and choose to not save the family when prompted. When prompted, choose to overwrite the existing version and its parameter values. You should now see the revised door family containing the nested door handle family.

REVEAL CONSTRAINTS

The Reveal Constraints display mode makes it easy to temporarily highlight (in red) all constraints in the active view. For example, this makes it easy to distinguish a locked dimension (constraint) from a regular dimension. After creating constraints in steps 8 and 10, you can highlight them by enabling this display mode from the View Control Bar's dimension lock icon.

Modifying 2D Families

In addition to 3D families that contain model geometry, Revit Architecture has categories of 2D families that consist of detail or annotation elements. These 2D families are handled differently than 3D model families. For example, tag families are treated as annotation, meaning they will resize according to the view scale. A 3D model family in Revit does not resize and is treated as physical geometry with real-world dimensions.

In the following exercises, you will work with the most common types of 2D families (tags, profiles, detail components, and title blocks) to better understand their functionality and use cases: you will edit and make some changes to an existing tag family; then you will load the family back into the project.

Exercise 6.8: Edit a Tag Family

To begin, open the file c06-ex-6.8start.rvt. The example file opens to the South elevation view; note the furniture tag. You will edit and modify this existing tag for your project (Figure 6.33).

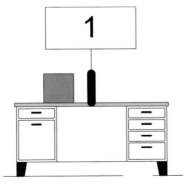

FIGURE 6.33 Existing furniture tag

1. From the Project Browser under Families, expand Annotation Symbols.

2. Find the Furniture Tag (M_ Furniture Tag) family, right-click it, and then select Edit from the context menu.

3. In the Family Editor, click the Create tab, and activate the Line tool.

4. Choose one of the arc draw tools and add lines to both sides of the tag.

5. Delete the vertical lines, leaving just the horizontal lines and new arc lines (Figure 6.34). Adjust the horizontal lines if needed.

FIGURE 6.34 New furniture tag shape

6. Click Load Into Project from the ribbon to reload the tag into the project and overwrite the existing tag.

    Notice that the tag instance has updated. The finished tag should look similar to Figure 6.35. Any tags of the same type in the project will also update to reflect the changes.

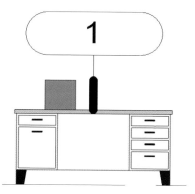

FIGURE 6.35 Completed furniture tag

In the following exercise, you will edit and make changes to a profile family, which you will use to generate geometry for the railing.

Exercise 6.9: Edit a Profile Family

To begin, open the file c06-ex-6.9start.rvt.

1. In the Project Browser under Families, click to expand Profiles, and then right-click Rectangular Handrail. Choose Edit from the context menu. Rectangular Handrail opens in the Family Editor.

2. Because you want to keep your existing handrail profile intact, from the Application button, choose Save As ➤ Family, and name the new profile **L Shaped Handrail**.

3. There are some parameters that you want to maintain in this family. To make them visible, go to the Visibility/Graphic Overrides dialog box (type VV on your keyboard), and select the Annotation Categories tab. Select all the options, as shown in Figure 6.36, and click OK to close the dialog box.

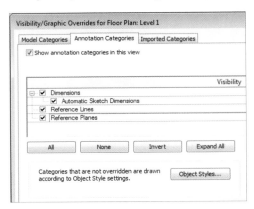

FIGURE 6.36 Adjusting the Visibility/Graphic Overrides properties of the view

At this point, the profile view resembles the image in Figure 6.37.

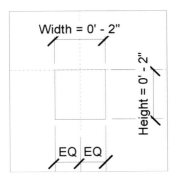

FIGURE 6.37 The profile with parameters visible

4. Drag the existing vertical line associated with the Width parameter upward. Then on the Create tab on the ribbon, click the Line tool, and add the new remaining profile lines so they resemble the lines in Figure 6.38. Load the profile into your project; the L Shaped Handrail profile family is now listed in your Project Browser under Families, along with the other profile families.

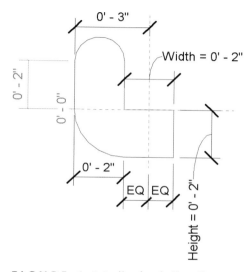

F I G U R E 6 . 3 8 New handrail profile

5. Next, you need to create a new railing type and associate it to your stair. In the Project Browser under Families, expand Railings ➤ Railing, and right-click Handrail - Rectangular. Select Duplicate from the con-text menu. The copy is named Handrail – Rectangular 2; rename it **L Shaped Handrail.**

6. Now you need to modify the properties of the railing to include the new handrail profile. To do so, right-click the L Shaped Handrail type you just renamed in the Project Browser, and select Type Properties, or just double-click the L Shaped Handrail type.

7. In the Type Properties dialog box, select Edit from the Rail Structure (Non-Continuous) option. Doing so opens the Edit Rails (Non-Continuous) dialog box (Figure 6.39). Click the drop-down arrow for the Profile cell to activate the list drop-down, and select the L Shaped Handrail: $2'' \times 2''$, as shown in Figure 6.39.

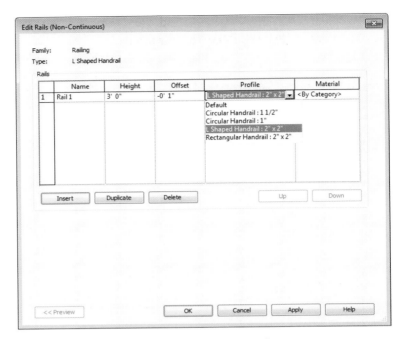

FIGURE 6.39 Selecting the profile for the railing

8. Click OK twice to return to the project. The new profile has been associated to the duplicate railing. All you need to do is swap out the default stair railing for the new one! Select the handrails assigned to the stair, and then choose L Shaped Handrail in the Type Selector in the Properties palette (Figure 6.40).

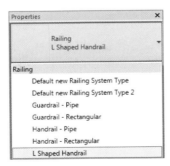

FIGURE 6.40 Selecting the new railing

In the following exercise, you will edit and make changes to an existing break line family that needs to be updated for your project.

Exercise 6.10: Update Detail Components

To begin, open the file c06-ex-6.10start.rvt. The example file should open to the starting view Callout of Section 1.

Text added directly inside a detail component (or standard component family) does not appear in the project.

1. In this detail callout view there is a Break Line family you need to modify (Figure 6.41). Select the break line, and click Edit Family from the ribbon to open the family in the Family Editor.

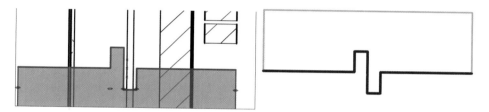

FIGURE 6.41 Selecting and editing the break line

2. Select the break line in the Family Editor, and then click Edit Boundary from the ribbon.
   This element is not a line (see Figure 6.41). It's actually a masking region (kind of like a white solid hatch) that is used to obscure geometry in your project. Some of the boundary line styles are set to Medium Lines, and some are set to Invisible Lines.

3. Before you begin to modify the masking region, you should be aware of any constraints established in the family. Press VV on the keyboard. Switch to the Annotation Categories tab, and check both the Dimensions and Reference Planes options. Click OK to close the dialog box.

Notice that the original boundary of the masking region remains displayed in the background for reference.

4. In the View Control Bar, change the scale of the view to 1 1/2″ = 1′-0″ (1:10) so the dimensions are more legible. Use Zoom To Fit to see the extents of the constraints (Figure 6.42).

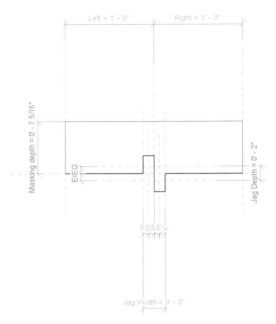

FIGURE 6.42 The masking region with all constraints displayed

5. Delete the squared jag lines shown in Figure 6.43.

6. From the Create tab in the ribbon, click the Line tool, and make sure Subcategory is set to Medium Lines at the right end of the ribbon. Draw new jag lines, as shown in Figure 6.44. Make sure the lines you draw snap to the midpoints of the previous jag lines and the end points of the remaining straight lines.

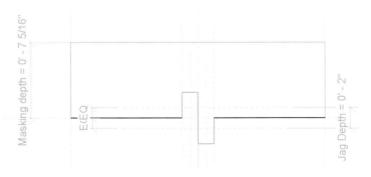

FIGURE 6.43 Delete the existing jag lines in the masking region

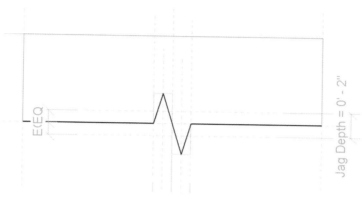

FIGURE 6.44 Sketch new jag lines in the masking region boundary

7. Click the green check mark in the Mode panel of the ribbon to finish the sketch.

8. Go to the Modify | Detail Items tab's Properties panel, and click the Family Types button. Change the Jag Depth value to 0′-6″ (150 mm), and then click Apply. The size of the jag in the masking region should change. Try a few different values for Jag Depth to make sure the masking region flexes correctly. Click OK to close the dialog box.

9. Click Load Into Project from the ribbon to reload the break line into your project and overwrite when prompted. Your break line will be updated in the Callout of Section 1 view to reflect the new shape.

In the following exercise, you will modify a title block family. Title blocks are used to organize your project views on sheets and are considered 2D families, similar to tags and detail components.

Exercise 6.11: Modify the Title Blocks

To begin, open the file c06-ex-6.11start.rvt.

1. Open sheet A101 from the Project Browser. Select the title block, and then choose Edit Family from the ribbon.

2. You need to create a new line type for use in a grid. Go to the Manage tab's Settings panel, and click Object Styles. When the Object Styles dialog box opens, click New under Modify Subcategories. Use the New Subcategory dialog box to create a new line called **Grid Lines**, as shown in Figure 6.45. From the Subcategory Of drop-down, select Title Blocks. Then click OK.

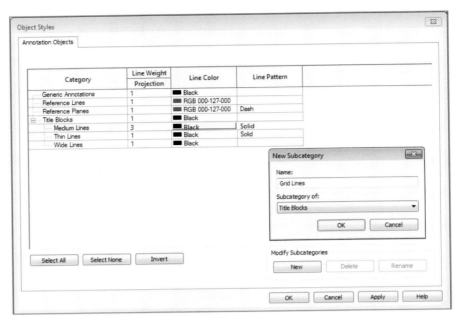

FIGURE 6.45 Adding a new subcategory

3. Select the Line Color option, and modify the color to a light blue. Click OK twice to exit the Object Styles dialog box and return to the family.

4. You're ready to draw the grid lines. Go to the Create tab's Detail panel, and click the Line tool. Select the Grid Lines subcategory at the right end of the ribbon.

5. Draw five vertical lines and four horizontal lines. Add a continuous dimension to each set of lines so there are two (the dimensions will not show up in the project environment). Click the EQ option, and all the lines become equally spaced (Figure 6.46).

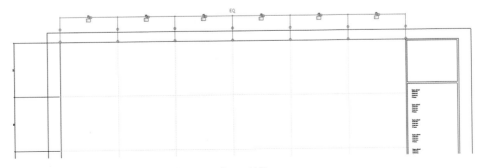

FIGURE 6.46 Adding and dimensioning grid lines

TURNING THE GRID ON AND OFF GLOBALLY

If you were to reload this sheet in the project, you'd be able to control the visibility of the grid as you would any other object: via Visibility/Graphic Overrides. But it's useful to be able to turn the visibility of the grid on and off throughout the project, not just one sheet at a time. You can do this by associating a type parameter to the grid lines you've just created. Then when you've finished using the grid line to set up your project views, you can turn it off with one click!

6. Select all the grid lines you just created. In the Properties palette, click the Associate Family Parameter button to the right of the Visible check box to open the Associate Family Parameter dialog box.

7. Click Add Parameter to open the Parameter Properties dialog box. In the Name field, type **Grid Visibility**. Click the Type radio button, and set Group Parameter Under to Graphics, as shown in Figure 6.47.

> Notice that the parameter type is set to Yes/No automatically since you selected the lines first.

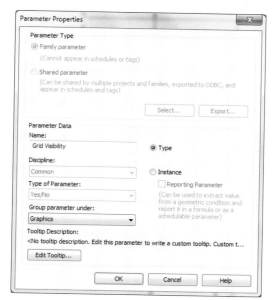

FIGURE 6.47 Creating a visibility parameter

> Notice that the Visible property is now inactive because it is being controlled by the new Grid Visibility parameter. This is how you expose properties of individual family elements in the project environment.

8. When you've finished, click OK to close both dialog boxes.

9. Click Load Into Project to reload the title block into your project, overwriting the parameters of the existing title block.

10. Select the title block in the project, and click Edit Type in the Properties palette to open the Type Properties dialog box (Figure 6.48).

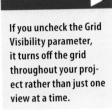

If you uncheck the Grid Visibility parameter, it turns off the grid throughout your project rather than just one view at a time.

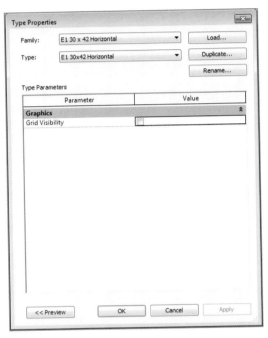

F I G U R E   6 . 4 8   The Grid Visibility parameter in the Type Properties dialog box

11. Deselect the parameter. When you click OK, the grid is no longer visible in the title block.

Family Tips and Best Practices

The following are some additional tips and best practices for modifying and working with families:

Name your reference planes   After adding new reference planes, make sure to assign them a name in the Properties palette's Name field. This makes it much easier to keep track of each reference plane and allows selection by name when you are editing the work plane.

Edit work planes   When working in the Family Editor, you may at times need to move a work plane–based element (such as an extrusion) from one work plane to another. When selecting the element, the Edit Work Plane option becomes available on the ribbon. You can select from a list of levels and reference planes to move the element to. This is another reason to name reference planes; if Name is blank, it will not appear under the Specify A New Work Plan ➤ Name list.

It is much easier to troubleshoot a potential issue before adding additional geometry into the family.

Flex reference planes before adding geometry   When creating new geometry in a family or adding a parameter to existing reference planes, be sure to properly flex the family before adding geometry. Think of reference planes as the framework for the geometry. First add reference planes, and then add dimensions between the reference planes as needed. Once the dimensions/parameters are in place, the values should be adjusted to ensure that the reference planes adjust properly.

Use the wall closure option   For wall-hosted families (such as door and windows), reference planes can be used to determine the point where the wall layers will wrap around the family insert. You can see the difference in Figure 6.49 with Wall Closure checked and unchecked.

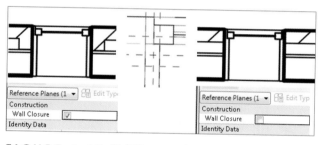

FIGURE 6.49 Wall Closure options

Deal with filled regions blocking lines in the title block   This is a common scenario when adding filled regions and lines in a title block family.

1. In the Family Editor, the filled region is added first, and the lines are added second (so the display order appears as expected with the lines on top).

2. Load the title block into the project, and the filled region now overstrikes the lines. One workaround is to start a new Revit generic annotation family and cut and paste the filled regions into the generic family.

While the display order may appear incorrect in the title block family, it should appear (and print) correctly in the project.

3. Last, load the generic annotation family into the title block family and locate as needed.

Know when objects in a family cannot be deleted   Notice that when you start a new family using a default template, some of the existing elements cannot be deleted (such as some reference planes). Why is this? Any geometry that is included as part of the family template cannot be deleted when a new family is created.

Use a "super" masking region   By default, masking regions mask model geometry in the project environment, but they do not mask annotation elements such as text, dimensions, tags, or detail lines. If you want to mask model and annotation elements, create a generic annotation family, and add a masking region in the family. When loaded into the project, the generic annotation family will mask both types of objects.

Use the family parameter Lock option   For parameters in a family (Family Types dialog), there is a column with an option to lock. If you lock a parameter in the family, any labeled dimension with that parameter applied will be locked. This means you will be unable to change the value in-canvas. This also means you won't be able to dynamically flex the family in-canvas (such as dragging a reference plane with a labeled dimension attached). This is good to keep in mind if you run into odd behavior when flexing the family; make sure to first confirm whether the parameter is locked.

Now You Know

In this chapter we expanded on the principles that we covered in Chapter 5. There is still much more that could be covered, but the lessons learned in this chapter have covered the essentials. In this chapter you've learned about editing 2D and 3D families. You created new families and edited existing families, including assigning a new family category. You learned about modifying the family insertion point, the room calculation point, and the visibility of geometry for specific detail levels. You also learned where to create new object styles, and even how to nest other families. And finally, you've learned to edit the wide range of 2D families such as masking regions, title blocks, detail components, tags, and profiles.

CHAPTER 7

Schematic Design

Design inspiration comes from any source, at any time. Some designers like to sketch by hand; others use digital tools to create a 3D sketch. When design sketches are digital, the transitions between concept design, schematic design, and design development are simplified.

When you bring a 3D sketch into the Autodesk® Revit® Architecture platform, you start with 3D volumes, primal elements called *masses*, to make sure your form and square footage are correct before modeling walls and floors. Once you've confirmed that your building mass can contain the building program, you will use the mass as an armature on which to place building elements.

In this chapter, you'll learn to:

▶ **Import a 2D image**

▶ **Scale an imported image**

▶ **Use a 3D sketch from FormIt**

▶ **Create mass floors to measure floor area**

▶ **Update mass to update area**

▶ **Create floors from a mass**

▶ **Create walls from a mass**

▶ **Create a curtain system**

▶ **Create a roof from a mass**

Importing a 2D Image

To create a 2D *digital* sketch, Autodesk released Autodesk® SketchBook® Pro on Apple's iPad (also available on PC and Mac), which allows you to sketch directly on a tablet using a stylus, or your finger, as you would use a pen or pencil. The sketch in Figure 7.1 was created on an iPad, but the following steps apply to any scanned image—from either a magazine or trace paper.

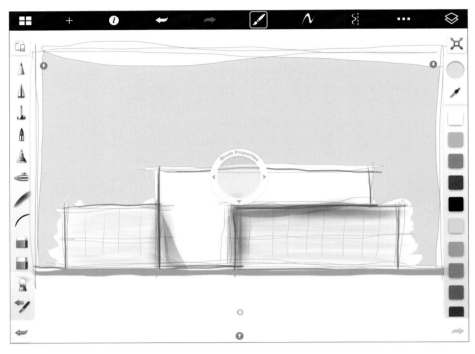

FIGURE 7.1   A 2D sketch from Autodesk SketchBook Pro for iPad

Exercise 7.1: Import and Scale a 2D Image

To begin, go to the book's web page at www.sybex.com/go/revit2016essentials, and download the files for Chapter 7. Open the file c07-ex-07.1start.rvt.

Image

1. On the home screen, select Architectural Template to open the default Revit Architectural template. Open the East elevation by double-clicking East in the Project Browser.

2. On the Insert tab, find the Import panel and click the Image button. Select the Massing_Image.png file from the Chapter07 folder. Click the Open button.

3. You may need to zoom out to see the preview graphic consisting of blue grips and an *X*. This preview indicates the size of the image. Click the mouse to place the image. Use the arrow keys to nudge the

image so that the ground plane of the building sketch roughly aligns with Level 1, as shown in Figure 7.2.

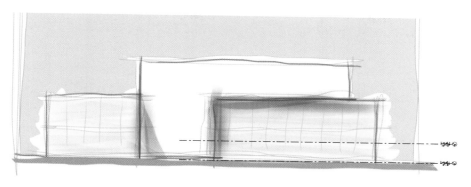

Three clicks are necessary to scale the image correctly; you must click the shared base point, the image reference point, and then the model reference point.

FIGURE 7.2   The imported image. Note the location of the levels relative to the ground plane in the image.

4. Zoom in to the Level symbols. Select the level line for Level 2. On the Properties palette, change the Elevation parameter from 10'-0" (3.04 m) to 15'-0" (4.57 m); this height is more consistent with commercial construction.

5. The image is a bit out of scale for the Revit model. Select the image and choose the Scale tool from the Modify panel. Refer to Figure 7.3 for the eventual goal.

FIGURE 7.3   The scaled image

Each image you import in Revit Architecture can be seen only in the view in which it's placed. In other words, an image placed in the East elevation view is only viewable in the East elevation view.

6. Hover the mouse over Level 1 until it highlights blue and then click. This is the shared base point.

7. Move your mouse straight up so the cursor roughly aligns with the second floor of the sketch; then click. This is the image reference point.

8. Finally, move you mouse straight down so the cursor aligns with Level 2 of the model; then click. This is the model reference point. After this last click, the image scales to look similar to Figure 7.3.

9. Once the imported image is scaled and in the right place, it is best to pin the image so it doesn't accidentally move. Select the image and click the Pin tool from the Modify panel.

This concludes Exercise 7.1. You can compare your results with the sample file c07-ex-07.1end.rvt available in the files you downloaded for this chapter.

Designing with a 3D Sketch

Autodesk has also released a 3D digital sketching application called Autodesk® FormIt®. This conceptual design app is accessible on Chrome or Firefox web browsers—and also on iPad and Android mobile devices! This is a conceptual design and modeling tool that allows you to create building forms and then export the geometry to Revit for further development. Read more at http://formit.autodesk.com.

The FormIt apps are fun, intuitive, and free. The FormIt web app is great for mouse clicking to pull faces in a more fluid and user-friendly way than Revit's conceptual massing environment. Figure 7.4 was created in FormIt Web in roughly 10 minutes! FormIt is like a napkin sketch, but in 3D.

When you save your 3D sketch in FormIt, the app syncs with the Autodesk® 360 Drive cloud storage service and converts the FormIt sketch to an RVT (.rvt) file. The conversion process takes the building geometry, group hierarchy, building levels, building location, and sun angle and creates a Revit file without losing this data. You can then download the RVT file, open it in Revit, and begin design development in Revit without remodeling!

For the following exercises, we'll use the Trapelo_sketch file we created in FormIt and converted to Revit. We encourage you to play with FormIt, create your own 3D sketch, and follow these steps again in the future, but with your own design. We included the Trapelo_sketch.axm file that can be opened in FormIt (after you place it in your A360 Drive FormIt folder!) so you can use it for your own explorations.

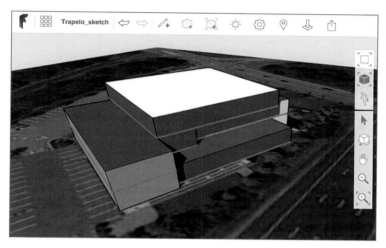

FIGURE 7.4   A FormIt 3D sketch in FormIt Web

Exercise 7.2: Use a 3D Sketch from FormIt

To begin, open the file c07-ex-07.2start.rvt from this chapter's download.

1. The file c07-ex-07.2start.rvt is the file that was created for you by FormIt. When you move your mouse over the model, notice that there are four large mass elements. Hover your mouse longer over one of the masses. The tooltip that appears tells you the name of the mass in FormIt. The tooltip also indicates that these are mass families in Revit. See Figure 7.5.

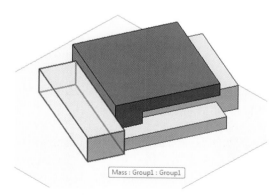

FIGURE 7.5   The FormIt group as a loaded mass family in Revit

Show Mass
Form and Floors

You can insert SketchUp files into Revit but not as easily as FormIt files. When you click the Import CAD button on the Insert tab, the file navigation dialog appears. Change the Files Of Type drop-down filter to show files whose names end in .skp.

2. Masses in Revit are a special category of family that allows you to use special modeling tools and requires special visibility properties. Click the View tab, and then click the Visibility/Graphics button from the Graphics tab (or type the keyboard shortcut **VG**). Now type **M** to quickly navigate to the categories that start with *M*. Uncheck the button to the left of the Mass category, and click OK. The masses all disappear!

3. Go to the Massing & Site tab of the ribbon and find the Conceptual Mass panel to the far left. Click the lower half of the button labeled Show Mass by View Settings. Then choose the second option, Show Mass Form And Floors. Your masses should appear again! This setting is only "per session," meaning that the next time you open this Revit file, your mass will only be visible if you have it checked ON in the Visibility/Graphic Overrides dialog.

4. Type **VG** again and note that the Mass category is still disabled but your masses are visible. This is what we mean by the "special visibility properties" of masses. Check the box so that your mass will be visible in this view in the next exercise.

This concludes Exercise 7.2. You can compare your results with the sample file c07-ex-07.2end.rvt available with the files you downloaded for this chapter.

Visibility of Mass Elements

The visibility of the Mass element can be tricky. The Massing & Site tab of the ribbon has a drop-down menu with two important options we need to clarify. The first option, Show Mass By View Settings, depends on the setting of the Mass category in the Visibility/Graphic Overrides dialog. This means you can enable visibility of the mass on a per-view basis. The second option, Show Mass Form And Floors, enables you to see the mass in all views but only per session—the visibility of the mass is not saved. If you choose this option, the mass probably won't be visible the next time you open the file.

Exercise 7.3: Create Mass Floors

To begin this exercise, open the file c07-ex-07.3start.rvt.

1. Refer back to the FormIt image in Figure 7.4. Note the blue horizontal lines. These blue lines are "levels" that you create in FormIt, and they translate into Revit levels automatically.

Mass
Floors

2. Select any one of the four mass elements in the sketch. At the far right of the ribbon is a panel labeled Model. Find the Mass Floors button and click it.

3. A dialog appears listing Levels 1 through 5 with a check box next to each. Check each one of the boxes. Click OK and note the orange lines that appear on your Revit mass.

4. Now select (or multi-select by holding down the Ctrl key while you click) each of the other three masses. Click the Mass Floors button, and check all of the boxes. Your entire model has Revit mass floors applied. See Figure 7.6.

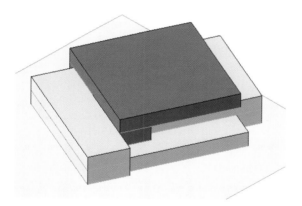

FIGURE 7.6 Your Revit model with mass floors

5. Look in the Project Browser and find the Schedules/Quantities node. Under it you will find a view, Mass Floor Schedule, that was created automatically when you opened an RVT (.rvt) file created by FormIt.

6. Open the Mass Floor Schedule view by double-clicking it. The schedule is organized to show you which levels are applied to which Mass.

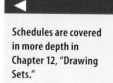

Schedules are covered
in more depth in
Chapter 12, "Drawing
Sets."

The most important data for architects at this phase is the Floor Area (column 4). Revit sums up the area in your building and keeps this area total up to date when you make changes. This is valuable information to have early on in schematic design.

This concludes Exercise 7.3. You can compare your results with the sample file c07-ex-07.3end.rvt that you downloaded earlier.

Exercise 7.4: Update a Mass

Open the file c07-ex-07.4start.rvt to start this exercise.

1. If the design changes, the 3D sketch changes and you'll need to update the Revit model. Select the Mass: Group1: Group1 element, as shown earlier in Figure 7.5.

2. Click the Edit Family button on the Mode panel on the ribbon. The mass element opens in the Conceptual Mass Editor in Revit. This environment is similar to the Family Editor, but it is specific to masses.

3. Select the south-/frontmost face of the mass (use the ViewCube in the upper-left corner for reference) and note the blue dimensions that appear. Click the blue dimension that's labeled 40'-0". Type 80'-0" into the small input box that appears, and watch as the face updates exactly (see Figure 7.7). This is a more accurate way to edit your mass than merely dragging the face.

4. Click the Load Into Project button on the Family Editor panel of the ribbon. You should have only one file open, so Revit will assume you want to reload the updated mass into your open project. If you have other files open, you will need to specify c07-ex-07.4start.rvt.

5. Revit will display a dialog that asks if you want to "overwrite the existing version" or "overwrite the existing version and its parameter values." Either option works in this case because you didn't set or change any parameter values. Choose the first option. Notice that your model updates with the 80' wide Group1 mass.

6. Now open the Mass Floor Schedule view again and review your Floor Area total. It used to be 55841 SF; now it is 66602 SF. You can continue to adjust your building masses in Revit to achieve the desired design while hitting your required area count.

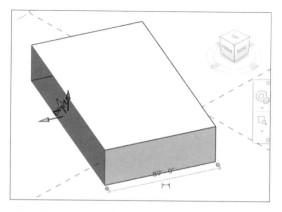

FIGURE 7.7 The updated mass in the Conceptual Mass Editor

This concludes Exercise 7.4. You can compare your results with the sample file c07-ex-07.4end.rvt that you downloaded earlier.

Creating Revit Elements from a Mass

Once your mass has approximately the right area and aesthetic shape, you can start to advance from the conceptual design phase to early design development. The mass itself has very few properties aside from area and volume. You need to add building elements like floors, walls, curtain systems, and roofs to enclose and define your building. Revit uses the mass as an armature to place these real model elements upon.

Exercise 7.5: Create Floors from a Mass

To start this exercise, open the file c07-ex-07.5start.rvt.

1. Go to the Massing & Site tab, find the Model By Face panel, and then click the Floor tool.

2. Do a box selection to select the mass floors of each of the four mass elements. With the cursor in the upper-left corner of the canvas, click the left mouse button and drag the mouse to the lower-right corner of the canvas. You will see a box encompass your entire model. Release the left mouse button when all mass floors are highlighted.

3. After selecting all seven mass floors, click the Create Floor button in the ribbon. Now you have real Revit floors that will be displayed in all views! See Figure 7.8. The benefit of creating floors from mass floors

You can change the *type* of floor you want to create before you make floors by face. Choose from the Type Selector drop-down after you start the Floor By Face command but before you click the Create Floor button.

Floor

is that you don't need to spend time sketching a custom shape. Revit automatically generates the floor outline for you.

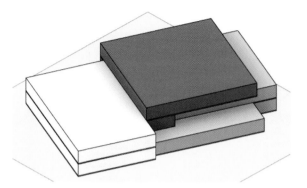

FIGURE 7.8 Mass floors are used to make real Revit floors

This concludes Exercise 7.5. You can compare your results with the sample file c07-ex-07.5end.rvt.

Exercise 7.6: Create Walls from a Mass

Open the file c07-ex-07.6start.rvt to begin this exercise.

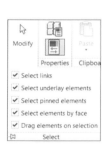

1. To make the next steps easier, turn on Face Selection. (You may want to turn this feature off for the other sections of this book because it is *not* the default setting for the other exercises.) Find the Modify button on the far-left side of the ribbon (it looks like an arrow). Click the Select button underneath it. Check the box next to Select Elements By Face.

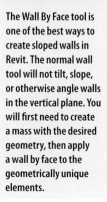

The Wall By Face tool is one of the best ways to create sloped walls in Revit. The normal wall tool will not tilt, slope, or otherwise angle walls in the vertical plane. You will first need to create a mass with the desired geometry, then apply a wall by face to the geometrically unique elements.

Wall

2. Go to the Massing & Site tab, find the Model By Face panel, and then click the Wall tool. You will place the solid walls into your design now. You'll place glass walls in the next exercise. Hover your mouse over one of the first-floor walls, shown in Figure 7.9. Click to place a new wall.

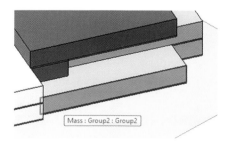

FIGURE 7.9 Place the solid walls by face

3. It is difficult to graphically differentiate the mass elements from the Revit walls because they are essentially right on top of each other. To show which walls have been created and which still need to be placed, adjust the graphics by changing the visual style to Shaded.

4. Open the Visibility/Graphic Overrides dialog by typing the shortcut **VG**. Find the Floors category, and uncheck the box next to it.

5. Also in the Visibility/Graphic Overrides dialog, find the Mass category and click into the cell in the column titled Transparency; then click again to make the Surfaces dialog appear. Set the Transparency value to **50**. Click OK.

6. Also in the Visibility/Graphic Overrides dialog, expand the Mass node. Uncheck the box next to the Mass Floor subcategory. Click OK to confirm all of these changes to the Visibility/Graphic Overrides dialog.

7. Make sure the Show Mass By View Settings button is enabled on the Massing & Site tab.

8. Now the mass and walls are distinguishable. Click the Massing & Site tab, choose the Wall By Face tool, and click to place walls until the volume in the middle of the mass looks like it does in Figure 7.10.

Show Mass by View Settings

This concludes Exercise 7.6. You can compare your results with the sample file c07-ex-07.6end.rvt.

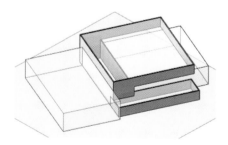

FIGURE 7.10 Create solid walls using the Wall By Face tool

Curtain
System

Exercise 7.7: Create a Curtain System

To begin this exercise, open the file c07-ex-07.7start.rvt.

1. To place the glass walls on the mass, you'll use a different tool, called the Curtain System. Go to the Massing & Site tab and click the Curtain System button.

The Curtain System tool is similar to the Curtain Walls tool (Chapter 2), but curtain systems are specific to massing and allow you to place many curtain walls at once.

 Edit Type

2. Let's change the spacing of the grids from the defaults. Click the Edit Type button in the Properties palette. Click the Duplicate button, and rename the type to 10′ (3.04 m) × 5′ (1.524 m) - Trapelo. Click OK to confirm the new name.

3. Change the Grid 1 Spacing parameter from 10′-0″ (3.04 m) to 5′-0″ (1.524 m). Change the Grid 2 Spacing parameter from 5′-0″ (1.524 m) to 10′-0″ (3.04 m). Click OK to confirm these changes to the Curtain System type.

Before making type property changes, it is almost always best practice to duplicate the type and rename the new type. This way you don't accidentally change other model elements that are defined by that type property.

4. Click the vertical faces that will become glass walls (look ahead to Figure 7.11). You can use the ViewCube to rotate the view to see the vertical faces on the other side of the building. One word of caution—it is easy to click horizontal faces of the mass (like floors or roofs), so be careful clicking! If you do accidentally select the wrong face, just click it again to remove it from the selection set.

Create
System

5. You cannot select faces from different masses. When you have the desired faces selected for one mass, click the Create System button from the ribbon. Then repeat the procedure on the other mass. Click Esc to close the tool. Your model should look like Figure 7.11.

This concludes Exercise 7.7. You can compare your results with the sample file c07-ex-07.7end.rvt.

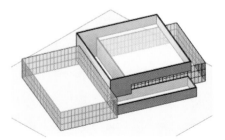

FIGURE 7.11   Curtain systems added to the mass

Exercise 7.8: Create a Roof from a Mass

Open the file c07-ex-07.8start.rvt to begin this exercise.

1. The last building element needed to enclose the design is the roof. Click the Massing & Site tab, and choose the Roof By Face tool.

Roof

Create Roof

2. Click the horizontal surface that needs a roof element on one of the masses. Then click the Create Roof button from the ribbon. Repeat this procedure on the next mass.

3. Type the keyboard shortcut **VG** to access the Visibility/Graphic Overrides dialog box. Turn the Floors category back on.

4. Uncheck the Mass category in the same dialog. This will hide the mass elements because we no longer need them for creating real Revit elements.

5. Click OK. Your finished schematic design should resemble Figure 7.12.

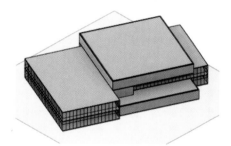

FIGURE 7.12   Finished schematic design

This concludes Exercise 7.8. You can compare your results with the sample file c07-ex-07.8end.rvt.

CREATE MASSES DIRECTLY IN REVIT

In the previous exercises you used a Revit model created by FormIt as your mass geometry. That is not the only way to progress from the schematic to the conceptual design. Revit has robust geometry-creation tools within the massing environment, including extrusions, blends, sweeps, swept blends, and revolves. After you've created basic forms in Revit, you can use Boolean operations to cut voids or add to your initial form.

(Continues)

CREATE MASSES DIRECTLY IN REVIT *(Continued)*

We don't have the time or space to go into all of the Revit massing tools. However, modeling more complex masses is something that you'll likely want to learn and experiment with. You may want to investigate the book *Mastering Revit Architecture 2016* (Sybex, 2015) for insight into these tools.

NOW YOU KNOW

Masses are an essential part of the early conceptual design process when you're using Revit. Working with other software tools like Autodesk FormIt or Autodesk SketchBook Pro is supported and even encouraged to get the design right before moving into design development. The information gleaned from simple massing studies in Revit can inform building orientation and building program validation. The nice part of the Revit massing workflow is that you can add walls and floors to the mass faces, thus allowing your conceptual design to maintain its building intelligence into the early stages of design development and throughout the design process.

CHAPTER 8

Rooms and Color Fill Plans

In the previous chapters of this book, we discussed creating physical elements such as walls, floors, roofs, stairs, and railings; however, one of the most important elements in architecture is the spaces bounded by those physical elements. In the Autodesk® Revit® Architecture software, you have the ability to create and manage rooms as unique elements with extended data properties. By keeping room names and areas coordinated, you can potentially free hours of manual effort for more productive and meaningful design-related tasks. Once rooms are tagged, you'll be able to create coordinated color fill plans that automatically reflect any data about the rooms in your project. Any changes to the rooms are immediately reflected throughout the entire project.

In this chapter, you'll learn to:

▶ **Define rooms in spaces**

▶ **Add a room tag**

▶ **Modify a room boundary**

▶ **Delete a room object**

▶ **Generate color fill room plans**

▶ **Modify a color scheme**

▶ **Add tags and color fill to sections**

Defining Rooms in Spaces

Rooms are unique types of objects because they do not have a clear physical representation like other model elements such as furniture and doors. Their horizontal extents are automatically determined by bounding objects in the form of walls, columns, or boundary lines that you can customize. These planar boundaries will determine the extent of the room object and thus the area of each defined room. As an additional option, you can allow Revit Architecture to calculate room volumes. The volumetric or vertical extents of rooms are determined by floors, ceilings, and roofs.

To access these calculation options, find the Room & Area panel on the Architecture tab. Click the panel title to expose the special commands, and select Area And Volume Computations (Figure 8.1).

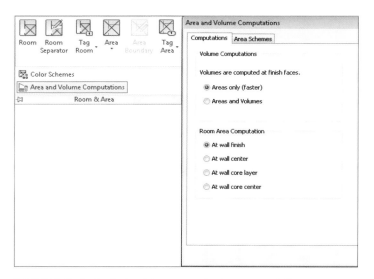

FIGURE 8.1 Customizing area and volume computations

The area and volume settings are shown at the right of Figure 8.1. In addition to setting the volume computation option, you have the ability to customize the area computation as it relates to walls. This is important to understand because it will affect the area values calculated and displayed in room tags.

Room Tags

Before you begin placing room objects, you should understand the distinction between rooms and room tags. The *room* is the spatial object that contains all the metadata about the space. The *tag* merely reports those values. In many cases, you can change the values in the room tag and the room properties will update (and vice versa). But whereas deleting the room will delete the tag, the opposite is not true. You can delete a room tag and the room will remain. Tags are simply 2D view–specific elements that attach to modeled objects or, in this case, the room object.

Because rooms do not represent physical objects, they have two unique properties to help you visualize and select them. One is a reference—a pair of invisible, crossing vectors that are usually near the middle of the space. You can find these by moving your mouse pointer around in a space. The reference will highlight when your mouse pointer is over one. The second unique property of a room is an interior fill. You can make these properties visible in the Visibility/Graphics settings, found under the View tab in the Graphics panel for any view (Figure 8.2).

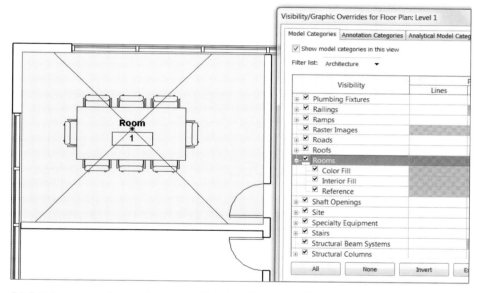

FIGURE 8.2 Room references and interior fill in the Visibility/Graphics settings

Room Boundaries

Rooms will automatically fill an enclosed area and their area will always be recalculated when bounding objects are defined and adjusted. Elements such as walls, floors, columns, and ceilings have a Room Bounding property that lets you customize this behavior to suit your designs. You can find this property in the Properties palette when you select one of the aforementioned model elements.

Room Separation Lines

There are times when you have a large, central open space, as in the following exercise, and you'll need that space to be subdivided and tagged into smaller

functional areas. You don't want to add walls to carve the large space into smaller areas, especially if they don't exist in the program; fortunately, there's a better option. You can draw spatial dividers known as *room separation lines*. Room separation lines are model lines that show up in 3D views. The great thing about them is that they allow you to create spaces without using 3D geometry.

Deleting Rooms

While using the Room command, you can place a room and a room tag simultaneously; however, deleting a room completely from a project takes multiple steps. If you simply delete a room tag, the room object remains in the space. You can add another tag to the room object later or tag it in a different view.

If you delete a room object, the definition of the room remains in your project until you either place another room using the same definition or delete it in a room schedule. We'll explore this behavior later with a quick exercise in which you will delete a room object, observe the unplaced room in a schedule, and then replace the room object in the floor plan.

In the following exercise, you will place rooms and room tags in a floor plan of a project in progress.

Exercise 8.1: Add Rooms and Room Tags

From the book's web page (www.sybex.com/go/revit2016essentials), download and open the project file c08-ex8.1start.rvt. Make sure the Level 1 floor plan is activated and set the scale to 1/4″ = 1′-0″ (1:50).

To add a room to your project, follow these steps:

You don't have to tag rooms as you place them, but by default, Tag On Placement is selected, as highlighted in the Modify | Place Room tab.

1. Go to the Architecture tab's Room & Area panel, and select the Room tool.

2. Hover over an enclosed space, and notice that the room boundary becomes highlighted, indicating the space in which you're about to place a room object (Figure 8.3).

3. Click to place a room in the upper-left space on the Level 1 floor plan. Notice that the default room tag indicates only the room name and number (Figure 8.4), but more options are available.

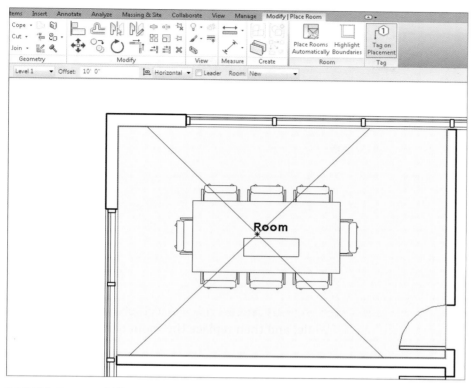

FIGURE 8.3 Adding a room and a room tag

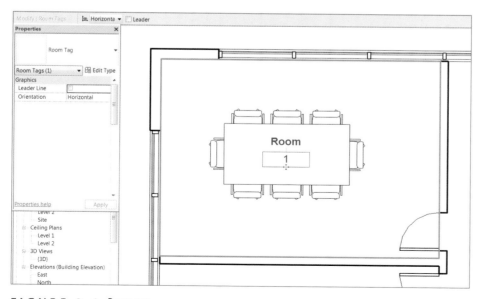

FIGURE 8.4 Room tag

4. Click the Modify button or press the Esc key to exit the Room command, and then select the room tag.

5. Choose the Room Tag With Area option from the Type Selector in the Properties palette. The room tag shows the area based on your project units (Figure 8.5). In this case, the room is 230 square feet (21 square meters).

The area feature of the room tag is incredibly helpful because you can constantly confirm that your spatial program requirements are being maintained as your design develops. As locations of walls are modified, the room object will adjust accordingly and display the recalculated area values.

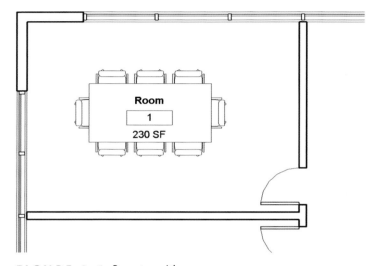

FIGURE 8.5   Room tag with area

6. Select the first room you created by finding the set of invisible crossing vectors, and examine its properties in the Properties palette. You can modify the room name and number here by editing the settings under Identity Data or by directly editing the Name and Number values in the room tag. It doesn't matter where you modify the data because it is all stored in the room object. This makes it easy to create various plan diagrams to suit your needs.

You can change the automatic numbering of rooms by editing the room number of the first one placed and then continuing to place others.

7. Change the name of the room to **Small Meeting**, and change the number to **101**.

8. Place some other rooms within the floor plan, and observe how the numbering scheme has changed.

9. Select the wall at the right edge of the Small Meeting room, as shown in Figure 8.6, and move it 2′-0″ (600 mm) to the left.

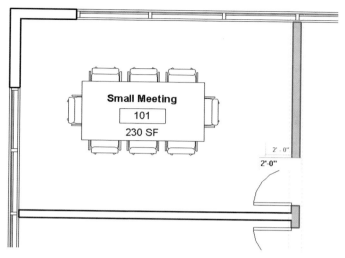

FIGURE 8.6   Moving the wall

Notice that the moment you release the wall, the room updates with the new area information, which is immediately reported by the room tag (Figure 8.7).

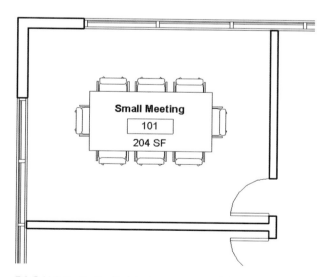

FIGURE 8.7   Updated room space and tag

You have two options to place the room objects. The Room tool lets you place each room manually. This approach is fine for a small project, but on larger projects you can save time by using the Place Rooms Automatically tool to automatically place rooms in your floor plan.

10. Continue to add rooms and tags to populate the Level 1 floor plan, as shown in Figure 8.8. If you're placing rooms manually, the rooms will

be numbered as you place them, so place the rooms according to the numeric sequence shown in the figure, starting with room 102.

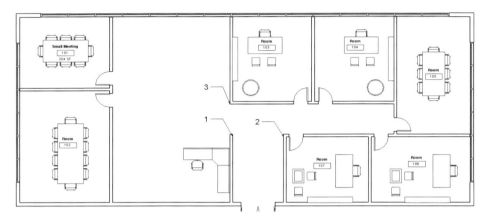

FIGURE 8.8 Adding rooms and tags

Place Rooms Automatically

11. As an alternative, to place rooms automatically, first select the Room tool under the Architecture tab's Room & Area panel, and then select the Place Rooms Automatically tool. Notice that Revit Architecture automatically reports how many room objects were created. Click Close to finish the command.

You can compare the file in its finished state by downloading the file titled c08-ex8.1end.rvt on the book's web page.

Exercise 8.2: Modify a Room Boundary

From the book's web page (www.sybex.com/go/revit2016essentials), download and open the project file c08-ex8.2start.rvt. Make sure the Level 1 floor plan is activated.

Follow these steps to subdivide the open space in the project into three functional spaces:

1. Start to add a tag to the large central open space and notice that the space will be tagged as a single room (Figure 8.9). In this exercise you want this space to be divided into smaller functional areas. Do not place a room object in this area.

2. Return to the Room & Area panel on the Architecture tab of the ribbon, and select Room Separator.

You can turn off room separation lines in the Visibility/Graphic Overrides dialog box for a view under the Lines category.

3. Draw a line between the wall intersections labeled 1 and 2 in the sample file.

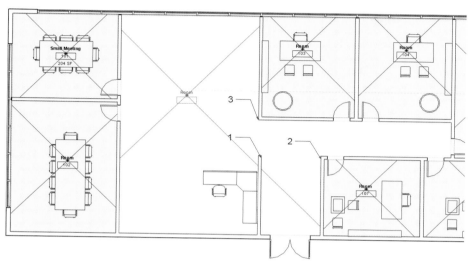

FIGURE 8.9 Tagging a large space

By default, these lines are thin and black, but you can change the settings to make it easier to distinguish the lines from other elements. You will modify the Room Separator line style to be more visible in a working view, but it will be turned off in your sheet views.

4. Go to the Manage tab's Settings panel, click the Additional Settings drop-down menu, and select Line Styles. Maximize lines to view all available line styles in the sample project.

5. Change the default values for the <Room Separation> lines as follows:

▶ Line Weight: 5

▶ Color: Blue

▶ Line Pattern: Dot 1/32″ (Dot 1 mm)

6. Click OK to finalize these changes.

7. Sketch another room separator in the sample file between the wall intersections labeled 1 and 3.

8. Add rooms and room tags to the subdivided open space, as shown in Figure 8.10.

Additional Settings

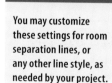

You may customize these settings for room separation lines, or any other line style, as needed by your project.

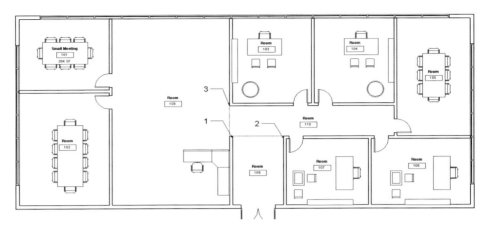

FIGURE 8.10 Adding room separation lines

Compare your completed floor plan to the example file c08-ex8.2end.rvt, available for download from the book's web page.

Exercise 8.3: Delete a Room Object

In this exercise, we will explore what happens when you delete a room object, observe the unplaced room in a schedule, and then replace the room object in the floor plan.

From the book's web page (www.sybex.com/go/revit2016essentials), download and open the project file c08-ex8.3start.rvt. If you completed Exercise 8.2, you can begin the following steps where you left off:

1. From the Level 1 floor plan, delete the Small Meeting room in the upper-left corner by selecting and deleting the room object. A warning appears in the lower-right corner of the application. This warning tells you that the room you just deleted will remain in the project and can be removed or added back by deleting it from or adding it to a room schedule.

2. Go to the View tab's Create panel, click the Schedules drop-down menu, and click Schedule/Quantities.

3. Select Rooms from the Category list, and click OK.

4. Add the following fields to the room schedule in this order:

   ▶ Number

   ▶ Name

   ▶ Area

5. Click OK. One room in the schedule displays Not Placed in the Area column.

6. To replace the room you just deleted, return to the Level 1 floor plan, and start the Room command again. This time, open the Room drop-down menu on the Options Bar. You see any unplaced rooms available in your project (Figure 8.11).

7. Select the unplaced room from the list, and place the room back in the floor plan.

There are filters in the ribbon to *show, hide,* or *isolate* not-placed or unenclosed rooms when you are viewing a room schedule. These filters are useful when you want to perform quality control on your project and quickly clean up not-placed rooms.

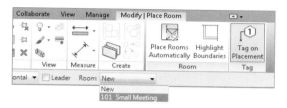

FIGURE 8.11 Place rooms with unplaced room definitions.

8. Return to the schedule you created by locating the Schedules/Quantities category in the Project Browser and opening the Room Schedule.

9. Highlight the name field for the first unnamed room object, and modify the value to read **Large Meeting**. Practice renaming all the remaining rooms, either in the schedule or in the floor plan, as shown in Figure 8.12, giving the spaces names that correspond to their function.

	<Room Schedule>	
A	**B**	**C**
Number	Name	Area
101	Small Meeting	204 SF
102	Large Meeting	323 SF
103	Office	214 SF
104	Office	216 SF
105	Small Meeting	277 SF
106	Office	208 SF
107	Office	173 SF
108	Waiting	700 SF
109	Entry	111 SF
110	Hallway	159 SF

FIGURE 8.12 Renaming rooms in a room schedule

Compare your completed exercise to the example file c08-ex8.3end.rvt, available for download from the book's web page.

Certification
Objective

Generating Color Fill Room Plans

Creating color fill plans in Revit Architecture is easier to accomplish than in most other design applications. Because color fills are associated with the elements of your building design, they will constantly update as existing information is modified or new information is added. This allows you to focus on communicating rather than coordinating your design information—as if resolving your design isn't already hard enough!

In the following exercises, we will explore how to add a color scheme to your floor plan and section and how to modify the values. By default, solid fill colors will be automatically assigned to each unique value in a color scheme. Fortunately, you can completely customize the colors and fill patterns for the scheme.

Exercise 8.4: Add and Modify a Color Scheme

From the book's web page (www.sybex.com/go/revit2016essentials), download and open the project file c08-ex8.4start.rvt.

Color Fill
Legend

1. Go to the Annotate tab's Color Fill panel, and select the Color Fill Legend tool.

2. Click anywhere in the white space of the drawing area and a dialog opens that allows you to select the space type and color scheme (Figure 8.13).

3. Set Space Type to Rooms and Color Scheme to Name. Click OK.

You can create any number of color schemes based on the data in your project model. For example, you could create color fill legends according to department or custom parameters such as floor finish, occupancy type, and even ranges in area.

F I G U R E   8 . 1 3   Defining the color fill legend

4. To edit the color assignments, select the color fill legend in the plan view. You can then select the Edit Scheme tool from the contextual ribbon. You can also access the same settings in the Properties palette for the current view. Just find the Color Scheme property, and click the button in the parameter field.

5. Select the Edit Scheme tool, which opens the Edit Color Scheme dialog, where all the values are available for editing (Figure 8.14).

In the Edit Color Scheme dialog, you can edit the color as well as the fill pattern. Changing the fill pattern is helpful if you want to create an analytic fill pattern for a black-and-white or grayscale print.

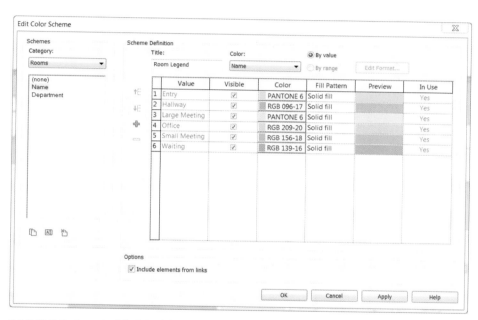

FIGURE 8.14 Edit Color Scheme dialog

6. With the Edit Color Scheme dialog box open, select the Color field in the row for Small Meeting. The Color dialog box opens.

7. Modify the color values to **Red 203**, **Green 242**, and **Blue 222**. The fill color automatically updates to reflect your changes (Figure 8.15). All rooms that share the same name also share the same color fill. Color fills were automatically created based on assigned room names. If a room is renamed, the color fill should change accordingly.

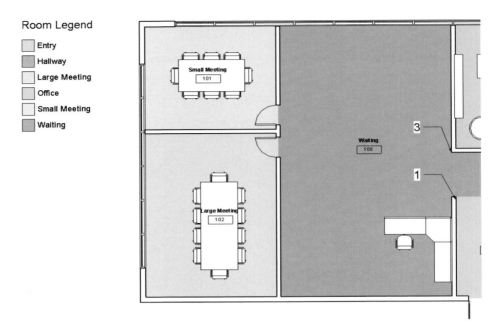

FIGURE 8.15   Resulting color fill

8. Continue modifying the color values in your color scheme until you are satisfied with its appearance (Figure 8.16).

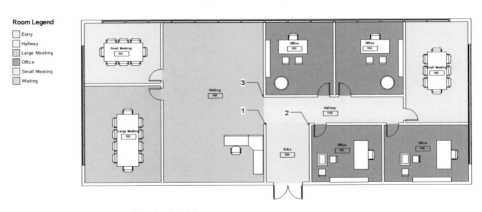

FIGURE 8.16   Updated color fill

Compare your completed floor plan to the example file c08-ex8.4end.rvt, available for download from the book's web page.

Exercise 8.5: Add Tags and Color Fills in Section

Room tags and color fills are not just for use in floor plans. They can be utilized in sections as well. Let's examine this functionality with a quick exercise. From the book's web page (www.sybex.com/go/revit2016essentials), download and open the project file c08-ex8.5start.rvt. If you completed Exercise 8.4, you can begin the following steps where you left off:

1. Activate the Level 1 floor plan. Go to the View tab's Create panel, and select the Section tool.

2. Create a section across the project plan view, as shown in Figure 8.17.

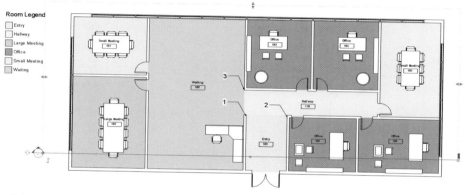

FIGURE 8.17 Creating the building section

3. Press the Esc key to deselect the section you just created. Double-click the section head to open the new view. Figure 8.18 illustrates the new building section. Although all the geometry is shown correctly, it would certainly help to tag the spaces with their room names.

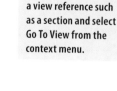

You can also right-click a view reference such as a section and select Go To View from the context menu.

FIGURE 8.18 Resulting building section

You have two options to tag the room objects. Room Tag lets you place each tag manually. This approach is fine for a small project, but on larger projects you can save time by using the Tag All Not Tagged command to automatically place tags in the current view.

4. Select the Tag All tool on the Annotate tab's Tag panel. Doing so opens the Tag All Not Tagged dialog, allowing you to tag numerous element categories in a view simultaneously. You need to tag only rooms in this exercise, so select the Room Tags category, as shown in Figure 8.19, and then click OK.

FIGURE 8.19   Adding room tags with the Tag All Not Tagged tool

5. To move a tag that may be overlapping element geometry, click the Modify button in the ribbon (or press the Esc key), select a tag, and drag it using the grip that appears near the selected tag (Figure 8.20). You can also grab and drag a tag directly without selecting it first.

FIGURE 8.20   Room tags shown in section

6. Return to the Annotate tab's Color Fill panel, select the Color Fill Legend tool, and place the legend in the section view.

7. Once again, set Space Type to Rooms and Color Scheme to Name, and click OK. The rooms are filled with the same pattern and color in the section view as the color fill in the plan view, as shown in Figure 8.21.

You can set the color fills in the section view to describe department or other values, while the room tags display the room name.

Room Legend
☐ Entry
☐ Large Meeting
■ Office
☐ Waiting

FIGURE 8.21   Room colors in the section view match the plan colors

8. Notice in Figure 8.21 that the color fill is obscured by some of the model elements such as doors and furniture. This is because the color fill can be placed as a background or foreground in any view. Find the Color Scheme Location parameter in the Properties palette for the settings of the current view. Change this setting to Foreground, and observe how the color fill display is modified.

Compare your completed section to the example file c08-ex8.5end.rvt, available for download from the book's web page.

Now You Know

In this chapter you have learned how to define rooms within spaces and add room tags to those spaces. You also learned how to modify the boundary of a room object based on your project's program and delete a room object if necessary. In addition, you created a color fill plan and section by adding a color scheme to your views and modifying the color values.

There's a lot of wonderful functionality with regard to rooms, room tags, and color fills that we haven't been able to cover in this brief chapter. Instead, we focused on typical uses to get you up to speed so you can be confident and productive as quickly as possible.

CHAPTER 9

Materials, Visualization, Rendering

Being able to visualize an architectural building before completion is one of the many advantages of building a 3D model. The Autodesk® Revit® Architecture platform offers various opportunities for you to visualize your design in exciting ways. We'll discuss how to set the material properties for your building information model, create compelling presentation graphics, and then produce beautiful renderings. As you become a skilled Revit user, you will also become a visualization expert.

In this chapter, you'll learn to:

▶ **Define a material**

▶ **Assign a material to walls**

▶ **Apply presentation graphics to an elevation view**

▶ **Apply presentation graphics to a 3D axon view**

▶ **Make an exploded axon**

▶ **Render a model**

▶ **Create an interactive rendering**

▶ **Render a model using the cloud**

Materials

Materials have many applications within Revit Architecture. In this chapter, we'll talk about the Graphic and Appearance tabs of the Material Editor to help you create and control the visualizations of your design. First we'll discuss how to create materials in your model. Then we'll apply a material to a brick wall.

Exercise 9.1: Define a Material

To begin, go to the book's web page at www.sybex.com/go/ revit2016essentials and download the project files for Chapter 9. Open the file c09-ex-09.1start.rvt.

Materials

1. Go to the Manage tab of the ribbon and click the Materials button. This will open the Material Browser, where you define your materials.

2. The Material Browser dialog has a list of material names in the list on the left, and there's a very helpful search box at the top of this list. Type the word **Brick** into the search field, and the list will filter.

The Graphics tab has a Shading property. These settings are displayed only when a view's Visual Style is set to Shaded or Consistent Colors.

3. Click the Masonry - Brick material and notice that the properties in the Graphics tab on the right update, as in Figure 9.1. The Graphics tab of the material's properties uses shaded views and not rendered views. You can choose a unique color for the brick by clicking the Color button. You can also redefine the surface pattern. The brick color and pattern look good, so leave them as is.

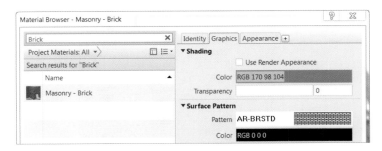

FIGURE 9.1 Search results for *Brick* and the Graphics tab

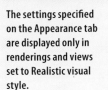

The settings specified on the Appearance tab are displayed only in renderings and views set to Realistic visual style.

4. Now click the Appearance tab and you'll see a small rendered preview of the brick material (Figure 9.2). Below this preview are properties that affect the way this material looks in renderings. Above the pre-view image are buttons related to the material asset. Click the icon with arrows (the swap icon), which allows you to replace the asset with a different material map.

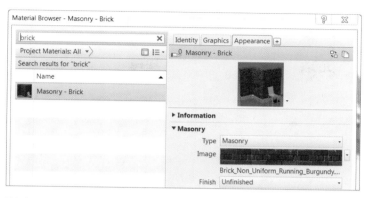

FIGURE 9.2   The Appearance tab and the swap icon

5. The Asset Browser dialog appears and it also has a search field at the top. Type **Brick** and you'll see a variety of options (Figure 9.3). You should drag the column widths so you can see the material asset names. Double-click the Non-Uniform Running - Red brick material.

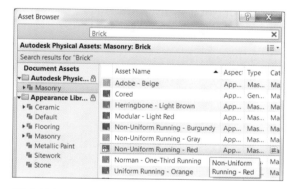

FIGURE 9.3   The Asset Browser

6. The preview in the Appearance tab updates. Click the Graphics tab again, and check the Use Render Appearance box (Figure 9.4). The shaded color updates to reflect an average color sample from the render appearance! This is very helpful for consistency between different visual styles. Click OK to exit.

Duplicating a material before modifying it is a safe way to edit it without affecting all model elements that use the original material. The same is true when editing a material render appearance asset.

▶

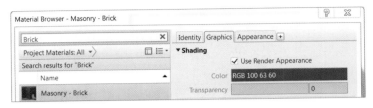

FIGURE 9.4 The Graphics tab after step 6

This concludes Exercise 9.1. You can compare your results with the sample file c09-ex-09.1end.rvt, included in the chapter's download.

Exercise 9.2: Assign a Material

To begin, open the project file c09-ex-09.2start.rvt.

1. Make sure you're in the 3d Cover Shot view.

2. Change your visual style to Shaded by using the icon on the View Control Bar below the drawing area.

3. Select the generic gray wall (Figure 9.5). Then, in the Properties palette, click the Edit Type button to open the Type Properties dialog box for the wall you have selected, Basic Wall 8 1/2″ (21 cm) Masonry.

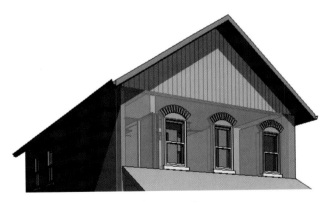

FIGURE 9.5 Select the gray wall.

Remember that changing the type properties of a wall (like editing the wall material) affects all segments of that wall type throughout the entire model.

▶

4. Find the Construction header. Below it, find the Structure label and click the Edit button to edit the structure of the wall. The Edit Assembly dialog box will appear. In the Material column, click in the cell with the text Default Wall. Notice that a small button appears in the cell. Click the button.

5. The Material Browser appears. Type **Brick** in the search field at the top of the list. Double-click the Masonry - Brick material that appears in the list on the left; this is the material you edited in the previous exercise. Click OK to close the Edit Assembly dialog, and click OK again to close the Type Properties dialog. The drawing updates dramatically by replacing the generic gray material with a red brick shading!

6. You've now applied your new material called Brick to all the walls of the type Basic Wall 8 1/2″ (21 cm) Masonry throughout your model. You can follow the same steps to apply materials to floors, roofs, and other walls in your projects.

This concludes Exercise 9.2. You can compare your results with the sample file c09-ex-09.2end.rvt included in the chapter's project files.

DESIGNING WITH GENERIC ELEMENTS

Developing your building design from generic ideas to specific elements plays an important role in your Revit Architecture workflow. When you're creating your design, it's not practical to invest time defining wall layers and material properties until the design is more refined. If you get too specific too soon, you might become frustrated.

Generic elements and materials help convey the intent of your design and allow your ideas to stay flexible. They'll help you emphasize *where* something is, as well as *what* something is, without getting into the details of how it's constructed. Designing from generic to specific will speed up your design process.

Graphic Display Options

Now that you understand the basics of assigning building materials to your model elements, you will open an example file that has materials and views already set up. You'll use this model to create a presentation drawing of an elevation and a 3D isometric drawing. You won't use renderings yet, just the techniques available in the Graphic Display Options dialog box.

Exercise 9.3: Presentation Elevation View

To begin, open the file c09-ex-09.3start.rvt.

1. Find the Elevations node in the Project Browser. Now find the view titled East. Right-click the view's name and choose Duplicate View ➢ Duplicate (Figure 9.6). This will make a copy of the view without copying annotation elements.

FIGURE 9.6 Duplicate a view from the Project Browser.

2. Find the newly created view in the Project Browser, named East Copy 1, right-click, and then chose Rename. Type a new name, **East - Presentation**.

3. Now you'll turn off the reference planes in the view. Select one of the green dashed reference planes, right-click, and choose Hide In View ➢ Category (Figure 9.7). All of the reference planes are now hidden.

FIGURE 9.7 Hide the category in the view.

4. Next you'll turn off the Level markers in the view. Select one of the Level datum graphics, right-click, and choose Hide In View ➢ Category. Notice that all of the Level markers are now hidden.

5. Now you are ready to embellish the presentation drawing with visual effects found in the Graphic Display Options (GDO) dialog box. First, make sure you have nothing selected. Look to the Properties palette, then click the Edit button next to the Graphic Display Options view parameter.

6. Click the Smooth Lines With Anti-Aliasing check box. This effect improves the line quality in the view dramatically. It has a negative performance impact, so use it in presentation views only.

Click the Reveal Hidden Elements light bulb on the View Control Bar to see hidden elements and categories. You can select any hidden element and choose Unhide Category from the ribbon. This will make the element visible again.

7. Expand the Shadows section. Click the Cast Shadows and Show Ambient Shadows check boxes. Click the Apply button at the bottom of the dialog to see the effect these have on the model.

8. Expand the Sketchy Lines section, and click the Enable Sketchy Lines check box. Slide the Extensions control to 7, and click Apply.

9. Expand the Lighting option, and find the Shadows slider. Slide this to the left to make your shadows lighter. Click Apply and adjust until you're satisfied with the darkness of the shadows.

10. Expand the Background section, and choose Gradient from the options. Click Apply. After following all of these steps, you should see something similar to Figure 9.8. Click OK to close the GDO dialog.

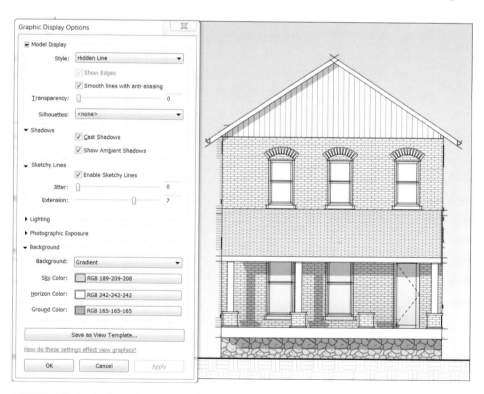

FIGURE 9.8   Elevation presentation view and GDO settings

11. The visual effects are all set, but the crop region needs to be adjusted. Select the edges of the view crop. Note the blue drag controls that

appear in the middle of the edges. These can be dragged so that the elevation is framed as you desire.

12. Once you have the elevation centered in the crop region, you can turn off the crop region. The control for the crop region visibility is on the View Control Bar at the bottom of the drawing area. Click the Hide Crop Region button (the one with the lightbulb!). Now you have an elevation view ready to be placed on a sheet.

This concludes Exercise 9.3. You can compare your results with the sample file c09-ex-09.3end.rvt available with the project files for this chapter.

Exercise 9.4: Presentation 3D View

To begin, open the file c09-ex-09.4start.rvt.

1. Open the 3D view titled 3D Isometric in the Project Browser. The view is locked so that you cannot accidentally change the angle. You can unlock the view by clicking the Unlocked 3D View button on the View Control Bar, next to the Hide Crop Region button.

2. Click the Visual Style button on the View Control Bar (the white cube), and choose the Shaded option. Then click the Visual Style button again, but this time click the Graphic Display Options text at the top of the list. This is a handy shortcut to the GDO dialog.

3. Check the Smooth Lines With Anti-Aliasing, Cast Shadows, and Show Ambient Shadows check boxes. Turn on Enable Sketchy Lines and set the Extension slider to 7. Set the Background option to Gradient. Click Apply to see these effects.

4. Expand the Lighting option, and adjust the Shadows, Sun, and Ambient Light controls. The Sun and Ambient Light sliders make an impact when your visual style is set to Shaded or Realistic. Set each of these values to 40, and click OK. You may need to zoom in a bit to see the surface patterns; then your view should look like Figure 9.9.

5. Select the large brick wall that is blocking your view into the house. Right-click and choose Override Graphics In View ➤ By Element. Click the arrow next to Surface Transparency, and use the slider to set the value to 40. Click OK, and deselect the wall by pressing the Esc key twice.

6. You can see into the house, but the brick surface pattern is still obscuring the view. Select the wall again, right-click, and choose Override Graphics In View ➤ By Element. Expand the

Surface Patterns control, and uncheck the Visible parameter as in Figure 9.10. Click OK, and then press Esc to deselect the wall.

FIGURE 9.9   3D Isometric with GDO effects

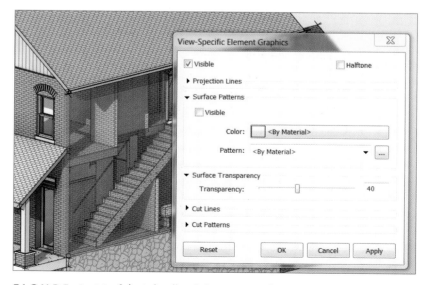

FIGURE 9.10   Selected wall and element overrides

This concludes Exercise 9.4. You can compare your results with the sample file c09-ex-09.4end.rvt available in the chapter's project files.

Exercise 9.5: 3D Exploded View

To begin, open the file c09-ex-09.5start.rvt, which is included with the files you downloaded for this chapter.

Displacing elements is a view-specific override much like hiding an element in a view affects that one view only. The changes made using Displacement will not affect the model or any other views of the model.

1. Open the view named 3D Exploded View. Select the large brick wall, and click the Displace Elements button on the View panel of the Modify tab.

2. A widget appears on the wall with green, red, and blue arrows. This widget allows you to "displace" the selected set of elements. Click and drag the red arrow away from the house. Release the mouse button to place the wall. With the wall still selected, look in the Properties palette for the X Displacement value. Set this value to 25′-0″ (7.6 m).

3. Since the windows are hosted in the wall, they move with it. You can displace these elements farther from the wall. Hover your mouse over a window, and tap the Tab key until the window highlights. Select the window, then hold down the Ctrl key and click the other two windows so you have all three selected. Click the Displace Elements button again. In the Properties palette, set the X Displacement value for the windows to 20′-0″ (6 m).

4. Click any of the displaced windows, and from the ribbon, choose the Path tool. Hover your mouse over one of the corners of your displaced windows. Click to add a dashed line back to where the element originated; repeat for the other corners. If you accidentally add a path line you don't want, you can select it and click Delete on the keyboard.

5. Now you can apply graphic effects from the GDO, using steps from the previous exercises, to make a beautiful and informative presentation drawing. Your results may look like Figure 9.11.

This concludes Exercise 9.5. You can compare your results with the sample file c09-ex-09.5end.rvt, which is included with the files you downloaded.

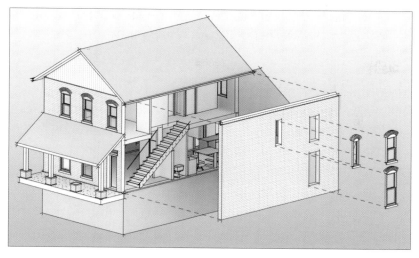

FIGURE 9.11   Finished exploded view

Rendering

The technique of computer rendering is a complex science that has been simplified and tailored for architects in Revit Architecture. There are many expert renderers in the architecture field, and we recommend this tutorial as an initiation to the activity of rendering.

Exercise 9.6: Render a View

To begin, open the file c09-ex-09.6start.rvt from the chapter's project files.

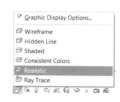

1. Open the view named 3D Cover Shot. Get a quick preview of the render appearance of the materials used in the scene by switching to the Realistic visual style using the View Control Bar.

REVISIT MATERIALS FOR RENDERING

If you're unsatisfied with any of the materials used, you can refer to Exercises 9.1 and 9.2 to change the material's Appearance properties (not the material's Graphics properties) to make the material more suitable for renderings.

2. Open the Rendering dialog by clicking the teapot icon in the View Control Bar or by clicking the Render button on the View tab. This dialog does not have an OK or Cancel button. It has a big Render button at the top. Click Render now.

3. Congratulations, you've just made a Revit rendering! Now let's refine the quality of this image. First, change the Quality setting to Medium, and click Render again. Then, change the Quality setting to High, and click Render again. Note that changing the Quality setting improves the rendering but lengthens the time it takes to finish the rendering. Change the Quality setting back to Medium for the rest of this exercise.

4. Click the Sun Settings button in the Lighting group. The dialog that opens allows you to specify the location of the sun during your rendering. Change the time from 10:15 a.m. to 1:15 p.m. (Figure 9.12), and click OK. Click Render again to see how this iteration changes the rendering.

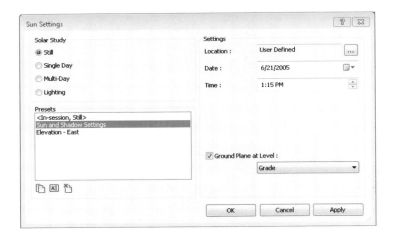

FIGURE 9.12 Sun Settings dialog box

5. Click the Adjust Exposure button. The very first slider control in this list allows you to lighten or darken the image. Adjust the Exposure Value parameter to 13. The other sliders are useful if you want to adjust the colors of your image without using photo-editing software. Click OK, and notice the changes made— without having to re-render!

6. Find the Resolution control in the Output Settings group. So far in this tutorial you've been rendering at screen resolution, so the rendering will finish faster. Click the Printer radio button. When switching to print output, you can specify the DPI. The higher the DPI, the longer the rendering takes. To have crisp edges in your finished rendering, set DPI to 150.

7. Once this rendering finishes (Figure 9.13), click the Save To Project button. This will prompt you to name the image. The image will be saved in your Project Browser under the Renderings branch. You can also click the Export button, which will save your rendering to your computer's hard drive as a BMP, JPG, PNG, or TIF file.

FIGURE 9.13 The finished rendering

You can continue to test different rendering quality settings and background options—even choosing a different rendering engine! Rendering is an iterative process; working from a generic low quality toward high DPI is a fast way to reach a finished presentation image. If you want to select a wall or change a material, you can click the Show The Model button at the bottom of the dialog to switch from a static rendered image back to the model view.

This concludes Exercise 9.6. You can compare your results with the sample file c09-ex-09.6end.rvt in the downloaded files for this chapter.

Exercise 9.7: Interactive Rendering

To begin, open the file c09-ex-09.7start.rvt from this chapter's project files.

1. In the Project Browser, find the 3D Views node, right-click the 3D Cover Shot view, and choose Duplicate View ➢ Duplicate. Rename the new view **Interactive Rendering**.

2. Change the visual style of the new view to Ray Trace using the View Control Bar. Ray Trace is a temporary, interactive rendering mode, where you can use the navigation wheel to pan, zoom, and orbit your model.

3. The rendering in Ray Trace mode will automatically start. At first, the image will be low quality and low resolution, but it will improve quickly the longer you let the view idle. When you begin navigating your model, the rendering will restart as soon as you stop navigating and let the view idle.

4. To change the rendering settings for Ray Trace mode, you need to access the GDO. You can type the keyboard shortcut **GD** or click the Visual Style menu on the View Control Bar. Make sure to change the Background setting to Sky. You can also brighten the scene using the Manual option of Photographic Exposure. Finally, you can change the sun location in Sun Settings; click OK. In the GDO dialog, click Apply to preview the changes, and then click OK when you're satisfied.

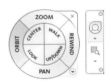

5. Click the navigation wheel icon, and use the Orbit command, the Walk command, and the Pan command to move the camera to various vantage points. The Look command is especially useful on interior scenes. When you find an interesting camera angle, you can stop there and let the Ray Trace rendering improve for a few seconds (Figure 9.14).

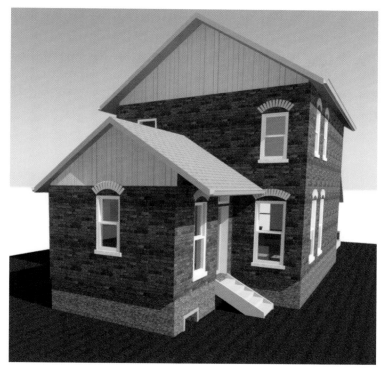

FIGURE 9.14   A Ray Trace rendering after 15 seconds

6. You can save the image to the Renderings node of your Project Browser. Just click the Save button from the ribbon. Name the rendering **Back of House**. Finally, click the close button on the ribbon to exit Ray Trace mode.

This concludes Exercise 9.7. You can compare your results with the sample file c09-ex-09.7end.rvt, which is included with the files you downloaded for this chapter.

Exercise 9.8: Cloud Rendering

Autodesk offers a very reliable and fast service that will render your Revit views in the cloud, thus allowing you to continue working while your renderings process somewhere else.

To begin, open the project file `c09-ex-09.8start.rvt`.

1. To use the Rendering cloud service, click the Render In Cloud button on the View tab. You will be asked to sign in using your Autodesk® 360 account. Create an account if you don't have one. After logging in, you should see a Render In Cloud dialog box with a few informational steps for cloud rendering; click Continue.

2. The Cloud Rendering Service provides an interface for you to select which views you'd like to have rendered. First, expand the 3D View drop-down menu, then check Interactive Rendering and 3D Cover Shot boxes—or choose to render all five of the 3D views.

3. There are other options below, but as long as you set Render Quality to Standard and Image Size to Medium (1 Mega Pixel), the renderings do not cost any cloud credits; they are free! See Figure 9.15.

FIGURE 9.15   Render In Cloud options

When the Render In Cloud Exposure property is set to Native, the Revit view's rendering setting for Exposure will be used instead of the default cloud-rendering Exposure setting.

4. Click the Start Rendering button at the bottom of the dialog. Revit will process for a few moments as your model is uploaded to the cloud service. Then you'll be able to continue working, while the renderings finish.

5. In a few minutes, you will get an email, or your communication center will notify you that your renderings are ready. Click the Render Gallery button on the ribbon and review your new rendered images.

6. You can get these renderings back into your Revit project by saving them from the cloud onto your desktop. Then duplicate the Back Of House view from the Renderings node of the Project Browser. Rename the copied view **Cloud Cover Shot**. Delete the old rendering, and import one of the new renderings as an image file to the blank drafting view.

This concludes Exercise 9.8. You can compare your results with the sample file c09-ex-09.8end.rvt, which is included with the files you downloaded earlier.

Now You Know

In this chapter, you learned how to create presentation graphics in elevation and 3D views and then render in three different ways. You applied various Graphic Display Options settings to achieve a sketchy design look. You also used the Displace Elements tool to create exploded axonometric views. Using these techniques, you can visualize your model in interesting, customizable ways: for presentations, for working on a detail, or for communicating construction methods.

CHAPTER 10

Worksharing

Understanding the multi-user Autodesk® Revit® Architecture workflow is essential to working with a project team simultaneously.

You may be familiar working with other team members in typical CAD software, where the drawing files are structured separately to support a one-user-per-file workflow.

Revit Architecture reinforces a more advanced approach. Because the Revit model is a database, each element inside it can be independently tracked. Revit will track each element and which user (if any) has ownership of that element. Because of this, Revit allows multiple users to work in the same model—saving separate drawings for floor plans, elevations, and sections is no longer required.

In this chapter, you'll learn to:

▶ **Understand worksharing options**

▶ **Enable worksharing**

▶ **Create a central model and a local file**

▶ **Create worksets**

▶ **Adjust workset visibility**

▶ **Use worksharing display modes**

▶ **Understand editing requests**

▶ **Review worksharing best practices**

Worksharing Options

There are three primary options for working with multiple team members in Revit Architecture:

Model-Based　This is the default out-of-the-box workflow for Revit Architecture. Multiple team members access a model saved on a standard file storage location.

Revit Server   This is a modified version of model-based worksharing where the project model (or models) is saved to or accessed by a dedicated instance (or instances) of Revit Server. One benefit of this approach is that multiple offices may be working with the same project model. Revit Server instances can be set up in each office, and each will cache a version of the model locally, subsequently speeding up save or open times.

For additional information on Revit Server, visit the web page at `http://knowledge.autodesk.com/` and search for "Revit Server."

Autodesk® A360 Collaboration for Revit®   This is similar to the Revit Server approach, where instead of a physical Revit Server, the project model (or models) is saved in the cloud via Autodesk A360. One benefit of this approach is that no configuration or setup is required (as there is with Revit Server) and different companies can easily work as a team with the same project model(s).

For additional information on Autodesk A360 Collaboration for Revit, visit the web page at

`www.autodesk.com/products/collaboration-for-revit/overview`

In this book, we will focus on the standard file-based worksharing, which is available out of the box to all Revit Architecture users. Generally speaking, most of the worksharing commands are the same regardless of which configuration your project team is using.

Configuring Worksharing

When you create a new project in Revit Architecture, the default state of the model will allow only one simultaneous user. For projects that require multiple simultaneous users, worksharing can be enabled to accommodate this collaboration. Revit identifies each user in the project by the username specified in the Application menu ➤ Options ➤ General ➤ Username. It is critical that each user working in the model have a unique username (Figure 10.1).

FIGURE 10.1 **Username setting in Options**

It is important to note that Revit initially sets your username to match your Windows login name. Should you edit the username, it will no longer match and your override will be maintained. Should you sign into Autodesk 360, Revit will automatically change your username to match your Autodesk ID.

In the following exercise, you will open an existing project, enable worksharing, and save it as the new central model.

Exercise 10.1: Enable Worksharing

To begin, go to the book's web page at www.sybex.com/go/revit2016essentials, download the files for Chapter 10, and open the file c10-ex-10.1start.rvt.

1. With the example file now open, navigate to the Collaborate tab and select the Worksets tool. The initial Worksharing dialog box (Figure 10.2) appears, outlining the worksets that project elements will be assigned to.

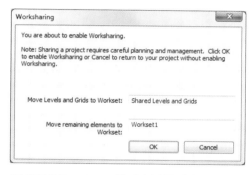

FIGURE 10.2   The initial Worksharing dialog box

> The first time you click the Worksets tool, it enables worksharing. Clicking the tool afterward allows you to access and modify worksets.

2. By default, datum objects are moved to a workset called Shared Levels And Grids. Project content that is not view specific (geometry and rooms) is all assigned to Workset1. Click OK to continue.

THE CENTRAL MODEL

In a real-world project, the next step would be to save your central model to a location so the entire project team could access it. Team members never work in the central model directly; instead, they create and work in local files. Local files communicate directly with the central model, so it needs to be in a location accessible to all.

3. The Worksets dialog box (Figure 10.3) opens next. Your username appears in the Owner field. Currently, you own everything in the project since you enabled worksharing. Click OK to continue.

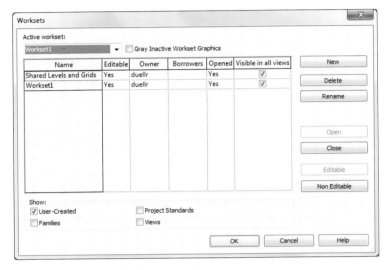

FIGURE 10.3 Worksets dialog box

> Before you save the model, think about where you need it to be located. When the central model is saved, it will include the file location as part of the project, so it can't be easily moved afterward.

4. Next, you want to save the project as the central model. Navigate to Application ≻ Save As ≻ Project. Before clicking Save, click the Options button. In the File Save Options dialog, you can confirm that this will be the central model. You will have other options, such as the maximum number of backups that Revit Architecture will maintain for the central model (Figure 10.4). Confirm that Make This A Central Model After Save is checked, and click OK to close the File Save Options dialog.

FIGURE 10.4 File Save Options dialog

5. In the Save As dialog, enter the filename **c10-ex-10.2start.rvt**. You will use this central model for the start of the next exercise. Click Save to create your central model (Figure 10.5).

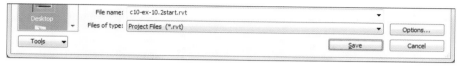

FIGURE 10.5 Save the central model

6. After the save completes, from the Collaborate tab click the Relinquish All Mine tool. This will release ownership of all model elements and is an important step to allow other users to work with the model.

Relinquish All Mine

7. Close the central model. You should not be prompted to save or relinquish any elements because you have already done so in the previous step.

In the following exercise you will create a local file using the newly saved central model from Exercise 10.1.

Exercise 10.2: Create a Local File and Worksets

To begin, ensure that Exercise 10.1 has been completed. You will utilize the central model you previously saved to create your local file. This is important because in order to create a local file, you must not have changed the central model location (since the initial save includes the model location).

1. Click Open in the Application menu and browse to your central model, c10-ex-10.2start.rvt.

2. Select the model but don't double-click or click Open just yet.

3. Ensure that the Create New Local option is checked, as shown in Figure 10.6.

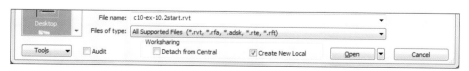

FIGURE 10.6 Creating the local file

Selecting this option will not open the central model directly but instead will create a local file (Figure 10.6).

By default, your local file is saved in your Documents folder with a suffix based on your Revit username. In this author's case, the username is duellr. So, the local file is saved in the Documents folder as c10-ex-10.2start_duellr.rvt.

4. Now click Open to create a local file that communicates directly with the central model. This is the same process you would use when working on real-world projects.

   Next, you'll create several worksets that can be used to organize your model elements.

5. Open the Worksets dialog box from the Collaborate tab ➤ Worksets.

6. Click New, and then create three additional worksets, called **Core**, **Exterior**, and **Interior** (Figure 10.7).

   Keep in mind that worksets are not layers and little granularity is required. Generally, worksets should be used as collections of objects for both organization and visibility control.

7. Click OK to close the dialog.

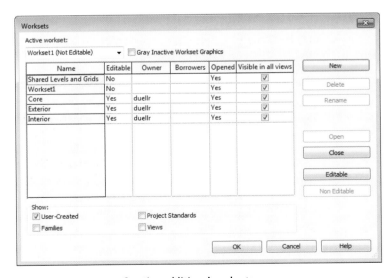

FIGURE 10.7 Creating additional worksets

8. Open the Visibility/Graphic Overrides dialog box for the view (type the keyboard shortcut **VG**).

Notice that there is now an additional Worksets tab that didn't exist before worksharing was enabled. This tab allows you to turn off the visibility of elements based on their workset assignment. When you've finished examining this tab, close the local file before starting the next exercise. You can specify to not save the project and relinquish all elements and worksets when prompted.

WORKSET VISIBILITY

Worksets can be used as an additional method to control the visibility of elements in a view. The default setting for workset visibility is Use Global Setting (Visible) under the view's Visibility/Graphic Overrides ➤ Worksets tab. On a view-by-view basis, you can override the Visibility setting should you need to show or hide elements on individual worksets.

In the following exercise, you will assign model elements to worksets and adjust the workset visibility settings of the view.

Exercise 10.3: Assign Elements to Worksets and Control Visibility

To begin, make sure that you've downloaded the file c10-ex-10.3start.rvt, but don't open it just yet.

1. From the Revit Application menu, click Open, and then browse to c10-ex-10.3start.rvt and select the file. Check Detach From Central and click Open. This will allow you to open an existing central model to resave it in a new location.

   Worksharing
   ☑ Detach from Central

2. When the Detach Model From Central dialog displays, choose Detach And Preserve Worksets. This will preserve all worksets in the model. After the model opens, click the Save button and save as c10-ex-10.3start.rvt. If you're saving the file in the same location as the original model, when prompted that the workset file already exists, click Yes.

3. The model should open the Level 1 floor plan view. Open the Visibility/Graphic Overrides dialog box for the view (type the keyboard shortcut **VG**) and click the Worksets tab. Change the Visibility setting for the Core, Exterior, and Interior worksets to Hide (Figure 10.8). Click OK to close the dialog.

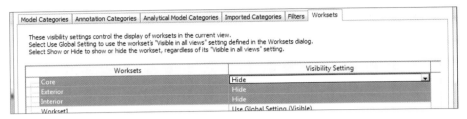

FIGURE 10.8 Workset Visibility setting

Filter

4. Draw a window around the elements as shown in Figure 10.9. While the elements are selected, click the Filter tool from the Selection contextual panel. Uncheck Room Tags and click OK to close the Filter dialog (Figure 10.9).

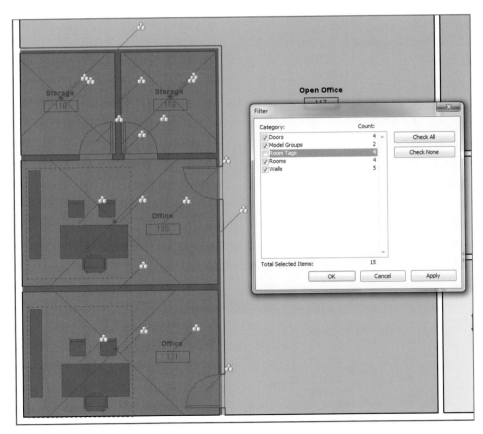

FIGURE 10.9 Element selection and filter

5. From the Properties palette, locate the Workset parameter. This indicates the element's workset assignment. With the multiple elements still selected, change this value from Workset1 to **Core**. Notice that the elements are no longer visible, since in step 3 you set this workset to be hidden.

6. Next, you will assign some interior elements to the Interior workset. Draw a selection window from the lower right to the upper left inside the exterior walls. Windowing from this direction will include every element you cross or include within the window you draw. (If you windowed from left to right, it would select *only* the elements fully contained within the selection box (Figure 10.10).

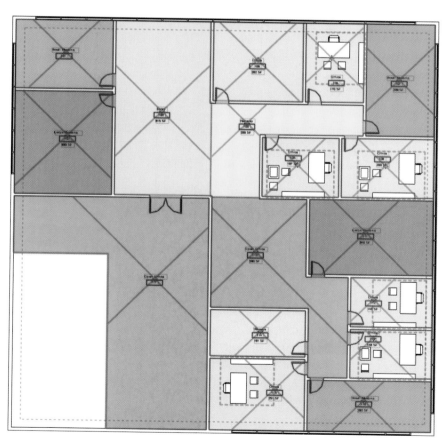

FIGURE 10.10 Selecting and assigning the Interior workset

7. With the multiple elements still selected, use the Filter tool again to uncheck Room Tags and <Room Separation>. Change the Workset value from Workset1 to **Interior.**

8. For the final selection set, select everything remaining in the view, and use the Filter tool. Click Check None; then check only Walls and click OK. In the Properties palette, change the workset from Workset1 to **Exterior.**

9. By this step the only items visible are two room separation lines. Select them and assign them to the Interior workset. Now no geometry should be visible in the Level 1 view. Open the Visibility/Graphic Overrides dialog for the view, and reset the visibility settings back to Use Global Setting (Visible), as shown in Figure 10.11. Click OK to return to the view, and all elements should once again be visible.

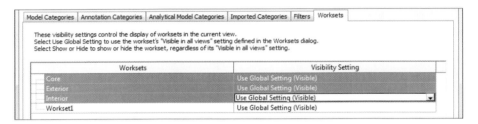

FIGURE 10.11 Resetting the Visibility settings

At this point you can close this model and save your changes when prompted. The next section elaborates on the options available when working in local files and interacting with the central model (such as saving your changes).

Saving to the Central Model

When working in your local file there are several options available for saving your changes back to or interacting with the central model. The following worksharing-specific options are available on the Synchronize panel of the Collaborate tab (Synchronize And Modify Settings and Synchronize Now are available in the Synchronize With Central flyout):

Synchronize Now   This option is probably used more frequently than the other options. Consider creating a keyboard shortcut so you don't have to return to the Collaborate tab as you work when you want to save to the central model.

Synchronize Now saves your local copy and syncs it with the central model as well as updates your file with any changes from the central model. Any borrowed elements are also relinquished by default. But if you have an entire workset checked out, it's not checked back in. It will still be editable by you after the save completes.

Synchronize And Modify Settings　　Synchronize And Modify Settings provides more specific control when saving the central model with Synchronize Now. The dialog box shown in Figure 10.12 displays the central model location and gives you options to relinquish worksets, compact the central model, and save your local file (after the sync with the central model is complete).

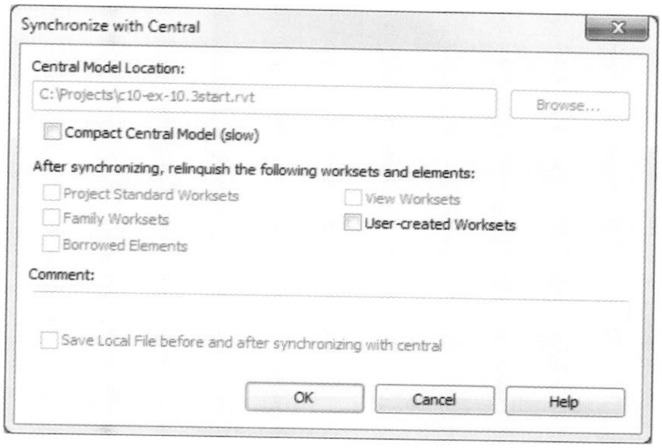

FIGURE 10.12　**Synchronize And Modify Settings**

Reload Latest　　The Reload Latest option lets you reload the latest version of the central model in your local project. However, it doesn't publish any of your work in the central model.

Relinquish All Mine　　Relinquish All Mine allows you to check in elements that you may have borrowed but did not change. If you've made changes, you have to either sync them with the central model or discard the changes without saving. You cannot relinquish elements in a file that has been modified.

If you select this option, Revit Architecture will ask you what to do with the elements you've borrowed or worksets you have enabled (Figure 10.13). If you relinquish the elements and worksets, other people will be able to modify them in their local files. If you keep ownership, the changes you've made will be lost, but you'll still have the elements and worksets enabled.

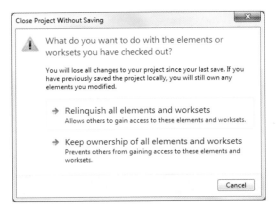

FIGURE 10.13   Relinquishing elements and worksets

When you have no elements or worksets enabled in a project, you can confirm this by opening the Worksets dialog box, shown in Figure 10.14.

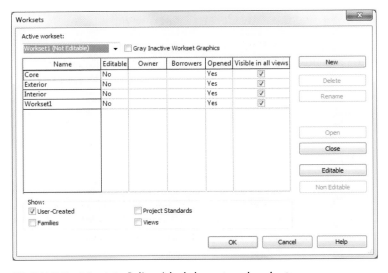

FIGURE 10.14   Relinquished elements and worksets

In the following exercise, you will utilize some of the previously outlined tools by simulating two users working with the same central model. You will work by adding elements and saving changes as one user and then switching to and adding elements as another user. One user can save their changes, and then another user can reload those changes into their model.

Exercise 10.4: Two-User Workflow

To begin, make sure that you've downloaded the file c10-ex-10.4start.rvt, but don't open it just yet.

1. With no project open, navigate to the Application menu ➤ Options ➤ General ➤ Username. Enter **UserA** as your username and click OK to close Options.

2. Open c10-ex-10.4start.rvt, navigate to the Collaborate tab, and select the Worksets tool. Click OK to dismiss the initial worksharing dialog and click OK to close the Worksets dialog.

3. Save the project. Because it is the first time worksharing has been enabled, Revit will ask you to confirm that you want to save this as the central model. Click Yes to save the central model.

4. Now you will save a local model to work in. You can select the Create New Local check box or choose Save As (while you have the central model open) to save a local file. Navigate to the Application menu, choose Save As, and name this local file **UserA.rvt**.

5. Close the local file and specify to relinquish elements and worksets when prompted. Again, with no project open, navigate to the Application menu ➤ Options ➤ General ➤ Username. Enter **UserB** as your username and click OK to close Options.

6. Select c10-ex-10.4start.rvt but don't open it just yet. Uncheck Create New Local first and then click Open to open the central model. Once again, navigate to the Application menu ➤ Save As option, and this time name this local file **UserB.rvt**.

   At this point you have created two local files: the first associated with UserA and the second associated with UserB. You can use this approach to simulate two users working with the same central model.

7. From the Level 1 floor plan view, notice the area of the floor plan to the right noted with UserB model text. Draw some walls, doors, and furniture inside this area of the floor plan.

8. When you're finished, you'll want to save your changes back to the central model so other users will be able to load the changes you made. Click the Synchronize Now tool to save your changes back to the central model. When the save completes, close the

UserB.rvt local file. If prompted, specify to relinquish elements and worksets (Figure 10.15).

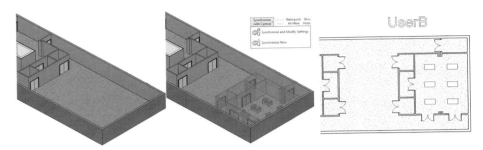

FIGURE 10.15   UserB local file changes

9. Again with no project open, navigate to the Application menu ➤ Options ➤ General ➤ Username. Enter **UserA** as your username and click OK to close the Options dialog. You are now working as the other user.

10. Open the UserA.rvt local file. Note that you do not see the most recent changes UserB added to the model because you have not used Reload Latest yet.

11. From the Level 1 floor plan view, notice the area of the plan to the left noted with UserA model text. Draw some walls and doors and place furniture inside this area of the floor plan.

12. When you're finished, you will save your changes to the central model and also update your local file with changes other users have saved to the central model. Click the Synchronize Now tool, which will perform both of these operations automatically (Figure 10.16).

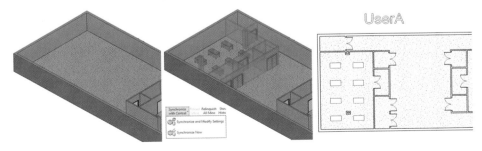

FIGURE 10.16   UserA local file changes

13. Revit saves your changes to the central model and updates your local file with the changes UserB made. This type of on-demand saving and

loading allows the project team to plan when users will interact with the central model, which greatly helps with performance. UserA now has the latest version of changes that have been published to the central model (Figure 10.17).

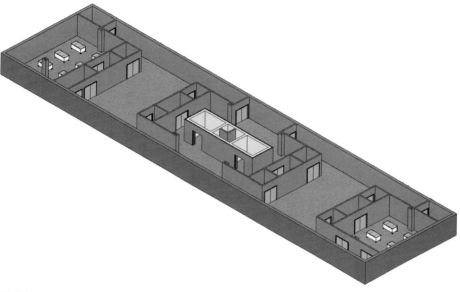

FIGURE 10.17 Latest version of the central model

In the following exercise, you will close and open worksets in an existing model to globally update visibility.

Exercise 10.5: Open and Close Worksets

To begin, make sure you've downloaded the file c10-ex-10.5start.rvt, but don't open it just yet.

OPEN OR CLOSE WORKSETS

In addition to setting the workset per-view visibility options, you can open or close a workset for an entire project. Doing so will globally turn on or off the visibility of everything on that workset for all project views regardless of the Workset Visibility setting for the view in which you're working. This is a great way to improve performance or turn off the display for entire portions of the model.

1. From the Revit Application menu, browse to `c10-ex-10.5start.rvt` and select the file. Check Detach From Central and click Open. This will allow you to open an existing central model to resave it in a new location.

2. When the Detach Model From Central dialog appears, choose Detach And Preserve Worksets. This will preserve all worksets in the model. After the model opens, click the Save button and save as `c10-ex-10.5start.rvt`. If you're saving in the same location as the original model, when prompted with The Workset File Already Exists, click Yes.

3. Open the Worksets dialog box under Collaborate ➤ Worksets (or click the Worksets button on the status bar). Notice that currently all worksets are set to Opened (the Opened column will read Yes or No accordingly).

4. In this example model there are five worksets: Doors-Windows, Exterior Walls, Furniture, Interior Walls, and Rooms. Select the Furniture and Rooms worksets and click the Close button (Figure 10.18). You can select multiple worksets at the same time by holding down the Ctrl key while selecting.

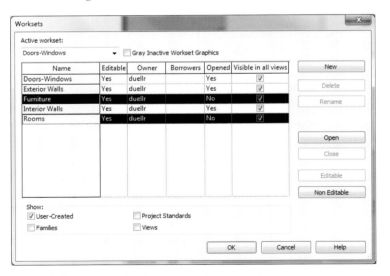

F I G U R E   1 0 . 1 8   Closing worksets in the model

5. Click OK to close the Worksets dialog. Notice in the Level 1 view that the rooms and furniture are no longer visible. Unlike with the Visibility/Graphic Overrides Worksets Visibility setting, closing or opening a workset will affect all views.

6. Open the {3D} view to confirm that all views are affected and note that the furniture is not visible. Open the Worksets dialog and additionally close the Interior Walls and Doors-Windows worksets. Click OK to return to the 3D view (Figure 10.19).

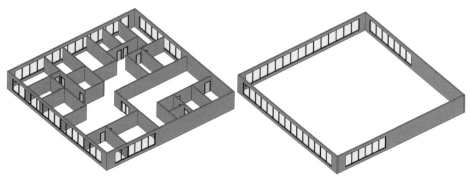

FIGURE 10.19 Worksets open and closed

7. At any point you can reopen worksets to make the elements on those worksets visible again. Open the Worksets dialog and select the Furniture and Interior Walls worksets. Click Open, and then click OK to return to the 3D view. Note that the furniture is visible again in this and any additional project views where it was previously. You can save and close this model when finished.

Worksharing Display Modes

Worksharing display modes are a great way to visually understand the current worksharing status of your project. For this example, all three authors of this book are accessing the central model saved on the server (from the three local files) at the same time. Furthermore, all of us have borrowed elements in the central file.

In Figure 10.20, the Worksets dialog box shows that no worksets are editable but that the user duellr has borrowed elements.

Name	Editable	Owner	Borrowers	Opened	Visible in all views
Core	No			Yes	✓
Exterior	No			Yes	✓
Interior	No		duellr	Yes	✓
Shared Levels and Grids	No			Yes	✓
Workset1	No		duellr	Yes	✓

FIGURE 10.20 Showing borrowed elements in the Worksets dialog box

Now let's look at the Worksharing Display Settings options available for worksharing display in a project: Checkout Status, Owners, Model Updates, and Worksets. If you would like to follow along, you can reopen your model from the previous exercise. These settings are based on the particular parameters in your project (number of worksets, active users, and so forth). To activate any of these settings, click on the bottom of the view window (View Control Bar), and choose one of the menu items from the list (Figure 10.21).

FIGURE 10.21   Worksharing Display Settings options

Activating any of the worksharing display modes on the menu toggles your visibility settings and applies an orange border to the view you're in, alerting you that you've activated the mode. To turn it back off, choose the Worksharing Display Off option from the same menu.

Let's set some of these modes active one at a time and view the results. Click the Worksharing Display button and choose Worksharing Display Settings. Start with the Checkout Status tab; the checkout status helps you distinguish between elements that are owned by you, others, or no one (Figure 10.22).

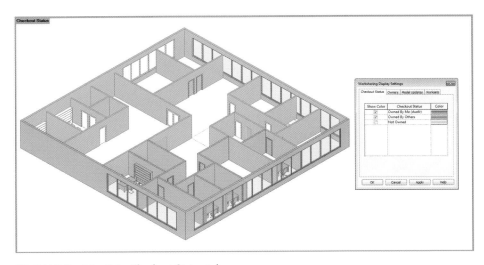

FIGURE 10.22   Checkout Status tab

Selecting the Owners display mode will show you exactly which elements belong to which users (Figure 10.23).

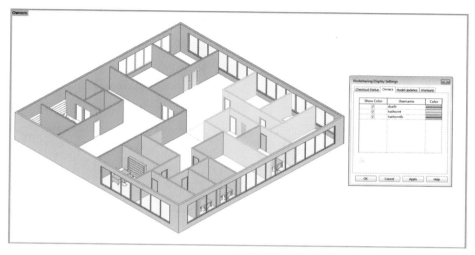

FIGURE 10.23   Owners tab

The Worksets tab helps you visualize elements based on the workset to which they're associated (Figure 10.24).

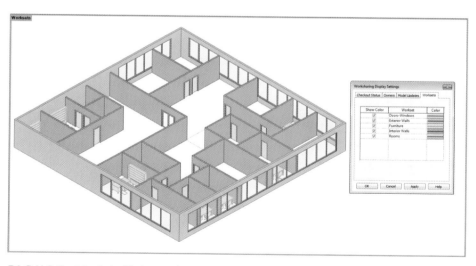

FIGURE 10.24   Worksets tab

Editing Requests

Eventually, while you're working on a project team, another user will own an element you need to modify. For you to modify that element, the other user will first need to relinquish it. Let's take UserA and UserB as a simple example for this scenario:

1. UserA attempts to modify a wall but receives an error dialog noting that UserB currently owns the element (Figure 10.25).

2. UserA clicks the Place Request button in the dialog so UserB will be notified (Figure 10.25).

FIGURE 10.25 Placing a request

3. While UserB is working in their local file, they receive a modal Editing Request Received dialog indicating that UserA has requested the wall element.

4. UserB clicks Grant, which will give editability to UserA for that wall element only (Figure 10.26).

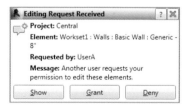

FIGURE 10.26 Granting a request

5. Last, UserA receives the confirmation dialog back that UserB has granted permission to edit the wall element (Figure 10.27).

In this example, no further action is required from UserA; UserA can start making modifications to the wall. The editing request serves as both a user notification system and an automated method to swap element ownership.

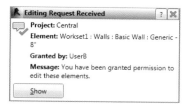

F I G U R E   1 0 . 2 7   Granted confirmation

Worksharing Best Practices

Now that you have a general understanding of how worksharing and worksets operate, take a moment to consider a few best practices.

Think of worksets as containers   Worksets aren't layers as in CAD. Think of them as containers for major systems in your building (interior, exterior, roof, core, and so on). You need to manage or be mindful only of objects that belong to user-created worksets, such as the following:

- ▶ Datum (levels and grids)
- ▶ Geometry (building elements that show up in multiple views)
- ▶ Rooms (the spaces that can be tagged)

Be mindful of the active workset   As you're creating datums, geometry, or rooms, be mindful of the active workset. And keep in mind that Revit Architecture automatically manages the worksets for everything else (views, families, and project standards), and these cannot be changed by the user.

Borrow elements on the fly   Don't check out worksets by making the entire workset editable. Instead, just borrow elements on the fly. This approach lets you avoid many conflicts that occur when one person needs to modify something you own (but don't really need) in the model. With the interconnected nature of buildings, you don't even need to deliberately make an element editable. All you have to do is modify an existing element and Revit Architecture will transparently borrow it for you. This works the same when adding new elements as well.

Associate linked files to their own workset   Associate any linked files to their own workset. Then you can open and close the worksets associated to those links. This strategy is much more predictable than loading and unloading links (which will have an effect on everyone working on the project). Opening or closing a workset affects only your local file.

Stay out of the central model   Stay out of the central model—don't move it, and don't rename it (unless you know what you're doing). Opening the central model restricts access by the files that are trying to connect to it. And if you break something in the central model, you'll break the connections that others have from their local file, which means they may end up losing their work (which in turn means your team will not like you).

Open and close worksets selectively   Selectively opening and closing worksets is a lot faster than opting to modify the visibility settings of multiple views or using hide/isolate on a view-by-view basis. If you're supposed to be working only on the core and internal areas of a multistory building, opening only the worksets associated to those areas will save a lot of computing power.

Now You Know

This chapter served as both an introduction and reference to multi-user collaboration in Revit Architecture. You enabled worksharing and saved a central model. Next, you created a local file, created and modified worksets, controlled element visibility using those worksets, and explored the options to save your work back to the central model. Moving forward, this chapter should also serve as a strong reference for more advanced collaboration topics such as worksharing display modes and editing requests. We concluded this chapter with some best practices for you to utilize on your real-world projects.

CHAPTER 11

Details and Annotations

So far, you have used Autodesk® Revit® Architecture software to create walls, doors, roofs, and floors; to define space; and to bring your architectural ideas into three-dimensional form. In each of these cases, the geometry is typically modeled based on a design intent, meaning that your goal hasn't been to model everything but rather to model enough to demonstrate what the building will look like. To this end, it becomes necessary to embellish parts of the model or specific views with detailed information to help clarify what you've drawn. This embellishment takes the shape of 2D detail elements in Revit Architecture that you will use to augment views and add extra information.

In this chapter, you will learn to:

▶ **Create a detail**

▶ **Enhance a detail with 2D elements**

▶ **Create a repeating detail component**

▶ **Annotate a detail**

▶ **Create a legend**

Creating Details

Even when you're creating details, Revit Architecture provides a variety of parametric tools that allow you to take advantage of working in *building information modeling (BIM)*. You can use these tools to create strictly 2D geometry or to augment details created from 3D plans, sections, or callouts. To become truly efficient at using Revit Architecture to create the drawings necessary to both design and document your project, you must become acquainted with these tools.

These view-based tools are located on the Detail panel of the Annotate tab (Figure 11.1). This small but very potent toolbox is what you will need to familiarize yourself with in order to create a majority of the 2D linework and components that will become the details in your project. To better understand how these tools are used, let's quickly step through some of them. You're going to use the Detail Line, Region, Component, and Detail Group tools because they will make up your most widely used toolkit for creating 2D details in Revit Architecture.

FIGURE 11.1 The Detail panel of the Annotate tab

Detail Line

The Detail Line tool is the first tool located on the Detail panel of the Annotate tab. This tool is the closest thing you'll find to traditional drafting in the Revit Architecture software. It lets you create view-specific linework using different lineweights and tones, draw different line shapes, and use many of the same manipulation commands you would find in a CAD program, such as offset, copy, move, and so on.

DETAIL LINES ARE VIEW SPECIFIC

Detail Lines appear only in the view in which they're drawn. They also have an arrangement to their placement, meaning you can layer them under or on top of each other or other 2D objects. This feature is especially important when you begin using regions, detail lines, and model content to create details.

Using the Detail Line tool is fairly easy. Selecting the tool changes your ribbon tab to look like Figure 11.2. This tab has several panels that allow you to add and manipulate linework.

FIGURE 11.2 The Detail Line toolset

This tab primarily contains three panels: Modify, Draw, and Line Style. You've seen the Modify panel before. It contains the host of tools you've used so far for walls, doors, and other elements. Here you can copy, offset, move, and perform other tasks. The Draw panel lets you create new content and define shapes, and the Line Style drop-down allows you to choose the line style you'd like to use.

Region

The next tool on the Detail panel of the Annotate tab is the Region tool. *Regions* are areas of any shape or size that you can fill with a pattern. This pattern (much like a hatch in AutoCAD) dynamically resizes with the region boundary. Regions layer just like detail lines do and can be placed on top of, or behind, other 2D linework and components. Regions also have opacity and can be completely opaque (covering what they are placed on) or transparent (letting elements show through).

There are two types of regions: filled regions and masking regions.

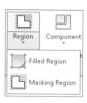

Filled Regions   *Filled regions* allow you to choose from a variety of hatch patterns to fill the region. They are commonly used in details to show things such as rigid insulation, concrete, plywood, and other material types defined by a specific pattern.

Certification
Objective

Masking Regions   *Masking regions*, on the other hand, come in only one flavor. They are white boxes with or without discernible border lines. Masking regions are typically used to hide, or *mask*, from a view certain content that you don't want shown or printed.

Component

The Component drop-down menu lets you insert a wide array of component types into your model. These are 2D detail components, or collections of detail components in the case of a repeating detail. Detail components are schedulable, taggable, keynotable 2D families that allow an additional level of standardization in your model.

Detail components are 2D families that can be made into parametric content. In other words, a full range of shapes can be available in a single detail component. Because they are families, they can also be stored in your office library and shared easily across projects.

To add a detail component to your drawing, follow these steps:

1. Select Detail Component from the Component drop-down menu list located on the Annotate tab.

2. Use the Type Selector to choose from detail components that are already inserted into the model.

If you don't see a detail component you want to insert in the Type Selector, try this:

1. Click the Load Family button on the Modify | Place Detail Component tab.

2. Insert a detail component from the default library or your office library.

> Some examples of where you'd use detail components are blocking, steel shapes, and brick coursing in section—just about any replicated 2D element that comes in a standardized shape.

Arranging Elements in the View

Knowing how to change arrangement is an important part of detailing so you don't have to draw everything in exact sequence. Arrangement allows you to change the position of an element, such as a line or a detail component, relative to another element. Much as with layers in Adobe Photoshop or arrangement in Microsoft PowerPoint, Revit Architecture allows you to place some elements visually in front of or behind others. Once an element or group of elements is selected and the Modify menu appears, on the far right you'll see the Arrange panel.

From here, you can choose among four options of arrangement:

▶ Bring To Front

▶ Bring Forward

▶ Send To Back

▶ Send Backward

Bring Forward and Send Backward are available selections using the drop-down arrows next to Bring To Front and Send To Back, respectively. Using these tools will help you get your layers in the proper order.

Repeating Detail Component

Repeating elements are common in architectural projects. Masonry, metal decking, and wall studs are some common elements that repeat at a regular interval. The Revit Architecture tool you use to create and manage these types of elements is called Repeating Detail Component, and it's located in the Component drop-down menu on the Detail panel under the Annotate tab.

This tool lets you place a detail component in a linear configuration in which the detail component repeats at a set interval; you draw a line that then becomes your repeating component. The default Revit Architecture repeating detail is common brick repeating in section. Creating elements like this not only lets you later tag and keynote the materials but also allows you some ease of flexibility over arraying these elements manually.

Before you create a repeating detail component, let's examine one such component's properties. Select Repeating Detail Component and choose Edit Type from the Properties palette to open the Type Properties dialog box shown in Figure 11.3.

Certification Objective

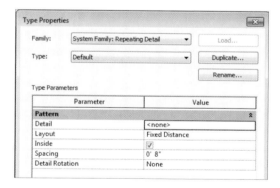

FIGURE 11.3 Type Properties dialog box for a repeating detail

Here's a brief description of what each of these settings does:

Detail   This setting lets you select the detail component to be repeated.

Layout   This option offers four modes:

>   **Fixed Distance**   This represents the path drawn between the start and end points when the repeating detail is the length at which your component repeats at a distance of the value set for Spacing.

Fixed Number   This mode sets the number of times a component repeats itself in the space between the start and end points (the length of the path).

Fill Available Space   Regardless of the value you choose for Spacing, the detail component is repeated on the path using its actual width as the Spacing value.

Maximum Spacing   The detail component is repeated using the set spacing, and the number of repeated components is set so that only complete components are drawn. Revit Architecture creates as many copies of the component as will fit on the path.

Inside   This option adjusts the start point and end point of the detail components that make up the repeating detail. Deselecting this option puts only full components between start and end points rather than partial components. As an example, if you have a run of brick, selecting the Inside check box will make a partial brick at the end of the run. If you want to see only full bricks (none that would be cut), deselect the option.

Spacing   This option is active only when Fixed Distance or Maximum Spacing is selected as the method of repetition. It represents the distance at which you want the repeating detail component to repeat. It doesn't have to be the actual width of the detail component.

Detail Rotation   This option allows you to rotate the detail component in the repeating detail.

Insulation

The best way to think of the Insulation tool is as a premade repeating detail. You'll find this tool on the Detail panel of the Annotate tab.

Selecting this tool allows you to draw a line of batt insulation, much like a repeating detail. You can modify the width of the inserted insulation from the Options Bar (Figure 11.4). The insulation is inserted using the centerline of the line of batt, and you can shorten, lengthen, or modify the width either before or after inserting it into your view.

F I G U R E 11.4 Modifying the insulation width in the Options Bar

Detail Groups

Detail groups are similar to blocks in AutoCAD and are a quick alternative to creating detail component families. Like modeled groups, these are a collection of graphics that contain detail lines, detail components, or 2D elements. While you will probably want to use a detail component to create something like blocking, if you plan to have the same blocking and flashing conditions in multiple locations, you can then group the flashing and blocking together and quickly replicate these pieces in other details. Like blocks in AutoCAD, manipulating one of the detail groups changes all of them consistently throughout the model.

There are two ways to make a detail group. Probably the most common is to create the detail elements you'd like to group and then select all of them. When you do, the Modify tab appears:

1. Click the Create Group button under the Create panel to make the group.

2. When you're prompted for a group name, name the group something clear like **Window Head Flashing** or **Office Layout 1** rather than accepting the default name Revit Architecture wants to give it (Group 1, Group 2, and so on).

The other way to create a detail group is as follows:

1. Go to the Annotate tab's Detail Group drop-down menu and click the Create Group button. You are prompted for the type of group (Model or Detail) as well as a group name.

   Model   Model groups contain model elements (elements that are visible in more than one view). Choose Model if you want elements to be visible in more than one view or if they are 3D geometry.

   Detail   Detail groups contain 2D detail elements and are visible only within the view you're in (you can copy or use them in other views). Choose Detail if you're creating a group containing detail lines or other annotations and 2D elements.

   When you select the elements, you're taken into Edit Group mode. A yellow transparency is overlaid on top of the view, and elements in the view appear gray.

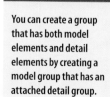

You can create a group that has both model elements and detail elements by creating a model group that has an attached detail group.

2. To add elements to the group, click Add and then choose your selected items (Figure 11.5).

FIGURE 11.5 The Edit Group panel

You can also remove unwanted elements.

3. When you've finished, click the green Finish check mark and your group will be complete.

You can place any group you've already made using the Place Detail Group button on the Annotate tab's Detail Group drop-down menu. Groups insert like families, and you can choose the group you'd like to insert from the Type Selector on the Properties palette.

Linework

Although not part of the Annotate tab, the Linework tool is an important feature in creating good lineweights for your details. Revit Architecture does a lot to help manage your views and lineweights automatically, but it doesn't cover all the requirements all the time. Sometimes the default Revit Architecture lines are heavier or thinner than you desire for your details. This is where the Linework tool comes in handy; it allows you to modify existing lines in a view-specific context.

To use the Linework tool, follow these steps:

1. Go to the Modify tab's View panel and click the Linework button, or use the keyboard shortcut **LW**.
   You will see the familiar Line Style Type Selector panel on the right of the tab.

2. Select a line style from the list.

3. Simply choose the style you want a particular line to look like; then select that line in the view.

The lines you pick can be almost anything: cut lines of model elements, families, components, and so on. Selecting the line or boundary of an element changes the line style from whatever it was to whatever you have chosen from the Type Selector. Figure 11.6 shows a before and after of the sill detail with the linework touched up.

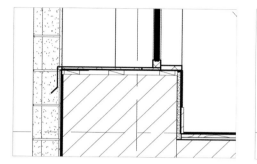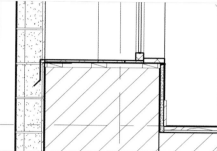

FIGURE 11.6 Before and after the Linework tool

You can also choose to visually remove lines using this tool. Doing so leaves the line in the view or as a part of the 3D element but makes it effectively invisible for the sake of the view. Do this by selecting the <Invisible Lines> line type. This is a good alternative to covering unwanted linework with a masking region.

You can return a line to its default lineweight by using the <By Category> line type.

Exercise 11.1: Enhance a Detail with Regions

Enhancing your model with 2D linework and components is an efficient way to add more information to specific views without modeling everything. It is not necessary to model flashing, blocking, or other elements shown only in large-scale format detail drawings. Using detail lines, regions, and detail components, you can enhance your views to show additional design intent.

From the book's web page (www.sybex.com/go/revit2016essentials), download the c11-ex11.1start.rvt file and open the view Exterior Detl, Typ, which you'll find in the Sections (Building Section) node of the Project Browser. In the following exercise, you will create a detail and enhance the detail using filled and masking regions to accurately represent built conditions within a typical window detail:

1. Use the Callout tool on the View tab to create a new detail of the second-floor window sill: create a new callout, and name it **Exterior Window Sill, Typ**. The starting view looks like Figure 11.7.

Callout

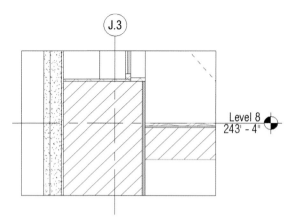

FIGURE 11.7 The window sill detail before embellishment

2. Click the Filled Region button under the Region drop-down menu on the Annotate tab. Choose <Invisible Lines> from the Line Style drop-down on the Modify tab, and create a box bounding the floor slab (Figure 11.8).

FIGURE 11.8 Modifying the boundary of the filled region

3. Select the top and bottom edges of the bounding box, which should align with the cut planes of the floor, and use the Line Style drop-down to change the lineweight to Medium Lines.

4. Click the Edit Type button in the Properties palette to open the Type Properties dialog box. Because there is no defined region type that is identical to existing materials, you need to make one. Click Duplicate, name the new region type **00 Existing**, and click OK.

5. Check to make sure these settings are in the Properties palette:

> Fill Pattern: Set this field to Drafting, and choose ANSI31.
>
> Background: Set this to Opaque.
>
> Line Weight: Set this to 1.
>
> Color: Set this to Black.
>
> Click OK when you've finished.

6. Click the green check mark ✔ to complete the sketch. Your finished filled region appears highlighted and slightly transparent.

7. Click off the region to see the finished product. The invisible line on the left doesn't cover the cut of the wall, and a thinner line remains.

8. Highlight the filled region again and use the Nudge tool (the arrow keys on the keyboard) to move the region over slightly to cover the remainder of the finished wall. The finished region looks like Figure 11.9.

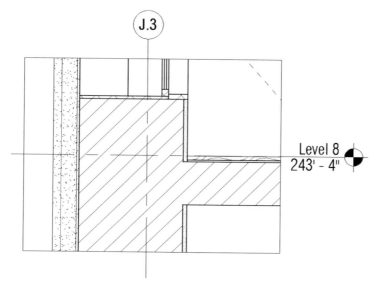

FIGURE 11.9 The finished filled region

9. Choose the Masking Region tool from the Region drop-down menu on the Annotate tab.

10. With Line Style set to Thin Lines, create a box 1″ (25 mm) deep under the window sill, creating a blank space where you will later add some other 2D components, such as blocking. (Figure 11.10.)

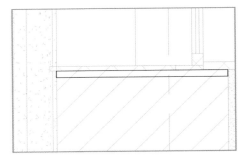

FIGURE 11.10 Adding a masking region

11. Click the green check mark to complete the sketch. The finished sill looks like Figure 11.11.

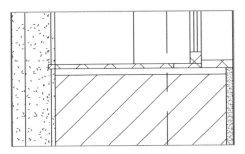

FIGURE 11.11 The completed sketch

Upon completion, your detail should resemble the c11-ex11.1end.rvt file, available in the download for this chapter. Save this detail; you'll return to it again in the next exercise.

Exercise 11.2: Add Detail Components and Detail Lines

The next step is to add some detail components for blocking and trim. From the Chapter 11 downloadable files, open the c11-ex11.2start.rvt file, or continue with your opened file if you've completed the previous exercise. Choose Application ➤ New ➤ Family, and choose Detail Item.rft. When you're creating detail components, as with any other family, you'll start with two reference planes crossing in the center of the family. This crossing point is the default insertion point of the family.

The first family, Blocking, is straightforward. You'll use Masking Region instead of the Lines tool so you have a clean, white box that you can use to layer over and mask other elements you might not want to see.

1. Select the Masking Region tool on the Create tab, and draw a box with the lower-left corner at the origin. The box should be 1″ (25 mm) high and 3″ (75 mm) wide.

2. Click the green check mark to complete the region.

3. On the Create tab, click the Line tool, and draw a line diagonally across the box to denote blocking. The family should look like Figure 11.12.

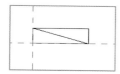

FIGURE 11.12
Creating a blocking detail component

4. Choose Application ➤ Save As ➤ Family, and name the family **06 Blocking**. Place it in a folder with the model.

5. Click the Load Into Project button at the far right on the ribbon to add the family to the model.

   If you have more than one project open, make sure you choose either your continued exercise file or the example file for this exercise, c11-ex11.2start.rvt.

6. To add the blocking detail component to your view, return to the Exterior Window Sill, Typ. detail, and select Detail Component from the Component drop-down menu on the Annotate tab.

The component you insert will become the default component; you can see the name 06 Blocking in the Type Selector.

7. Insert pieces of blocking at the left, right, and center of the sill (Figure 11.13).

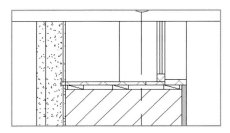

FIGURE 11.13 Inserting and placing the blocking

8. Create a new detail item using steps 1–3 for another detail component representing the baseboard (do not create a diagonal line to denote blocking), and use the dimensions 1″ (25 mm) wide by 6″ (150 mm) high.

9. Name the new family **06 Baseboard**.

10. Save the baseboard, and click Load Into Project, selecting the accurate project file if more than one file is open.

11. Navigate to the view Exterior Window Sill, Typ. if it's not already open, and place the baseboard at the corner of the gypsum board and finished floor. The detail looks like Figure 11.14.

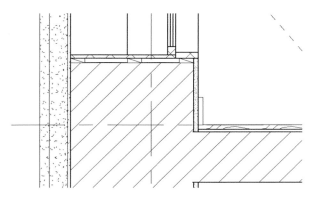

FIGURE 11.14 The sill detail with base

Sometimes, it is easier and more effective to simply use detail lines to create the necessary features in a detail. For these purposes, you want to create some flashing at the window sill.

12. Choose the Detail Line tool, and select Medium Lines from the Line Style drop-down menu.

Families offer more functionality and versatility down the line for faster documentation; you can make them taggable objects by using the Keynote tool.

13. Using the Detail Line tool, draw in some flashing for the window sill (Figure 11.15).

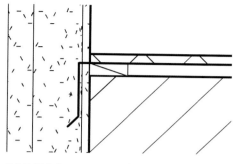

FIGURE 11.15 Adding flashing using detail lines

Compare your finished detail with the c11-ex11.2end.rvt file, available in the download from the book's web page. You'll return to this detail again for the next exercise.

Exercise 11.3: Create a Repeating Detail Component

In the following exercise, you will create a custom repeating detail for the sill detail you've been working on. The exterior of the building is terracotta brick and will have visible joint work every 8″ (200 mm). From the Chapter 11 downloadable files, open the c11-ex11.3start.rvt file, or continue with your opened file if you've completed the previous exercise. Follow these steps:

1. Select a new Detail Component family again. Choose Application ➤ New ➤ Family, and choose Detail Item.rft from the list.

2. Create a masonry joint 6″ (150 mm) long and 3/8″ (10 mm) high with a strike on one of the short ends (Figure 11.16) using a filled region with no hatch pattern.

3. Save the family as **04 Grout**, and load it into the project, selecting the correct open project file if more than one file is open.

FIGURE 11.16 The grout detail component

4. Click the Esc button to clear the active command. Back in the project file, in the Annotate tab's Detail panel, choose the Repeating Detail Component tool from the Component drop-down menu.

5. Choose Edit Type from the Properties palette, and then click the Duplicate button in the Type Properties dialog.

6. Name the new type **04 Terracotta Grout**, and click OK.

7. Change the properties of this new type to reflect the detail component you just created and its spacing. Change only the following fields:

> Detail: Set this field to 04 Grout, the family you just created.

> Spacing: Set this value to 8″ (**200** mm).

8. The Type Properties dialog box looks like Figure 11.17. Click OK when you've finished.

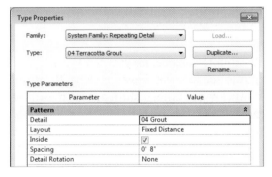

F I G U R E   1 1 . 1 7   **The repeating detail's type properties**

9. With the Repeating Detail command still active, draw a line all the way up the left edge of the exterior wall, starting at the base of the view, placing the new joint over the terracotta exterior.

10. Place one of the joints directly below the window sill by using the Nudge tool to shift the detail into the right location. This appears on top of the flashing you drew earlier, so you'll want to move the flashing to the front.

11. Select the flashing detail line, and choose Bring To Front from the Arrange panel. The completed detail looks like Figure 11.18.

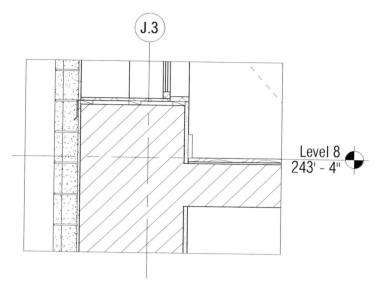

FIGURE 11.18 The finished window sill detail

Although this detail needs annotations before you can think about placing it onto a sheet, you can begin to see how you have used the 3D geometry of the model and were able to quickly add embellishment to it in order to create a working project detail. Compare your finished detail with the c11-ex11.3end .rvt file, available in the download from the book's web page. You'll return to this detail again for the next exercise.

Annotating Your Details

Notes are a critical part of communicating design and construction intent to owners and builders. No drawing set is complete without descriptions of materials and notes about the design. Now that you've created a detail, you need to add the final touches of annotations to communicate size, location, and materiality. The tools you will use for annotations are found on the same Annotate tab that you used to create details. These are the Dimension, Text, and Tag panels shown in Figure 11.19.

Certification
Objective

FIGURE 11.19 The Revit Architecture annotation tools

Dimensions

The Dimension panel is the first panel located on the Annotate tab. Revit Architecture provides you with a variety of options for dimensioning the distance between two objects, including Aligned, Linear, Angular, Radial, Diameter, and Arc Length dimensioning tools. The dimension tool you will use the most often is Aligned 🖊, located on the left side of the Dimension panel shown in Figure 11.19. It can also be found on the Quick Access toolbar. Using the Aligned Dimension tool is quite simple. Click once on the first reference object to start the dimension string, and click again on the second reference object to finish the dimension.

Tags

The Tag All tool is a quick way to tag everything in a view of a certain category. For example, you can tag all the windows shown in a floor plan with a single click.

Tags are 2D view-specific elements that attach to modeled or detail elements to report information based on that element's type or instance properties. Any modeled or detail element can be tagged; however, tags are most commonly used to identify your basic building blocks—doors, windows, wall types, and rooms. You can add tags to your project by navigating to the Tag panel located on the Annotate tab. When you select the Tag By Category tool and then select an object in your model, Revit Architecture will automatically assign the correct tag type to the associated material. From there, you can enter the appropriate information within the tag object.

Text

A
Text

Not all elements in Revit Architecture have materiality to them, and sometimes tags are not the best way to convey information. In these cases, you can use text. The Text tool is located on the Text panel of the Annotate tab.

When you're using text in your model, it's important to remember that text is not linked to any element or material; it's 2D view-specific information. If you label something with text or use text to call out notes, the text doesn't dynamically update as elements change in the model.

Exercise 11.4: Add Dimensions to Your Detail

In your detail, you have added aspects to the window family to reflect some of the details needed for construction. Now, with much of the linework and elements in the view, you need to annotate and add dimensions. From the Chapter 11 downloadable files, open the c11-ex11.4start.rvt file, or continue with your opened file if you've completed the previous exercise.

1. Select the Aligned Dimension tool, and place a dimension string from the grid line to the centerline of the wall, as shown in Figure 11.20.

Dimensions are dynamic in Revit Architecture and are easy to relocate.

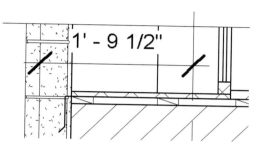

FIGURE 11.20 Adding a dimension string

2. Click Esc to clear the active command. Highlight the dimension string, and you see two sets of blue dots on either side. One set controls the length of the *witness line* (the line that extends from the actual element you dimensioned to the tick mark), and the other (on top of the tick mark) controls the witness line's location.

3. To place the dimension string in the accurate location, select the blue dot that controls the witness line location, and drag it to the exterior of the wall. The dimension automatically updates.

Certification Objective

4. Add another dimension string from the grid line to the back of the window jamb.

5. To relocate the text, grab the blue dot under the text and drag the text string to the right. Once the dimension text is outside the dimension string, Revit Architecture adds an arc associating the text to the dimension (Figure 11.21).

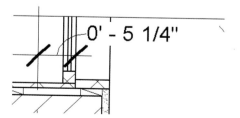

FIGURE 11.21 Modifying the text location

6. Add another dimension that locates the gypsum board relative to the grid line (Figure 11.22). By default, the exterior face of the gypsum board won't highlight to accept the dimension. With your mouse hovering over the right edge of the gypsum board, press the Tab key, and you can place the other side of the dimension string.

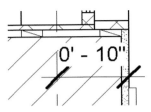

FIGURE 11.22 Dimensioning the wall location

7. To change the dimension text to eliminate the white masking region behind the text, highlight the dimension by left-clicking it, and select Edit Type from the Properties palette. The Type Properties dialog box for dimensions opens, as shown in Figure 11.23.

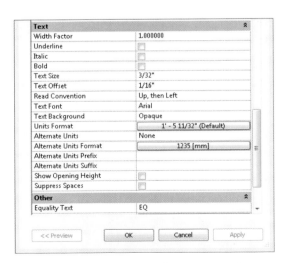

FIGURE 11.23 Dimension type properties

8. Scroll to the bottom to find the Opaque value next to the Text Background option. This controls that white box behind the dimension. Set it to Transparent, and click OK. The dimension now has a transparent background.

9. Add a dimension locating the window sill relative to the floor, as shown in Figure 11.24.

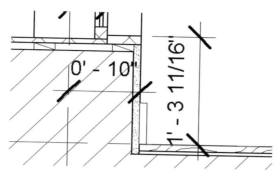

FIGURE 11.24 Dimensioning the window sill

10. To change the dimension string from the awkward length shown to a more reasonable value, you need to change the location of one of the two objects you've dimensioned. The floor probably isn't going to move, but you can reposition the window slightly. Select the window. The dimension string turns blue, and the numbers become very small (Figure 11.25).

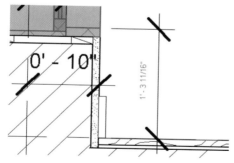

FIGURE 11.25 To change the dimension string value, change the location of the objects dimensioned by selecting the window.

11. Select the blue text, and type 1′ 4″ (400 mm) in the text box (Figure 11.26). Press Enter. The window pushes up just a bit and resets the dimension string.

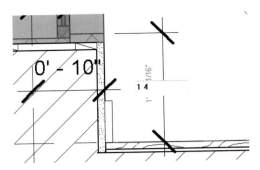

FIGURE 11.26 Entering a value into a dimension string

With all the dimensions on the detail, it should look like Figure 11.27. Compare your finished detail with the c11-ex11.4end.rvt file, available in the download from the book's web page. You'll return to this detail again for the next exercise.

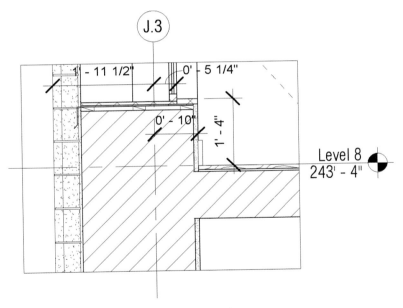

FIGURE 11.27 The dimensioned detail

Exercise 11.5: Add Tags and Text to Your Detail

From the Chapter 11 downloadable files, open the `c11-ex11.5start.rvt` file, or continue with your opened file if you've completed the previous exercise.

Now that you have embellished and dimensioned the detail, it's time to add some annotations in the form of tags and text. In this exercise, you'll tag the window as well as some of the materials in the detail to help identify these items to the contractor. Also, the shims you placed as part of the window family do not have a way to tag a material and need to be called out using text. Follow these steps:

1. Choose the Tag By Category button on the Annotate tab's Tag panel, and select the window.

   Revit Architecture displays the warning shown in Figure 11.28. It tells you that Revit Architecture has added a tag, but that it has fallen outside of your view. By default, Revit Architecture places tags in the center of the element being tagged. In this case, the tag resides in the middle of the window cut in section, which is above your crop box.

   FIGURE 11.28 The tag fell outside of the crop window

2. Click Esc to clear the active command. Select the box that defines the crop region for the detail. Doing so highlights the crop box and also an invisible, dashed box called the *annotation crop box*.

   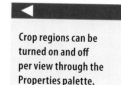

   Crop regions can be turned on and off per view through the Properties palette.

3. Drag the upper limit of the annotation box higher, and you will eventually see the Window tag you placed on the window (Figure 11.29).

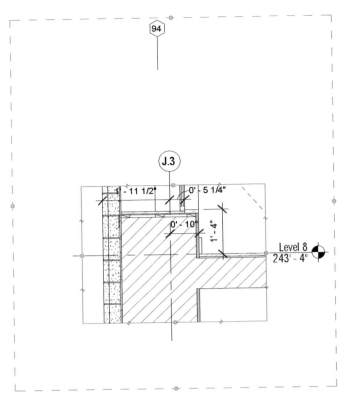

FIGURE 11.29 Extending the annotation crop window

Material tags let you tag materials consistently throughout the model. If you tag something like concrete once in the model, the material will remember the tag you used and show that same tag every time you tag it in any other view.

For materials that aren't already specified, Revit Architecture will display a question mark. Click the material tag, and enter the text describing that material. Changes made to this material will be broadcast throughout the model.

4. Highlight the tag, and in the Options Bar deselect the Leader check box that is shown checked (Figure 11.30). Doing so lets you drag the tag down—leader free—and place it in the crop region.

FIGURE 11.30 Removing the leader from the Window tag

5. Choose the Material Tag button from the Tag panel on the Annotate tab. With the tag selected, mouse over the vertical panel shown in Figure 11.31. The object has been prepopulated with 5/8″ GYPSUM BOARD as a tag through the material (from the Manage tab). Select the material, and place the tag. You may have to readjust your

annotation crop region again to have your material tags appear within your detail.

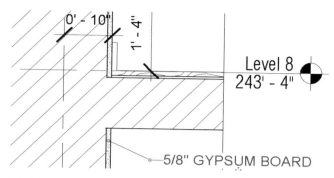

FIGURE 11.31 Using the material tag

6. Notice that by default the tag has no arrowhead. Select the tag, and choose Edit Type from the Properties palette. Here in the tag's Type Properties dialog, you can assign an arrowhead. Choose 30 Degree Arrow for the Leader Arrowhead property, and click OK (Figure 11.32).

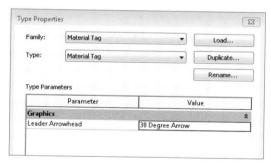

FIGURE 11.32 Adding an arrowhead to the tag

7. Choose the Text command on the Annotate tab. Doing so opens the Modify Text tab. The tools on the Format panel control the leaders, leader location, justification, and font formats, respectively.

8. For now, leave the selections at the defaults, choose a location on the screen, and click the left mouse button. Doing so begins a text box.

Type **1/2″ SHIMS** (Figure 11.33). Click the mouse to finish the text and hit Esc to clear the active command.

FIGURE 11.33 Adding text to the detail

9. Select the text you just created. To add a leader, click the Add Leader button ⁺A at the upper left of the Format panel.

10. Move the text and leader into position with the other notes. In this way, you can complete the annotations on the detail (Figure 11.34) and begin the next one.

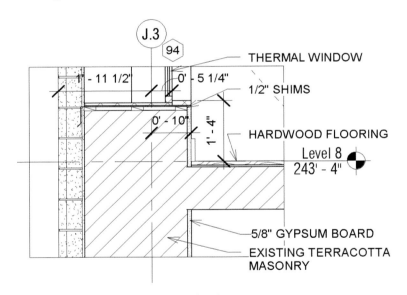

FIGURE 11.34 Finishing the detail

Compare your finished detail with the `c11-ex11.5end.rvt` file, available in the download from the book's web page.

Creating Legends

Legends are unique views in Revit Architecture because you can place them on more than one sheet, which is not typical for most view types. These can be great tools for things such as general notes, key plans, or any other view type you want to be consistent across several sheets. It's important to note that any-thing you place inside a legend view—doors, walls, windows, and so on—will not appear or be counted in any schedules. Legend elements live outside of any quantities present in the model.

The Legends tool is located on the View tab. You can create two types of legends from this menu: a *legend*, which is a graphic display, or a *keynote legend*, which is a text-based schedule. Both legend types can be placed on multiple sheets, but for the following exercise, you'll focus on the legend.

The simplest type of legend would include notes such as general plan or demolition comments that would appear in each of your floor plans. More complex legends include modeled elements, such as walls.

Legends by default are blank views; it's up to you to add content.

You can add modeled elements to the legend view by expanding the Families tree in the Project Browser and navigating to the chosen family. Once a modeled element is added to a legend, you'll notice three sections on the Modify | Legend Components settings in the Options Bar. This menu is consistent for any of the family types you insert.

Family   This drop-down menu allows you to select different family types and operates just as the Type Selector does for other elements in the model.

View   The View option lets you change the type of view from plan to section.

Host Length   This option changes the overall length (or, in the case of sections, height) of the element selected.

As part of the sample workflow, you may want to present some of the wall types as part of your presentation package to demonstrate the Sound Transmission Class (STC) of the walls and the overall wall assembly. Because these wall types will appear on all the sheets where you use them in the plan, you'll make them using a legend.

Exercise 11.6: Create a Legend

From the Chapter 11 downloadable files, open the c11-ex11.6start.rvt file, or continue with your opened file if you've completed the previous exercise.

1. Choose Legend on the View tab's Legends drop-down menu. Creating a new legend is much like creating a new drafting view.

   A New Legend View dialog box opens (Figure 11.35), where you can name the legend and set the scale.

2. Name this legend **WALL LEGEND**, and choose 1″ = 1′-0″ (1:10) for the scale. Click OK to create the legend.

FIGURE 11.35 Creating a legend

3. To add wall types or any other family to the legend view, expand the Families tree in the Project Browser and navigate to the Walls family. Expand this node, and then expand the Basic Wall node.

4. Select the Interior - Gyp 4 7/8″ wall type, and drag it into the legend view.

5. Change the view's detail level in the view's Properties palette from Coarse to Medium or Fine so you can see the detail in the wall.
   Remember, you can turn off the thicker lines in the view by clicking the Thin Lines button [icon] in the Quick Access Toolbar (QAT).

6. Highlight the inserted wall, and look at the Modify | Legend Components settings in the Options Bar (Figure 11.36).

FIGURE 11.36 Select a legend component to access its properties in the Options Bar.

7. Change View to Section, and change Host Length to 1′-6″ (500 mm).
   The wall now looks like a sectional element. By adding some simple text and detail components, you can embellish the wall type to better explain the elements you're viewing (Figure 11.37).

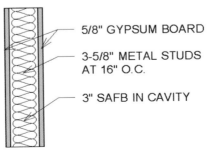

FIGURE 11.37 Add other annotations and detail components to embellish the wall-type section.

8. Continue the exercise by adding the Exterior - Brick wall type to the legend along with some additional text notes.

Compare your finished legend with the c11-ex11.6end.rvt file, available in the files you downloaded from the book's web page.

Now You Know

In this chapter you have learned to create a detail and enhance the detail with 2D elements—filled regions, masking regions, detail lines, and components—to more accurately represent built conditions. You have also learned to annotate the detail using dimensions, tags, and text to convey more information. In addition, you have created a legend to show typical wall assemblies in your project.

The process of embellishing a model to reflect the design intent and detailing gets easier with practice. Remember that you won't have all the geometry you need in the 3D model to show the level of detail you'll need for full documentation. By embellishing the callouts and sections with additional information, you can quickly add the detailed information you need to show.

CHAPTER 12

Drawing Sets

While the building industry moves toward a building information model as a contract deliverable, we still need to produce 2D documents for construction and permitting purposes. Using the Autodesk® Revit® Architecture software, you can create these sets of drawings with more accuracy than in the past.

In this chapter, you'll learn to:

▶ **Create a window schedule**

▶ **Create a room schedule**

▶ **Create a sheet list**

▶ **Customize schedules**

▶ **Arrange plan views on a sheet**

▶ **Activate and deactivate views**

▶ **Adjust crop regions**

▶ **Add schedules to a sheet**

▶ **Specify a sheet set for printing**

▶ **Adjust print settings**

▶ **Print documents**

Schedules

Schedules are lists of model elements and their properties. They can be used to itemize building objects such as walls, doors, and windows; calculate quantities, areas, and volumes; and list elements, such as the number of sheets, keynotes, and so on. Schedules are a valuable, spreadsheet-based way to view information about the building objects in a model. Once created, schedules are dynamically kept up-to-date when new elements are added or when changes occur to the model.

Understanding Schedules

In a non-BIM project workflow, creating schedules of building elements, areas, or other objects is one of the most laborious tasks for architects. When this process is performed manually, it can take a long time and is typically error prone. In Revit Architecture, schedules update automatically and are inherently accurate. Every building element you model in Revit has properties. For example, windows have properties like location, type, size, and material. All this information can be scheduled and quantified. As those windows are changed, the properties update in the schedule automatically so everything is always coordinated.

Because Revit Architecture is a bidirectional parametric modeling program, you are able to make changes to properties from a schedule view, thus updating the model. Continuing with the window example, you can change the material of a window in the schedule view and the Material tags and presentation views will instantly update.

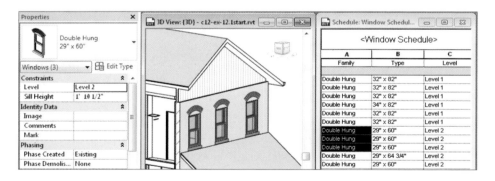

Exercise 12.1: Create a Window Schedule

To begin, go to the book's web page at www.sybex.com/go/revit2016essentials, download the files for Chapter 12, and open the file c12-ex-12.1start.rvt.

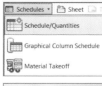

1. Go to the View tab, find the Create panel, click the Schedules button, and click the Schedule/Quantities button. The New Schedule dialog box opens.

2. Click in the Filter List drop-down in the upper-left corner, and uncheck all of the disciplines except for Architecture. This will filter out the categories in the dialog window below.

3. From the Category list, select Windows. Click in the Name field and title your schedule **New Window Schedule**, as shown in Figure 12.1. This project has multiple phases, so you want to make sure the phase is set to New Construction because you don't need to schedule the windows you're *removing*. Click OK to continue.

The lower-left corner of the Fields tab of the Schedule Properties dialog has an Include Elements In Links check box. Enabling this option allows you to schedule across multiple files; it can be a useful tool on larger projects.

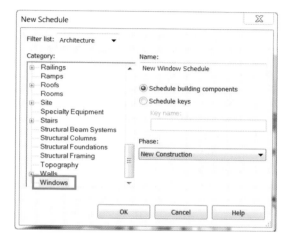

FIGURE 12.1 The New Schedule dialog

4. You should find yourself in the Fields tab of the Schedule Properties dialog. From the Available Fields column, choose Type, Type Mark, Width, Height, and Count; then click the Add button. The properties should now be listed in the Scheduled Fields column, as shown in Figure 12.2. If the order of the fields is incorrect, you can use the Move Up and Move Down buttons to reorder.

5. Click the Filter tab at the top of the dialog. Choose to filter by Type Mark, and then click Does Not Equal from the drop-down list to the right. Finally, choose A from the last column. This allows you to remove certain window types from your new window schedule when desired (Figure 12.3).

6. Click the Sorting/Grouping tab. From the Sort By drop-down, choose Type. Uncheck the Itemize Every Instance option, which is located at the bottom left of the dialog.

7. Click the Formatting tab, and select Count from the Fields list on the left. Change the Alignment setting to Right. Then choose the Type

Mark field from the list on the left and change Alignment to Center so all the letters will align nicely.

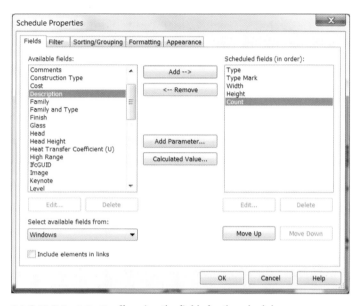

FIGURE 12.2   Choosing the fields for the schedule

FIGURE 12.3   Filtering the window schedule

8. Click the Appearance tab, check the Outline option, and choose Wide Lines from the drop-down (Figure 12.4). You will see this graphics formatting of the schedule only when it is placed on a sheet. We'll get to that later in this chapter.

FIGURE 12.4   Setting the appearance for the schedule

9. Click OK to commit all of these schedule properties changes. Revit opens your new schedule. In the schedule view, you can alter the column heading names by clicking inside the spreadsheet cells. Let's change the first column to **OPENING** and the second column to **TYPE**. Your schedule view should appear as shown in Figure 12.5.

A	B	C	D	E
OPENING	TYPE	Width	Height	Count
18" x 54"	D	1' - 6"	4' - 8"	1
18" x 64.75"	H	1' - 6"	5' - 4 3/4"	1
28" x 63.5"	C	2' - 4"	5' - 3 1/2"	1
29" X 48"	F	2' - 5"	4' - 0"	1
29" x 60"	E	2' - 5"	5' - 0"	6
29" x 64 3/4	G	2' - 5"	5' - 4 3/4"	1
34" x 82"	B	2' - 10"	6' - 10"	2
36" X 12"	J	3' - 0"	1' - 0"	2

<New Window Schedule>

FIGURE 12.5   The new window schedule

10. Now look in the Properties palette of the schedule view and find the Phasing header. Under it you will find the Phase Filter parameter. Set it to Show New and click Apply, or move your mouse into the schedule. Notice that the list of windows is much shorter now (Figure 12.6). Remember, in step 3 you set the phase of the schedule to New Construction; however, this phase setting does not customize the display of the elements in the schedule view. The Phase Filter view property is required to exclude model elements that were demolished in a previous phase.

A	B	C	D	E
OPENING	TYPE	Width	Height	Count
18" x 54"	D	1' - 6"	4' - 8"	1
28" x 63.5"	C	2' - 4"	5' - 3 1/2"	1
34" x 82"	B	2' - 10"	6' - 10"	1
36" X 12"	J	3' - 0"	1' - 0"	2

<New Window Schedule>

FIGURE 12.6   The new window schedule

This concludes Exercise 12.1. You can compare your results with the sample file `c12-ex-12.1end.rvt`, included with the files you download for this chapter.

MULTI-CATEGORY SCHEDULES

You can create schedules that include more than one category. Perhaps you want to schedule all the windows and doors together. The way to accomplish this is to choose the <Multi-Category> option from the top of the Category list in the New Schedule dialog. One limitation of choosing the Multi-Category option is that you cannot schedule host elements such as walls, floors, and ceilings when using this type of schedule.

Exercise 12.2: Create a Room Schedule

Creating other schedule types is fairly simple if you follow the guidelines we just discussed as you step through the tabs in the Schedule Properties dialog box. You have one schedule under your belt, so let's try another—this time you'll create a room schedule.

USING RIBBON COMMANDS IN A SCHEDULE VIEW

Schedules have their own special tab on the ribbon when you are in a schedule view.

A handy shortcut found in the Modify Schedules/Quantities tab is the Highlight In Model button on the far right of the ribbon. This button allows you to select any element in the schedule row and locate that element in the model. Let's say you want to locate a particular window from your window schedule. Click the row in the schedule, and click the Highlight In Model button; you will be taken to a different view with that window instance highlighted.

To begin this exercise, open the file c12-ex-12.2start.rvt from the files you downloaded for this chapter.

1. Let's try a different method for starting a new schedule. In the Project Browser, right-click the Schedules/Quantities node, and then select New Schedule/Quantities (Figure 12.7).

2. Choose Rooms from the Category list in the New Schedule dialog box, verify that the phase is New Construction, and click OK.

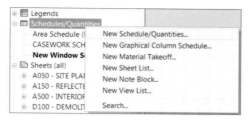

FIGURE 12.7 **Start a new schedule from the Project Browser**

3. In the Fields tab of the Schedule Properties dialog, add the following fields from the Available Fields column to the Scheduled Fields column (in order): Number, Name, Floor Finish, North Wall, East Wall, South Wall, West Wall, Area, Comments.

4. Click the Filter tab and for the Filter By option, choose Name, Does Not Equal, and type the word **Room** into the third field. This will filter out rooms that haven't been updated with a specific name representing their function (Figure 12.8).

FIGURE 12.8 **Filter out unnamed rooms**

5. On the Sorting/Grouping tab, choose the option to sort by number, and then make sure the Itemize Every Instance option is checked in the lower-left corner.

6. On the Formatting tab, select the Area field, and set the alignment to Right. Multi-select North Wall, East Wall, South Wall, and West Wall by holding down Ctrl when you click them; then set the alignment to Center. Click OK to get the schedule you see in Figure 12.9.

				<Room Schedule>				
A	B	C	D	E	F	G	H	I
Number	Name	Floor Finish	North Wall	East Wall	South Wall	West Wall	Area	Comments
100	LIVING ROO	WOOD					307 SF	a
101	DINING RO	WOOD					99 SF	a
102	OFFICE	WOOD					71 SF	a
103	1/2 BATH	WOOD					25 SF	a
104	KITCHEN						134 SF	
200	BEDROOM	WOOD					161 SF	a
201	BATH 1						39 SF	
202	BEDROOM	WOOD					121 SF	a
203	BATH 2						41 SF	
205	HALL	WOOD					95 SF	a

FIGURE 12.9 **Room schedule**

7. Now add a header to the four wall finish columns so you can visually group them. Click in the <Room Schedule> field (the brackets denote that this text is reporting the View Name parameter value). Find the Rows panel on the ribbon. Click Insert ➤ Below Selected. Notice that you now have a blank row of headers corresponding to the columns below them (Figure 12.10).

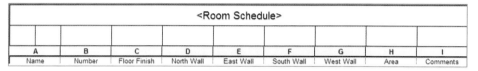

<Room Schedule>								
A	B	C	D	E	F	G	H	I
Name	Number	Floor Finish	North Wall	East Wall	South Wall	West Wall	Area	Comments

FIGURE 12.10   New row inserted

8. Hold down the Shift key, and click the four cells that are directly above the D, E, F, and G columns. With the four columns selected, click the Merge Unmerge button in the Titles & Headers panel of the ribbon. This gives you one large cell. Click in the cell and type **Wall Finishes**. Select the cells above A, B, and C using the Shift key to select them all, and then click Merge Unmerge; name this header **Room Information**. Merge the cells above columns H and I as well, and name this header **Area**.

9. You can add data about the room elements while in the schedule view. This is quite a bit easier than selecting the room elements individually in a floor plan and inputting data about the wall finishes. Click in the cell for the LIVING ROOM, North Wall, and type **Beige Paint**. When you click in another cell of the same column, you can choose the previous text from the drop-down. You can change all of the cells to Beige Paint if you like (Figure 12.11).

<Room Schedule>								
Room Information			Wall Finishes				Area	
A	B	C	D	E	F	G	H	I
Number	Name	Floor Finish	North Wall	East Wall	South Wall	West Wall	Area	Comments
100	LIVING ROOM	WOOD	Beige Paint				307 SF	a.
101	DINING ROOM	WOOD	Beige Paint				99 SF	a.
102	OFFICE	WOOD	Beige Paint				71 SF	a.
103	1/2 BATH	WOOD	Beige Paint				25 SF	a.
104	KITCHEN		Beige Paint				134 SF	
200	BEDROOM 1	WOOD	Beige Paint				161 SF	a.
201	BATH 1		Beige Paint				39 SF	
202	BEDROOM 3	WOOD	Beige Paint				121 SF	a.
203	BATH 2		Beige Paint				41 SF	
205	HALL	WOOD	Beige Paint				95 SF	a.

FIGURE 12.11   The finished room schedule

10. You can edit existing information, like the names of the rooms. Change the name of 1/2 BATH to HALL BATH by clicking in its cell, deleting the old text, and typing the new text. Now open Floor Plans, Level 1, and zoom into the bathroom; you'll notice that the room name has updated in the plan (Figure 12.12)!

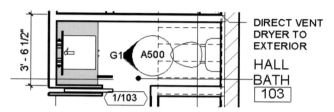

FIGURE 12.12   The updated room name in plan view

This ends Exercise 12.2. You can compare your results with the sample file c12-ex-12.2end.rvt, included with the files you download for this chapter.

Exercise 12.3: Create a Sheet List

The last kind of schedule we'll discuss is a sheet list, which creates a customized list of drawing sheets in your project. This can be especially useful on larger projects where the sheet list can get long.

To begin this exercise, open the file c12-ex-12.3start.rvt from the files you download for this chapter.

1. Select the Sheet List tool from the Schedules button on the View tab. The Sheet List Properties dialog box appears, open to the Fields tab.

2. Move the Sheet Number and Sheet Name fields from the list on the left to the column on the right.

3. On the Filter tab, choose to filter by sheet number. From the next drop-down, choose Begins With.

4. In the third field, enter the letter A. (Be sure to use an uppercase A, because Revit filters are case sensitive.) The filter should look like Figure 12.13.

5. On the Sorting/Grouping tab, choose to sort by sheet number, and make sure the Itemize Every Instance box is checked.

6. When you've finished, click OK to close the dialog box. You should have a schedule with only sheet numbers that begin with the letter A.

Creating a view list schedule can help you manage your project's views efficiently, especially when using the filtering built into schedules.

You can drag the right-most edge of column B to make room for the full sheet name if necessary.

F I G U R E   1 2 . 1 3   Create a filter for specific sheets

7. With the sheet list view still active, click the Insert Data Row button from the Rows panel of the Ribbon. You should see a row appear with a sheet name listed as Unnamed.

8. Change the name to **FLOOR PLANS** and the number to **A100** (Figure 12.14). You have created a placeholder sheet. These are useful when you are creating an outline sheet set and filling in sheet parameters, before you create an actual sheet with a titleblock in your project.

▶

You can also create new sheets by right-clicking the Sheets heading in the Project Browser.

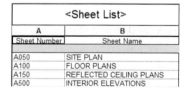

F I G U R E   1 2 . 1 4   The filtered sheet list

9. Click the View tab of the ribbon; then find the Sheet Composition panel and click the Sheet button.

10. In the New Sheet dialog box, choose the Sheets CD C1 22 × 34 : Sheets - CD - C1 titleblock and select A100 - FLOOR PLANS from the list of placeholder sheets below (Figure 12.15).

11. Click OK to create the new sheet. You'll notice in the new sheet that the sheet number and sheet name have been automatically set using the information you added to the sheet list when the sheet was a placeholder.

You can use the place-holder sheet feature to create a cartoon set, where the index of drawings may be planned in advance. As the design progresses and sheets are created, the design team can pick from the list of placeholder sheets.

▶

This ends Exercise 12.3. You can compare your results with the sample file c12-ex-12.3end.rvt, included with the files you downloaded for this chapter.

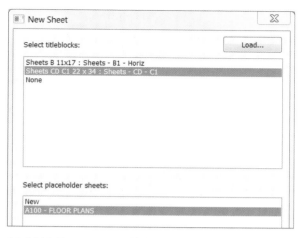

FIGURE 12.15 Add sheets using a placeholder

Placing Views on Sheets

Throughout this book, you have created several different kinds of views, including plans and elevations and perspectives. Eventually, you will need to lay out those views on sheets so they can be printed or converted to PDF and sent to clients or team members for review. Let's walk through laying out these views on sheets and see how each view can be further manipulated once it's placed on a sheet.

Exercise 12.4: Arrange Plan Views on a Sheet

To begin this exercise, open the file c12-ex-12.4start.rvt from the files you downloaded earlier.

   A series of views has already been created in the exercise file. Let's use the sheet you just made and place some views on it using a simple drag-and-drop procedure:

    1. Open the example file, and you should be on sheet A100. If not, expand the Sheets node of the Project Browser, and then double-click sheet A100 - FLOOR PLANS.

    2. Under the Views heading in the Project Browser, find Floor Plans, and expand the tree to locate the plan view Basement. Click the Basement view and drag the view out of the Project Browser and drop it onto sheet A100. Release the left mouse button and the outline of the view appears. Click anywhere to complete the placement of the view (Figure 12.16).

3. You can always adjust the location of the view on the sheet. The arrow keys on the keyboard are good for nudging the view.

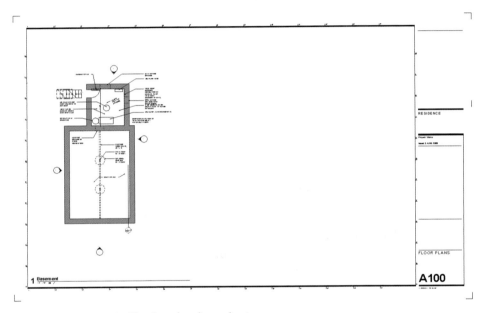

FIGURE 12.16   The view placed on a sheet

To adjust the text in the view tags, start by selecting the view itself, *not the tag element*.

4. Add the Level 1 floor plan view next by dragging and dropping it from the Project Browser onto the sheet. When you're placing another view on the sheet, you will see a dashed line in the center of the view. This is an alignment indicator (Figure 12.17); Revit is assuming you want the plan views to align on the sheet, and it is intelligent enough to aid you in this process. You can casually drag the views around on the sheet to find the alignment lines and ensure that your plans line up.

5. Add the Level 2 floor plan view to Sheet A100 next using the same alignment guide. After all three views are placed on the sheet, use the arrow keys to nudge them left or right so they are more or less evenly spaced on the sheet, as in Figure 12.18.

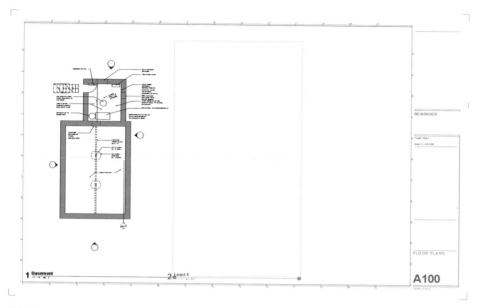

FIGURE 12.17 Aligning views on a sheet

6. Select the Basement view placed on the sheet. The view tag highlights in blue. Click the number 1, and change the value to A1 (as per the ConDoc drawing system, which locates the view port using the letters and numbers along the sides of the sheet).

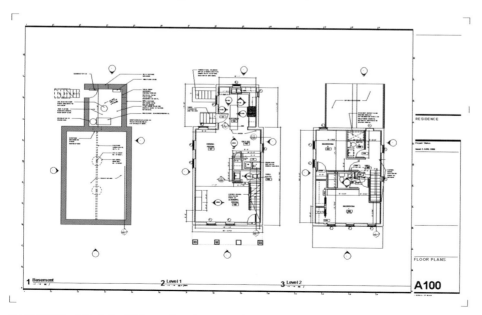

FIGURE 12.18 All three plan views on a sheet

7. Select the Basement view again. Using the blue circular grips on the view tag line, drag the left and right ends of the line. You will most likely need to zoom in to successfully drag the grips. Repeat steps 6 and 7 on the other two views. The numbers of the views should be A6 and A11. The results should be similar to Figure 12.19.

FIGURE 12.19 The edited view tags

8. To finish organizing your sheet, add a few detail lines to divide the views. Click the Annotate tab of the ribbon, find the Detail panel, and then click the Detail Line tool. This activates the Modify | Place Detail Lines contextual menu. On the Line Style panel at the far right, choose Wide Lines from the drop-down.

9. By default, the Line tool is active. You can select one of the nodes on the sheet between views and draw a vertical line between the Basement and Level 1 plans and again between the Level 1 and Level 2 plans (Figure 12.20).

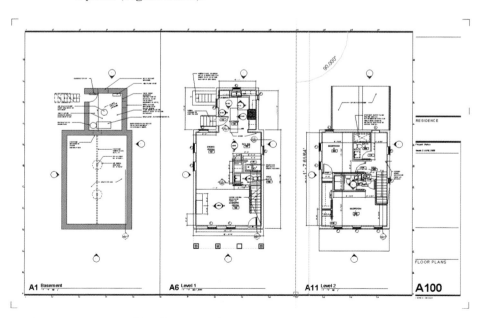

FIGURE 12.20 Adding lines to the sheet

10. With these dividing lines in place, some of the text annotations in the Basement view are crossing the dividing line onto the Level 1 floor plan you added to the sheet; see Figure 12.21.

The Revit workflow of activating a view to make changes in the context of a sheet is much like working in a model-space viewport while in paper space using the Autodesk® AutoCAD® software.

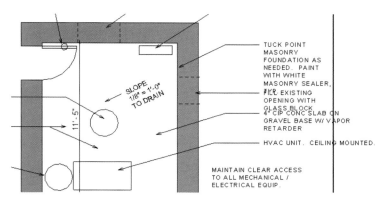

FIGURE 12.21   Text to be adjusted in the sheet view

11. Right-click the Basement view, and choose Activate View from the context menu (Figure 12.22). You can also double-click your mouse on the view to activate it.

FIGURE 12.22   Activate the Basement view

You must deactivate the view before moving on to other steps. The easiest way to do this is to double-click outside of the view port. Alternatively, you can choose the Deactivate View command from the right-click context menu.

12. With the view activated, notice that the other views on the sheet have become grayed out. Select the text box you want to adjust, and drag the right grip toward the left so the text wraps and no longer crosses the line (Figure 12.23).

13. To complete your edits, you need to deactivate the view. The easiest way to do this is to double click outside of the view port. Alternatively, you can choose the Deactivate View from the right-click context menu.

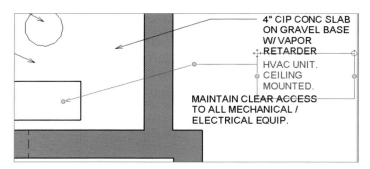

F I G U R E   1 2 . 2 3   Modifying the text box

This ends Exercise 12.4. You can compare your results with the sample file
c12-ex-12.4end.rvt, included with the files you download for this chapter.

Exercise 12.5: Adjust Crop Regions

One very important aspect of composing views on sheets is to adjust the size of
the view port so that only the most pertinent information is shown in the view.
This helps to make an accurate set of drawings for the builder and estimator.

Open the file c12-ex-12.5start.rvt you downloaded previously to get
started.

1. The file should open to sheet K100 – KITCHEN LAYOUT.

2. Zoom into view 1 called Kitchen. This is an enlarged plan of the
   kitchen layout, and it doesn't fit into the sheet boundary.

3. Select the view, and from the ribbon's contextual panel at the far
   right, click the Activate View button.

4. Once the view is activated, select the crop region bordering the view.
   Notice the blue, circular grips that appear at the midpoint of each
   edge (Figure 12.24). These are used for dragging interactively.

5. Drag the left grip so that the view fits inside the sheet boundary.
   Revit allows you to customize the shape of your view beyond a simple
   rectangle.

6. Make sure view is selected, and then click the Edit Crop button from
   the contextual panel on the ribbon. Now you are in a sketch mode
   where the crop region boundary lines are pink and the rest of the
   model is visible but grayed out. This is very similar to editing a floor
   sketch boundary. Note the Draw panel in the ribbon.

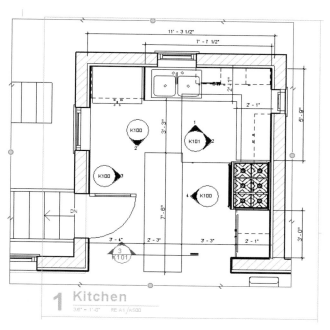

FIGURE 12.24 Crop region grips

7. Select the Line tool. Draw two pink lines and then trim them to form an L-shaped crop that excludes the kitchen door.

8. When your screen is similar to Figure 12.25 (take note of the pink lines), click the green check mark to finish editing the sketch.

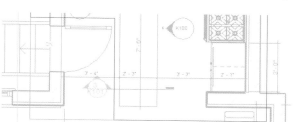

FIGURE 12.25 An L-shaped crop region

9. Now turn off the visibility of the crop region by clicking the Hide Crop Region button. The View Control Bar at the bottom of the canvas has many useful buttons; the one we care about has a crop symbol and a light bulb.

10. Click this, and notice that the crop region is no longer visible, but it is still masking unwanted areas.

11. Finally, right-click and choose Deactivate View. This is a simple example, but adjusting crop regions in the context of other views on sheets is an essential Revit skill you'll use often. The finished plan is shown in Figure 12.26.

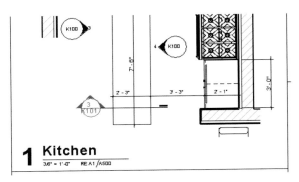

F I G U R E   1 2 . 2 6   Finished enlarged plan

This ends Exercise 12.5. You can compare your results with the sample file c12-ex-12.5end.rvt, included with the files you downloaded previously.

Exercise 12.6: Add Schedules to Sheets

With your sheet of floor plans and kitchen details composed, you can finish the sheet set by adding the schedules you created earlier. Adding a schedule to a sheet is like adding any other view—you drag and drop it from the Project Browser onto the sheet.

To begin, open the file c12-ex-12.6start.rvt.

1. The file should open to the sheet named G000 – COVER SHEET.

2. Find the Schedules/Quantities node of the Project Browser. Grab the new window schedule from the Project Browser; then drag and drop it onto an open area on the sheet. Look ahead to Figure 12.27 to see the result of this action.

3. Repeat this process for the room schedule and the sheet list. Notice that the dotted blue alignment line appears and helps you line up the left edges so the final layout looks like Figure 12.17. You can redefine the column width of your schedules on the sheet.

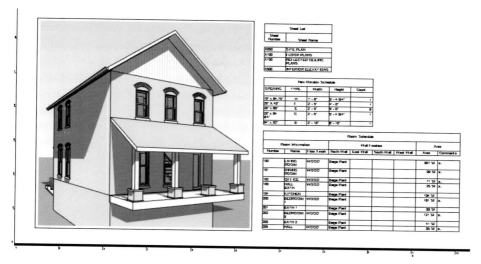

FIGURE 12.27 Place the schedules on sheet G000

4. Start by selecting the sheet list schedule. The schedule turns blue, and inverted triangle grips appear at the top of each column.

5. Grab one, and drag it left or right to change the column sizing.

This ends Exercise 12.6. You can compare your results with the sample file c12-ex-12.6end.rvt, included with the files you download for this chapter.

FIXING SCHEDULES THAT RUN OFF THE SHEET

You can *split* larger schedules to make them easier to read on the sheet. When you select a schedule, you'll notice a blue cut symbol. This cut symbol lets you break the schedule into parts while on the same sheet. This can be especially handy if you have a long schedule, such as a room or door schedule that has too many rows to fit on your sheet vertically. Selecting this break symbol splits the schedule in half (and you can split it in half again and again). If you choose to separate your schedule in this fashion, it retains all the necessary information and continues to automatically fill dynamically as a single schedule would. You can also change the overall height of the schedule once it is broken by grabbing the grips at the bottom of the schedule and dragging them up or down.

Printing Documents

You will eventually need to print or create PDFs of your documentation sheets from Revit Architecture. You'll find that printing from Revit Architecture is straightforward because the process resembles that used in other Windows-based applications.

Exercise 12.7: Explore the Print Dialog Box

Open the downloaded file `c12-ex-12.7start.rvt` to begin this exercise.

1. To begin printing, you do not need to be in any particular view or sheet. Click the Application menu button (the big R) and then select the Print button to open the Print dialog (or use the keyboard shortcut Ctrl+P). There are several groups of settings for us to discuss.

2. Choose the printer you want to use from the Name drop-down menu at the top of the Print dialog. This can be a physical printer or a virtual one (such as Adobe PDF).

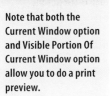

Note that both the Current Window option and Visible Portion Of Current Window option allow you to do a print preview.

3. The next group box is named File, and it appears only if you are printing documents to a file instead of a printer. If you're using a PDF printer, then name the output something specific, and browse to the file location you desire. You should choose to combine multiple selected views/sheets into a single file. This is a very important property to double-check *before* printing!

4. The Print Range settings allow you to specify what you want to print. The Current Window option prints the full extent of the current view, regardless of what is currently visible on your screen. The Visible Portion Of Current Window option prints only what you currently see in the frame of the open view. Note that both of these options allow you to do a print preview.

5. Click the Selected Views/Sheets option. Then click the Select button. This option allows you to choose multiple sheets or views to print at once. You cannot do a print preview, but you do end up saving time by batch printing (Figure 12.28).

6. The View/Sheet Set dialog opens. You should start out by clicking the Check None button. This will give you a clean slate.

FIGURE 12.28 The Print Range, Options, and Settings properties

7. At the bottom of the dialog is an important filtering check box. Uncheck the Views option so that you're viewing only sheets. There should be three sheets; let's check each of them.

8. Click the Save As button, and name the sheet set Exercise 12 (Figure 12.29). This will speed up the process if you ever need to reprint this same set of sheets. Click OK twice to return to the Print dialog.

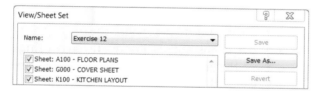

FIGURE 12.29 Specify the sheet set

9. Click the Setup button in the Settings group (refer back to Figure 12.28). The Print Setup dialog opens with options for print settings such as paper size, zoom, and orientation. You can also save these settings with a name so that you can reuse them later.

10. Choose your desired paper size. Then choose the desired zoom level; for this exercise choose 50 percent. To print the sheets to a specific scale, remember that every view is assigned a scale factor already; therefore, changing the zoom level in the print dialog, will affect the scale of the drawings. For example, if a floor plan is assigned a scale factor of 1/4″=1′-0″ (1:50) and you would like to generate a print of the plan at 1/8″=1′-0″ (1:100), set the zoom level to 50 percent. Sheets should be printed at 100 percent for full size or 50 percent for a half-size set.

If you add more sheets to your project, they won't automatically be added to this print set. You'll need to revisit this dialog box, add the sheets, and click the Save button.

The print settings can be transferred to other project files, if necessary, using the Transfer Project Standards tool located on the Manage tab in the ribbon.

11. Next, spend a few moments reviewing the options at the bottom of the dialog. Make sure to check Hide Ref/Work Planes, Hide Scope Boxes, and Hide Crop Boundaries. These three options let you decide whether to see elements that are usually only helpful references when modeling the project.

12. Check the Hide Unreferenced View Tags box. During the course of modeling your project, you usually create helpful working views that you don't end up using on sheets, such as elevations, sections, or detail callouts. If these views are not placed on any sheets, the view tags are blank and therefore unreferenced. This is a helpful way to avoid printing them.

13. Once your options are set, click the Save As button, and name the current setup **Exercise 12 - Half Size**; then click OK. As with the sheet set, you can reuse these settings on future prints. Your Print Setup dialog should look like Figure 12.30. Click OK to close this dialog.

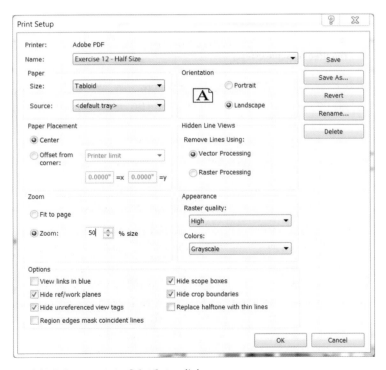

FIGURE 12.30 **Print Setup dialog**

14. Now you're back to the Print dialog. If you click OK, Revit will move forward with the printing process, sending the selected drawings to the printer listed at the top of the dialog. If you click Close, then the changes made in the dialog are saved and the dialog closes without printing.

15. In the case that your print set includes some views with shading or other graphics effects like shadows, Revit will show you a warning similar to Figure 12.31. This means that Revit will use raster processing instead of vector processing for these views. See the sidebar "Using Vector or Raster Print Processing" for some additional information about the differences between vector and raster processing.

FIGURE 12.31 Raster printing is required for some effects

This ends Exercise 12.7. You can compare your results with the sample file c12-ex-12.7end.rvt, which is included with the files you downloaded earlier.

USING VECTOR OR RASTER PRINT PROCESSING

Views in Revit Architecture can be displayed in several visual styles that can be printed: Wireframe, Hidden Line, Shaded, Consistent Colors, and Realistic.

The Hidden Line visual style is generally used for construction documents and can utilize vector processing, which is faster and creates sharper edges.

The Shaded, Consistent Colors, and Realistic visual styles are generally used for presentation views, and they require raster processing to handle color gradients, shadows, and other graphic effects. Raster is slower and creates pixelated edges, but it also creates output that is the same as the screen display. If you choose raster, you can specify low-, medium-, high-, or presentation-quality output in the Print Setup dialog.

Now You Know

This chapter illustrated how to move your Revit project from modeling to documentation using schedules, sheets, views, and printing. You learned how to quantify windows, rooms, and sheet elements in the model by using a schedule. Then you learned to place views, edit views, adjust crop regions, and compose sheets. Finally, you learned how to adjust the print settings to get your model information printed out.

CHAPTER 13

Workflow and Site Modeling

Understanding the Autodesk® Revit® Architecture software and how to use it is not a difficult challenge. The real challenge is determining how using Revit Architecture and building information modeling (BIM) will change your organization's culture and your project's workflow, especially if you're coming from a CAD-based environment. Revit Architecture can be more than just a different way to draw a line. In this chapter, we'll focus on the changes and provide some tools to help you manage the transition.

In this chapter, you'll learn to:

▶ **Staff a BIM project**

▶ **Model a site**

▶ **Create a building pad**

▶ **Purge unused families and groups**

▶ **Manage links and images**

▶ **Reduce number of views**

▶ **Maintain project warnings**

Understanding a BIM Workflow

Regardless of the workflow you have established, moving to Revit Architecture is going to change how you approach projects. You'll need tools to help the transition from your current workflow to one using Revit Architecture. To begin, we'll cover some of the core differences between a CAD-based system and a BIM-based one.

Moving to BIM involves a shift in how designers and contractors look at the design and documentation process throughout the entire life cycle of a project, from concept to occupancy. In a traditional CAD-based workflow, represented in Figure 13.1, each view is drawn separately with no inherent relationship between drawings. In this type of production environment, the team creates plans, sections, elevations, schedules, and perspectives and must coordinate any changes between files manually.

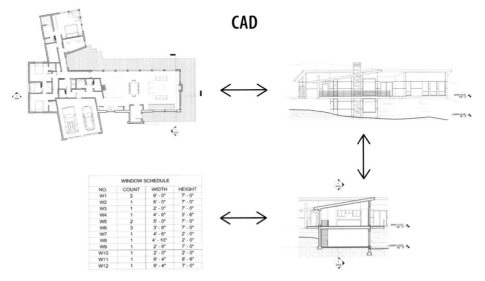

FIGURE 13.1 A CAD-based workflow

In a BIM-based workflow, the team creates a 3D, parametric model and uses this model to automatically generate the drawings necessary for documentation. Plans, sections, elevations, schedules, and perspectives are all by-products of creating an embellished BIM model, as shown in Figure 13.2. This enhanced documentation methodology not only allows for a highly coordinated drawing set but also provides the basic model geometry necessary for analysis, such as daylighting studies, energy, material takeoffs, and so on.

Using Revit Architecture becomes more than a change in software; it becomes a change in workflow and methodology. As various design specializations interact and create the building model (Figure 13.3), you can see how structure, mechanical, energy, daylight, and other factors inform design direction. You can also draw relationships between some of these elements that might not have been as obvious in a more traditional approach. Although some of these specialties (such as structure and mechanical) are historically separate systems, by integrating them into a single design model, you can see how they interact in relation to other systems within a building.

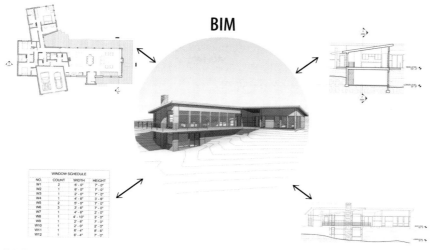

FIGURE 13.2 A BIM workflow

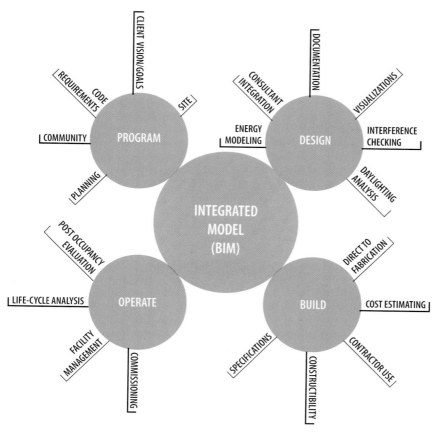

FIGURE 13.3 The integrated design model

Analysis such as daylighting can inform your building orientation and structure. Depending on your glazing, it can also affect your mechanical requirements (as solar gain). You can see some of these effects through a computational fluid dynamics (CFD) model (used to calculate airflow). Geographic information system (GIS) data will give you your relative location globally and allow you to see how much sunlight you will be receiving or what the local temperature swings will be during the course of a day. As you can see, all of these variables can easily affect building design.

Staffing a BIM Project

A common misconception of project management when teams are first moving from CAD to BIM is that staffing the project will be the same in both workflows.

As you rethink the process of design and documentation, one of the semantic changes you will need to address is staffing. When the workflow changes from CAD to BIM, staffing allocations, time to complete tasks, and percentage of work by phase are all affected as a by-product of the change of method.

In a CAD-based project, the level of effort during each of the phases is fairly well known. The industry has been using some metrics over the past several years that should be fairly familiar. There is modest effort and staffing in the conceptual design and schematic design phases, and this effort builds until it crescendos during construction documentation. At this phase, a CAD project can greatly increase the number of staff in an effort to expedite the completion of the drawing set. This staff increase can be effective because the CAD drawings are typically separate files and moving lines in one drawing won't dynamically change another.

In a BIM-based framework, there is still a gradual increase of staffing and effort through conceptual design and into the schematic phase, but the effort during schematic design is greater using BIM than in CAD. During schematic design and design development, the project team is still performing all the same tasks that occur in any design process: testing design concepts, visualizations, or design iteration. The increase in effort during the early design phases lets the team use the parametric nature of the model to significantly reduce the effort later during construction documents, allowing for a decrease in the overall effort over the project cycle.

Project Roles Using Revit Architecture

With such a significant change in the effort behind a BIM-based project flow, it's also important to understand how this can change the various roles and responsibilities for the project team. The changes in traditional roles can become a barrier to many projects successfully adopting BIM. Project managers need to be able to predict staffing and time to complete tasks throughout the project phases and have relied on the past precedent of staff and project types to do this. Because a BIM-based project can significantly alter the project workflow, many of the historic timetables for task completion are no longer valid. However, a BIM-based project can be broken down into a few primary roles that will allow you some level of predictability through the various project phases. Although the specific effort and staffing will vary between offices (and even projects), some general roles will need to be accounted for on every project.

There are three primary roles on every BIM project.

Architect   Deals with design issues, code compliances, clear widths, wall types, and so on

Modeler   Creates content in 2D or in 3D

Drafter   Deals with annotations, sheet layout, view creation, and detail creation

These roles represent efforts and general tasks that you need to take into account on any Revit Architecture project. We'll now cover each of these in a bit more detail and discuss how these roles interact with the project cycle.

On a large project, these roles could also represent individual people, whereas in a smaller project they might be all the same person, or one person might carry multiple roles.

Architect

The role of the architect is to deal with the architectural issues revolving around the project. As the model is being created, you will naturally have to solve issues such as constructability and wall types, set corridor widths, deal with department areas, and deal with other issues involving either codes or the overall architectural design. This role will be the one applying standards to the project (as in wall types, keynotes, and so on) and organizing the document set. This role will need to be present on the project from the beginning to ensure consistency of the virtual building creation and isn't necessarily limited to only one person.

This role also might or might not be a "designer." Although it is possible to do early design in Revit Architecture, many project teams prefer to utilize other tools such as Trimble SketchUp or even pencil and trace paper. The job of the architect is steering the creation of the building in Revit Architecture. This role includes the following tasks:

▶ Leading the creation of massing (if used) and major architectural elements and then building from within the model

▶ Designing around code requirements and other building logistics

▶ Ensuring constructability and detailing aspects of the design

Modeler

The role of the modeler is to create all the 2D and especially the 3D content needed in the project. This content includes all the parametric families for elements such as windows, doors, casework, wall types, stairs, railings, and furnishings. Typically, this role is the responsibility of less experienced staff who might not be able to fulfill the role of architect. These less experienced staff members tend to have longer periods of undisturbed time, making them better suited to deal with some of the longer, more involved tasks in modeling content. Finally, they also tend to have some 3D experience coming out of school. They might not have worked with Revit Architecture directly, but have possibly worked with Autodesk® 3ds Max® or Trimble SketchUp, and are thereby familiar with working in a 3D environment. This role includes the following tasks:

▶ Exchanging any generic elements used during early design stages for more specific building elements

▶ Creating and adding new family components and modifying existing components in the project

▶ Regularly reviewing and eliminating project warnings

Drafter

The role of the drafter is to create sheets and views and embellish those views with annotations or other 2D content. This role will be doing the bulk of the work needed to document the project. In earlier stages of the project, this role is typically assumed by either the architect or the modeler, but as documentation gets moving into high gear, it can quickly become the role of multiple people on a larger project. This role includes the following tasks:

▶ Keynoting

▶ Dimensioning

▶ Setting up sheets and views

▶ Creating schedules

For the purpose of staffing planning, we are discussing the ideal times to bring some of these various roles into the project. At the inception of a project design, a modeling role will be most useful. This person can help create the building form, add conceptual content, and get the massing for the building established. If you're using the conceptual modeling tools, the modeler can even do some early sustainable design calculations.

Once the design begins to settle down, you'll need an architect role to step into the project. Since the design is more resolved, it's a good time to begin applying specific materials and wall types and validating spatial requirements and the owner's program. The process of moving from the general "what" something is and "where" it is to the more specific "how" something is going to be assembled isn't new. It's the same process that was used to create both traditional and modern buildings (Figure 13.4).

FIGURE 13.4 Traditional and modern designs

During schematic design, you'll need to include the role of the drafter to begin laying out sheets and creating views. These sheets and views don't have to be for a construction document set yet, but you'll have to establish views for any schematic design submittals. If these views are set up properly, they can be reused later for design development and construction-document submittals as the model continues to gain a greater level of detail.

Adding Team Members to Fight Fires

In many projects, there comes a time when the schedule gets tight and project management wants to add more staff to a project to meet a specific deadline.

What you'd like to avoid, if possible, is adding staff during the construction-document phase. In a BIM/Revit Architecture workflow, this can sometimes cause more problems than it solves and slow down the team rather than help get work done faster.

In a 2D CAD environment, new team members would be added to help meet a deadline and would have the burden of trying to learn the architecture of the building, the thoughts behind its design, and how its various systems interact. In a Revit Architecture project, they have that same obligation, but they have the additional task of learning how the *model* goes together. The model will have constraints set against various elements (such as locking a corridor width) as well as various digital construction issues (such as how floors and walls might be tied together, what the various family names are, or workset organization). This ramping-up period consumes additional time.

Regardless of planning, deadlines escape the best of architects and project managers. It's a good idea to know when and how you can staff to make sure you meet deadlines. Keep in mind that any team members new to the project have to learn about *both* the design and the model they have been thrown into; follow these suggestions so new staff can help production and don't accidentally break anything along the way:

Create content, content, content   You will find that you are making model families or detail components until the end of the project. This process will help get the newbie engaged in a specific part of the project and also isolate them until they learn more about how the model has gone together.

Put them into a drafting role   Even if this isn't their ultimate role on the project, having staff new to the design help create views and lay out sheets will get them familiar with the architecture while still allowing the team to progress on the document set.

Start them to work on detailing   Every project can always use someone who knows how to put a building together. If you have someone new to the project and possibly even new to Revit Architecture, let them embellish some of the views already created and laid out on sheets. These views can be layered with 2D components, linework, and annotations.

Modeling a Site

In the previous sections of this chapter, you learned about the fundamental roles and workflow for your project team. Now let's talk about some tools. One set of tools you should become familiar with are the site tools. They allow you to create a context in which your building models can be situated. For example, a toposurface will create a hatched area when you view your building in a section, and it will function as a hosting surface for site components such as trees, shrubs, parking spaces, accessories, and vehicles (Figure 13.5).

FIGURE 13.5 A toposurface can host components such as trees, entourage, and vehicles.

The site tools in Revit Architecture are intended only to be used for the creation of basic elements, including topography, property lines, and building pads. Although editing utilities are available to manipulate the site elements, these tools are not meant to be used for civil engineering like the functionality found in Autodesk® AutoCAD® Civil 3D®.

In the following sections, you'll learn about the different ways to create and modify a toposurface and how to model a building pad in a toposurface.

Toposurface

As its name suggests, a toposurface is a surface-based representation of the topography context supporting a project. It is not modeled as a solid in Revit Architecture; however, a toposurface will appear as if it were a solid in any section cut view, as in the 3D view with a section box enabled shown in Figure 13.6.

Certification Objective

Toposurface

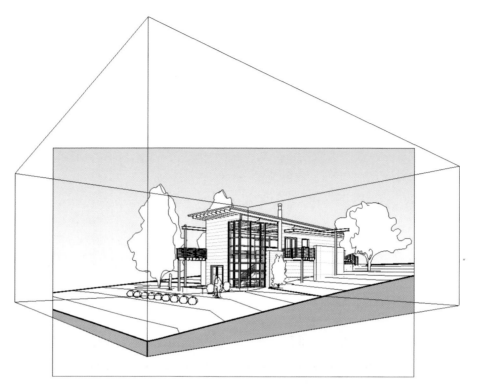

FIGURE 13.6 A toposurface appears as a solid in a 3D view only if a section box is used.

You can create a toposurface in three ways: by placing points at specific elevations, by using a linked CAD file with lines or points at varying elevations, or by using a points file generated by a civil-engineering application. You'll create a site from an imported CAD file in the first exercise.

A common workflow you may encounter when creating the topography context involves the use of CAD data generated by a civil engineer. In this case, the engineer must create a file with 3D data. Blocks, circles, and contour polylines must exist in the CAD file at the appropriate vertical elevation to be used in the process of generating a toposurface in Revit Architecture.

Building Pad

Certification
Objective

Building
Pad

A *building pad* in Revit Architecture is a unique model element that resembles a floor. It can have a thickness and compound structure, it is associated with a level, and it can be sloped using slope arrows while you're sketching its boundary. The building pad is different from a floor because it will automatically cut through a toposurface, defining the outline for your building's garden level or basement.

Exercise 13.1: Model a Toposurface

In the following exercise, you will download a sample DWG file with contour polylines. You must link the file into your Revit Architecture project before creating the toposurface. Here are the steps:

1. Create a new Revit Architecture project using the Architectural template.

2. Download the file c13-ex13.1Site.dwg from this book's web page, www.sybex.com/go/revit2016essentials.

3. Activate the floor plan named Site in the Project Browser.

4. Go to the Insert tab in the ribbon, and click the Link CAD button. Select the c13-ex13.1Site.dwg file, and set the following options:

   ▶ Current View Only: Unchecked

   ▶ Import Units: Auto-Detect

   ▶ Positioning: Auto – Center To Center

   ▶ Place At: Level 1

   Certification Objective

5. Click Open to close the dialog box and complete the insertion of the CAD link. Open a default 3D view to examine the results (Figure 13.7).

FIGURE 13.7   Linked CAD file as seen in a 3D view

6. Click the Toposurface button on the Massing & Site tab in the ribbon.

7. In the Tools panel on the Modify | Edit Surface tab, select Create From Import and then choose Select Import Instance.

8. Click the linked CAD file, and the Add Points From Selected Layers dialog box appears (Figure 13.8).

9. Click the Check None button, and then select the layers C-TOPO-MAJR and C-TOPO-MINR.

All of the active layers in your CAD file will appear in this dialog box. To ensure that your CAD file will be usable for a 3D toposurface, isolate and rename the contour lines as their own linetype within the CAD file.

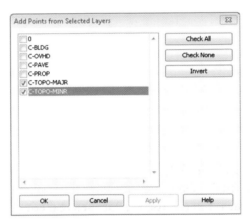

FIGURE 13.8 Select only the layers containing 3D contour information.

10. Click OK to close the dialog box. Revit Architecture may take a few seconds to generate the points based on the contour polylines in the linked file, but they will appear as black squares when they have all been placed.

11. If you want to use fewer points to define the toposurface, click the Simplify Surface button in the contextual ribbon, enter a larger value, such as 1′-0″ (300 mm), and click OK.

12. Click the Finish Surface button in the contextual ribbon to complete the toposurface. Change the visual style of the view to Consistent Colors to examine your results.

Upon completion, your toposurface should resemble the file `c13-ex13.1end .rvt`, available for download from the book's web page.

Exercise 13.2: Create a Building Pad

The process to create a building pad is virtually identical to that of creating a floor. Let's run through a quick exercise to create a building pad in a sample project:

1. Download the file c13-ex13.2start.rvt from this book's web page and open it.

2. Activate the floor plan named Site in the Project Browser. You see an existing topographic surface and a property line. Notice that reference planes were created to demarcate the required zoning setbacks from the property line. Foundation walls have been created in these reference planes.

3. Activate the Cellar floor plan from the Project Browser.

4. Go to the Massing & Site tab in the ribbon, and click the Building Pad button.

5. In the Properties palette, change the Height Offset From Level value to 0.

6. Switch to Pick Walls mode, if it's not already selected in the Draw panel of the contextual ribbon, and then click the inside edges of the four foundation walls. You can use the Tab+select method to place all four lines at once.

7. Click the Finish Edit Mode button in the contextual ribbon to complete the sketch.

8. Double-click the section head in the plan view to examine your results. Notice that the top of the building pad is at the Cellar level and the poche of the topographic surface has been removed in the space of the cellar (Figure 13.9).

You don't have to create a property line and walls before creating a building pad. You might create a building pad before any other building elements.

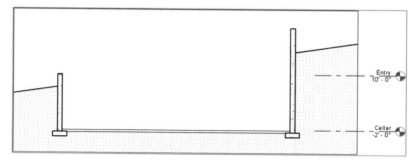

FIGURE 13.9 This section view illustrates how the building pad adjusts the extents of the topographic surface.

Upon completion, your building pad should resemble the file c13-ex13.2end .rvt, available for download from the book's web page.

ADJUSTING THE SECTION POCHE FOR TOPOGRAPHIC SURFACES

If you want to customize the settings for the fill pattern and depth of the poche, click the small arrow at the lower right of the Model Site panel on the Massing & Site tab of the ribbon to open the Site Settings dialog box shown here.

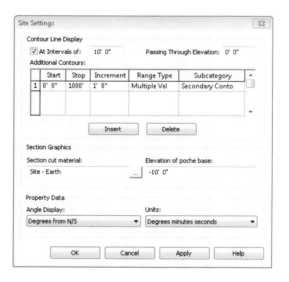

Performing Quality Control on Your Model: Keeping an Eye on File Size

You can take several measures to ensure that your model is a smooth-running and efficient machine. From time to time, ideally after major project milestones, someone on the project team should oversee the model to manage your model's file size and the number of warnings.

Watch the size of your file. It's a good metric for general file stability. A typical Revit Architecture file size for a project in construction documents will be between 100 MB and 250 MB (250 MB is on the high side of file sizes). Beyond that, you will find that the model will be slow to open and hard to rotate in 3D views, and other views, such as building elevations and overall plans, will also be slow to open.

Should your file become large or unwieldy, you have several ways to trim the file down and get the model lean and responsive again.

Purging Unused Families and Groups

On the Manage tab is a command called Purge Unused. This command removes all the unused families and groups from your model by deleting them. Many times in a design process you will change window types or wall types or swap one set of families for another. Even if those elements are not being used in the project, they are being stored in the file, and therefore when the file is opened, they are being loaded into memory. Depending on the stage of your project, you should periodically delete these elements from the model to keep your file size down.

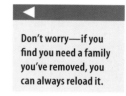

Don't worry—if you find you need a family you've removed, you can always reload it.

Select the Manage tab, and choose Purge Unused on the Settings panel. Depending on the size of your model and how many families you have loaded, it might take Revit Architecture a few minutes to complete this command.

Purge Unused

After Revit Architecture is done thinking, it will provide you with a list of all the families and groups in the file that are not actively in a view (Figure 13.10). At this point, you have the option to select the elements you want to delete or keep.

FIGURE 13.10 The Purge Unused dialog box

We don't recommend you use this command in the early stages of design, mainly because your file size won't be that large early on and purging at this stage would eliminate any preloaded families that you might have included in your template. During schematic design and design development, you are typically going through design iteration and will likely be adding and removing content regularly. It can become a hassle to have to constantly load or reload families into the model. If your model is not suffering from performance issues or the file size isn't unruly, it's not necessary to use the Purge Unused command.

Managing Links and Images

Another way to manage your project's file size is to remove all unused linked files and raster images from your model. If you've linked CAD files from your civil engineer or other consultants and no longer need them as a reference in your model, removing them will also unload that stored data from your model. In addition, if you've imported raster images into your project, deleting them can significantly reduce your file size. It is good practice to periodically remove these types of files from your model, especially after major deadlines, if they are not actively being used in your project.

To access these options, find the Manage Project panel on the Manage tab. Notice the Manage Links and Manage Images tools. These two commands allow you to remove any linked CAD files, Revit files, Point Cloud files, IFC files, and DWF files, as well as any raster images not required for your project. Click Manage Links to remove any unwanted files, browse to the appropriate tab, select the file to delete, and click Remove. Manage Images works similarly; click Manage Images, highlight the image you want to remove, and click Delete.

Cutting Down on the Number of Views

The ability to quickly create views in a model is one of the fast and easy benefits of using Revit Architecture. This ability can also be a detriment, though, if it is not managed. Beyond the hassle of having to sort through many views to find the one you need, having too many views in Revit Architecture can also impact your performance and file size.

Obviously, a number of views are needed in the model to create the construction documentation. In addition, you will find yourself creating views to study the design, deal with model creation, or view the building or project from a new angle. These types of working views will never make it to the sheet set, and some will be used only for brief periods.

HOW MANY WORKING VIEWS IS TOO MANY?

How many working views is too many to have in your model? The obvious answer is that when performance begins to suffer, you need to start looking at ways to make the model lean and speed up response times. Members of a project team that were new to Revit Architecture were complaining about a file being slow to open and manipulate. When we reviewed their model, the file size was around 800 MB! We were surprised that they were able to do any work at all.

One of the first things we did to get the file size down was look at all the views that were not on sheets. More than 1,200 views were not being used. Deleting those views, paired with a Compact File save (found in the File Save Options dialog box), reduced the file size to 500 MB. Although the file was still big, you can see the impact that keeping too many views has on file size.

Dealing with Warnings

An important way to troubleshoot your model is to use the Review Warnings tool. This tool will do very little to affect your overall file size, but it will alert you to problems in the model. Warnings should regularly be addressed to ensure file stability. To open the Review Warnings dialog box, shown in Figure 13.11, click the Warnings button on the Inquiry panel of the Manage tab. The dialog box lists all warnings still active in your project file.

Warnings

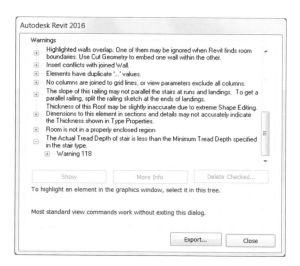

FIGURE 13.11   The Warnings dialog box

Errors and warnings are all essentially types of issues Revit Architecture has when it tries to resolve geometry, conflicts, or formulas that do not equate. Things that appear in this dialog box include instances of multiple elements sitting directly on top of each other, thereby creating inaccurate schedule counts; wall joints that do not properly clean themselves up; wall and room separation lines overlapping; stairs that have the wrong number of risers between floors; and so on. This dialog box shows you all the times the yellow warning box appeared in the bottom-right corner of the screen and you ignored it. Errors that go unchecked can compound to create other errors and can also lead to inaccurate reporting in schedules or even file corruption. Check the Warnings dialog box regularly as part of your periodic file maintenance, and try to keep the number of instances to a minimum.

Notice that the Warnings dialog box has an Export feature. Use this feature to export your error list to an HTML file so you can read it at your leisure outside the model environment (Figure 13.12). You can also pull this list into a Microsoft Word or Excel document so you can distribute the errors across the team to be resolved.

PhillipsPlace Error Report (12/18/2013 10:29:11 PM)

Error message	Elements
Highlighted walls are attached to, but miss, the highlighted targets.	Workset1 : Walls : Basic Wall : Interior - 4 7/8" Partition : id 230670 Workset1 : Floors : Floor : Wood Joist 8" - Attic : id 682650
Highlighted walls are attached to, but miss, the highlighted targets.	Workset1 : Walls : Basic Wall : Generic - 5" : id 260324 Workset1 : Ceilings : Compound Ceiling : TYPE B - GWB on Furring - Mark SLOPED : id 712355
Highlighted walls are attached to, but miss, the highlighted targets.	Workset1 : Ceilings : Compound Ceiling : TYPE A - 3/8" Laminated Drywall - Mark 8' - 3" : id 546901 Workset1 : Walls : Basic Wall : Generic - 6" : id 941926
Highlighted walls are attached to, but miss, the highlighted targets.	Workset1 : Floors : Floor : Wood Joist 8" - Attic : id 682650 Workset1 : Walls : Basic Wall : Interior - 4 7/8" Partition : id 722087
Highlighted elements are joined but do not intersect.	Workset1 : Walls : Basic Wall : Exterior - Existing Wood Shake : id 199956 Workset1 : Walls : Basic Wall : Interior - 5 1/2" Partition : id 212840
Highlighted elements are joined but do not intersect.	Workset1 : Walls : Basic Wall : Interior - 5 1/2" Partition : id 207075 Type : Workset1 : Walls : Chimney 5 : Chimney 5 : id 285404
Highlighted elements are joined but do not intersect.	Workset1 : Walls : Basic Wall : Generic - 15" : id 213525 Workset1 : Walls : Basic Wall : Interior - Type 4A -2 1/2" Furring Partition Foundation Wall : id 1319154
Highlighted elements are joined but do not intersect.	Workset1 : Walls : Basic Wall : Generic - 15" : id 214350 Workset1 : Walls : Basic Wall : Interior - Type 4A -2 1/2" Furring Partition Foundation Wall : id 1319064

FIGURE 13.12 Exporting errors and warnings

In the example shown in Figure 13.12, using the Phillips Place model, the file has 118 errors and warnings. How many errors in a file are too many? Much of that depends on your model, your computer's capabilities, the error types, and your deliverable. For instance, if you are delivering a BIM model to your client or to the contractor, you might have a zero-error requirement. In that case, no errors are acceptable. If you are still actively in the design phase of the project, however, you will always have some errors—it is an inescapable part of the iteration process. As you refine the drawings, errors will be resolved, and as you add new content to the model that is in need of resolution, new errors will be created. If you are not worried about a model deliverable, you can get away with having fewer than 1,000 errors in the project without too much trouble. That said, the cleaner the model, the smoother it will run.

Now You Know

In this chapter you have learned how to transition from a 2D CAD environment to a Revit Architecture BIM workflow and staff a BIM project. You have also learned to model a site and create a building pad—with some of the lesser-used (but just as important) tools in Revit Architecture. In addition, you have learned to perform quality control measures on your model—purge unused families and groups, manage links and images, reduce the number of views, and maintain project warnings—to ensure that your Revit Architecture projects are quick and responsive.

Using Revit Architecture means understanding BIM as a workflow and process at all levels in your office and at all phases of your project. Being prepared for a process change as well as a software change will help you become successful as you move into BIM.

CHAPTER 14

Repetition in Revit

This chapter provides an overview for the primary methods of repeating objects in the Autodesk® Revit® Architecture software. You will review each tool and the situations most appropriate to use one over another. Also included in this chapter are tips and shortcuts you can take advantage of when working in your projects.

In this chapter, you'll learn to:

▶ **Use component families**

▶ **Use groups**

▶ **Use assemblies**

▶ **Use Revit links**

▶ **Use tips and shortcuts**

Repeating Geometry

Revit Architecture has several tools to repeat geometry across your project. Each tool has variations in functionality, so it is important to understand which tool is appropriate and best suited for your requirements. You will review four different tools that can be used to repeat geometry, specifically focusing on features available for each tool.

Component Families

As outlined in Chapter 5, "Adding Families," and Chapter 6, "Modifying Families," component families are the core type of repeating object you will utilize. They can be constructed to be parametric by creating multiple types of the same family; think of one door with 10 types to represent variations in standard sizes. Component families can also be used with (and are a critical aspect of) groups, links, and assemblies.

In the following exercise, you will create two new family types with varying parameter values and then load and apply the new types to family instances in the project.

Exercise 14.1: Create and Apply Family Types

To begin, go to the book's web page at www.sybex.com/go/revit2016essentials, download the files for Chapter 14, and open the file c14-ex-14.1start.rvt.

1. Open the exercise file to the Level 1 floor plan view. There are several instances of the Cubicle_Standard furniture system family. Select any instance of this family and click Edit Family from the Modify | Furniture Systems contextual tab on the ribbon.

2. Once in the Family Editor, click the Family Types button from the Properties panel on the Create tab. Currently there is only one type, Type A. You need to create two additional types in order to accommodate larger sizes of the cubicle.

3. While still in the Family Types dialog, click New under Family Types. In the Name dialog, specify **Type B** and click OK. Repeat the same process to create a **Type C**.

   At this point you have three family types; next, you'll specify a different dimension for the two new types.

4. While still in the Family Types dialog, set Name to Type B. Change the Panel1 Length parameter value to 6'-6" (1980 mm). Next, set Name to Type C. Change the Panel2 Length parameter value to 8'-0" (2438 mm) (Figure 14.1).

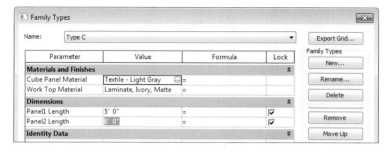

FIGURE 14.1 Family Types parameters

5. Click OK to close the dialog. You now have three types in the family, all with different dimensions. Update the version in the project by clicking Load Into Project And Close on the ribbon and specifying not

to save changes when prompted. For the Family Already Exists dialog, choose Overwrite The Existing Version And Its Parameter Values.

6. The existing family instances don't change just yet because they are all using Type A and we did not change any dimensions for it.

7. Select the eight cubicle instances in the upper-right area of the floor plan, and from the Type Selector, change the families from Type A to Type B. Notice that the size increases to match the 6′-6″ dimension you specified in the family (Figure 14.2).

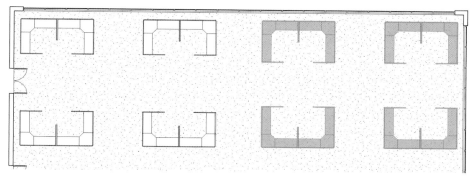

F I G U R E   1 4 . 2   **Type B family instances**

8. Select the 15 cubicle instances in the lower-right area of the floor plan, and from the Type Selector, change the families from Type A to Type C. Notice that the size increases even more to reflect the 8′-0″ dimension you specified in the family (Figure 14.3).

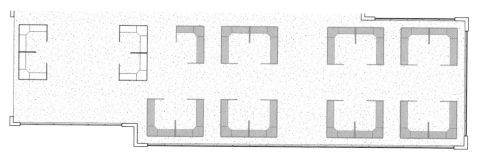

F I G U R E   1 4 . 3   **Type C family instances**

Component families can be saved outside the project as standalone RFA files and loaded back in or into other projects. This allows for the creation of shared libraries so the entire office or multiple offices can utilize the same components.

For each family type you can assign different parameter values, which allows you to repeat geometry in your project without creating a different family file and re-creating geometry for each variation.

Groups

Groups are collections of project objects such as system families, component families, or detail items. Model groups are collections of 3D geometries, whereas detail groups are strictly 2D. Groups are easily created by selecting the objects you want to include in the group and choosing Create Group on the ribbon.

Creating a group will generate a single element that contains a collection of objects (which also makes it easy to move everything together). A good use case for groups is a condominium or apartment project. For typical units or apartments that will appear more than once in the project, you can select the objects and create a group. This group can then be copied or inserted at multiple project locations. Edit one group type, and all instances will update to match.

In the following exercise, you will create a furniture layout and then create a group. Once the group is created, you will copy it to other areas in order to repeat the same furniture layout.

Exercise 14.2: Create and Edit a Group

To begin, open the file c14-ex-14.2start.rvt.

1. Open the exercise file to the Level 1 floor plan view. Notice that there is one round table family in the upper-left area of the plan. Create eight copies of the table family so there are three rows containing three tables each. Each table should be spaced 8'-0" (2438 mm) apart (Figure 14.4).

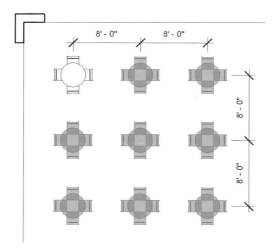

FIGURE 14.4   Table layout and spacing

2. Next, select all nine tables, and from the Modify | Furniture contextual ribbon tab, click Create Group. Revit will prompt you to name the group. From the Create Model Group dialog, specify a name of 9 Table.

3. Click OK and the group will be created. Clicking on any of the tables will now select the entire group; think of it as a container.

4. With the newly created group instance selected, create five copies of the group to the right of the original spaced at 24'-0" (7315 mm) apart. Then create three copies of the group under the original, also spaced at 24'-0" (7315 mm) apart. At this point, the floor plan view should look similar to Figure 14.5.

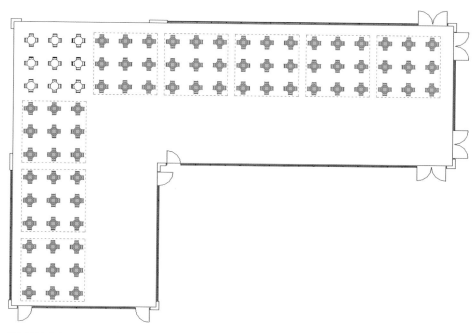

FIGURE 14.5 Overall group layout

5. Select any instance of the 9 Table group, and from the Group ribbon panel, click Edit Group. This will put you into group edit mode. Any changes you make in this mode will be applied to the other instances of the same group type.

6. Select the three vertical table instances in the center, and from the Type Selector, change the type from 36" Diameter to 60" Diameter.

The tables should now reflect the larger size and updated number of nested chair families.

7. From the Edit Group floating panel, click the Finish button. This will apply the changes you just made to every other group instance. Open the 3D view to see the revised furniture layout (Figure 14.6).

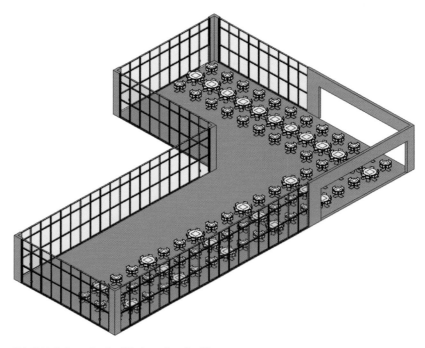

FIGURE 14.6   3D view of revised layout

Groups can also be saved out of a project as stand-alone project files (right-click the group type in the Project Browser and choose Save Group).

8. For the last modification, select any instance of the 9 Table group, and from the Group ribbon panel, click Edit Group. Select the center 60″ Diameter table instance and press the Delete key to delete it.

9. From the Edit Group floating panel, click the Finish button. This will delete the center table from every instance of the same group type.

10. At this point, do a Save As and name the example dataset **c14-ex-14.3start.rvt** so you can start the next exercise with this model.

In the following exercise, you will create a new group type based on one of the existing group types. You will then modify some of the group instances so they have slight variations from the other instances.

Exercise 14.3: Create Variation in Groups

To begin, open the file c14-ex-14.3start.rvt you saved in the previous exercise, or use the included exercise file.

1. From the Level 1 floor plan view, select the 9 Table group instance farthest to the right and click Edit Type from the Properties palette. Click the Duplicate button and specify the new name, **6 Table**.

2. Click OK to close the Name dialog, and click OK again to close the Type Properties dialog. At this point you have duplicated the group type and assigned this new group type to the selected group instance only.

3. Select the 6 Table instance you just created, and from the Group ribbon panel, click Edit Group. Delete the two 60″ Diameter table family instances and click Finish on the Edit Group floating panel. Figure 14.7 shows the newly created group type.

FIGURE 14.7   Newly created group type

4. Next, you will assign this new group type to some of the other group instances. Select the three groups in the lower area of the floor plan, and from the Type Selector, change the type to the new Table 6 type. Each group instance will update to reflect the new type.

    For situations where you don't want to create a new type for slight variations, you can also exclude elements from group instances. This is useful for when a group instance needs to be identical except for one variation.

5. There are five tables closest to the exterior doors you'll want to remove from group instances without having to create a new type. Move the cursor over any of the five tables shown in light blue in Figure 14.8 and press the Tab key until the table is preselected.

6. With the table preselected, left-click to select it. With the table selected, notice the symbol that appears; this is the toggle to include or exclude

members from the group instance. Click the symbol to exclude that group member.

7. Repeat this same process for the other four tables closest to the doors. Notice when you move the cursor over a group with excluded members, you see a ghosted outline indicating the previous table location (Figure 14.8).

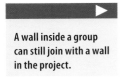

A wall inside a group can still join with a wall in the project.

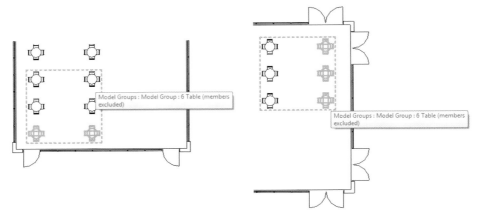

FIGURE 14.8   Excluded group instances

8. Should you need to restore the excluded group members, you can do so using two different approaches. You can select the entire group and click the Restore All Excluded tool from the Group panel of the ribbon. Alternatively, for cases where you need to be more precise, you can move the cursor over an element in the group and use the Tab key to left-click-select one of the excluded members and click the Restore Excluded Group Member To Group Instance symbol. Figure 14.9 shows both methods.

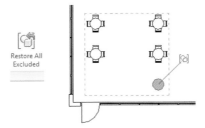

FIGURE 14.9   Restore group instances

Assemblies

Assemblies are collections of objects organized in the Project Browser—which can also contain assembly-specific views. Assemblies are similar in some aspects to groups but with some unique tools directed toward construction workflows. The main difference between an assembly and a group is that an assembly does not propagate change if it's modified (and no longer matches other instances). Instead, assemblies create a new type if there are no other matches.

In the following exercise, you will go create several assemblies to illustrate how Revit matches an existing assembly versus creating a new type. You will also edit an assembly to add additional elements.

Exercise 14.4: Create and Edit an Assembly

To begin, open the file c14-ex-14.4start.rvt.

1. Open the exercise file to the Level 1 floor plan view. Locate the model text labeled Step 2 and zoom in on this area of the floor plan.

2. Select the four brick walls and the structural column and click Create Assembly from the Create ribbon panel.

3. This will activate the New Assembly dialog. Revit Architecture automatically detects the category of elements in the selection set. Change Type Name to **Exterior Column**. Leave the Naming Category dropdown as is (Structural Columns). Click OK to create the assembly.

4. Next locate the model text labeled Step 4. Again, select the four brick walls and the structural column and click Create Assembly from the Create ribbon panel. This time the New Assembly dialog should appear with the grayed-out type name Exterior Column. Revit has detected that this assembly is identical to the last one you created and instead has inherited the name (Figure 14.10). Click OK to create the assembly.

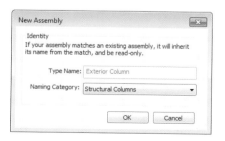

FIGURE 14.10   New Assembly dialog

5. For the next assembly, locate the model text labeled Step 5. Again, select the four brick walls and the structural column and click Create Assembly from the Create ribbon panel. Because the structural column is a different family, Revit creates a new assembly type. Change Type Name to **Exterior Column 2**. Click OK to create the assembly.

6. For the next assembly, locate the model text labeled Step 6. This assembly will be identical to the last one you created. Again, select the four brick walls and the structural column and click Create Assembly from the Create ribbon panel. This assembly will inherit the Exterior Column 2 type. Click OK to create the assembly.

For the next portion of the exercise, you will edit two of the existing assemblies.

7. Select the assembly Exterior Column 2 near the Step 5 text and click Edit Assembly from the Assembly ribbon panel. You are now in edit mode (assembly edit mode is similar to group edit mode). Select the structural column instance inside this assembly and change the type from W10X33 to W10X49.

8. Click Finish from the floating Edit Assembly panel. Revit will report that the edits match an existing assembly type (Figure 14.11).

FIGURE 14.11   Assembly match dialog

This is the main difference between an assembly and a group; instead of propagating the edit you made to the assembly type, Revit instead checks to see if this change matches any existing type. And if a match is found, it switches to that type instead.

9. Click OK to close the dialog. The assembly instance has been automatically swapped from the Exterior Column 2 type to the Exterior Column type.

10. For the last modification, you will edit the Exterior Column assembly instance near the model text Step 2. Select this assembly and click

Edit Assembly from the Assembly ribbon panel. Select any one of the brick walls and press the Delete key to delete it.

11. Click Finish from the Edit Assembly floating panel. Revit will check and confirm that the edit you just made does not match any existing types, so a new type is created (Figure 14.12). Click OK to close the dialog. Revit also attempts to keep the naming convention similar, so you now have a new type called Exterior Column 3. Open the default 3D view to see all of the types.

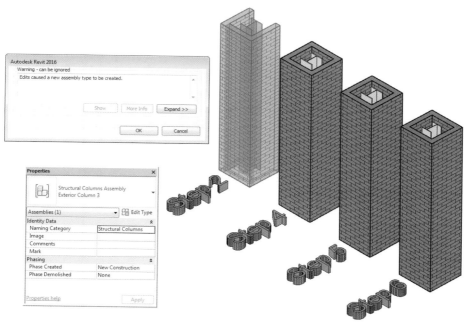

FIGURE 14.12   New Assembly Properties and Assembly Types

In the following exercise, you will utilize a feature specific to assemblies, the Create Views functionality.

Exercise 14.5: Create Assembly Views

To begin, open the file c14-ex-14.5start.rvt.

1. Open the exercise file to the Level 1 floor plan view. There are some generic masonry walls and two elevator families. Select all of this geometry and click Create Assembly from the Create ribbon panel.

2. In the New Assembly dialog, you can leave all of the settings as they are, including the assigned type name, Specialty Equipment 001. Click OK to create the assembly.

3. In the Project Browser, expand Assemblies and notice that your assembly is organized here. For the next step, you will create assembly views. Assembly views are specific to assemblies; they are essentially a set of Revit views, sheets, and schedules that are exclusive to the geometry of a particular assembly. Right-click on the Specialty Equipment 001 assembly from the Project Browser, and select Create Assembly Views.

4. In the Create Assembly Views dialog, check the options outlined in Figure 14.13, and change the Sheet option from None to E1 30 × 42 Horizontal. Click OK to create the assembly views.

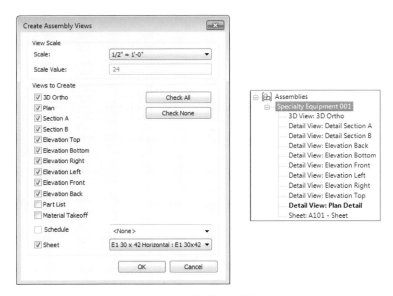

FIGURE 14.13   Create Assembly Views dialog

5. The assembly views are organized under the specific assembly for which they were created in the Project Browser. You can click the + sign to expand the list and see all assembly views.

6. For the last step of the exercise, you will populate the assembly sheet A101 with some of the assembly views. Open Sheet A101 by double-clicking it in the Project Browser.

7. Right-click Sheet A101 in the Project Browser and choose Add View. First, select Specialty Equipment 001: 3D View: 3D Ortho. Click Add View To Sheet. The viewport will be placed on the cursor. Simply move into position and left-click to place the view on the sheet.

8. Repeat step 7, but add the assembly views Plan Detail and Detail Section A. When you're finished, you should have a nicely organized sheet populated with your assembly views, similar to Figure 14.14, depending on how you organized the sheet.

You can't add as many object categories to assemblies as you can to groups. There are restrictions on some object categories (they cannot be added to the assembly) such as other assembled objects, annotation/detail items, groups, imports, links, model lines, masses, rooms, images, curtain systems, stacked walls, and curtain walls.

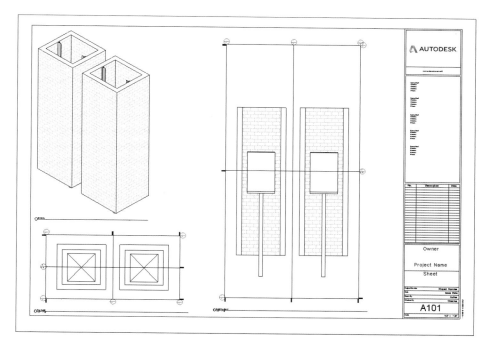

FIGURE 14.14 Assembly views on sheet

Revit Links

Revit project files can be linked into one another. This is useful not only to divide large projects or campus buildings but also to repeat geometry. For example, your project may have identical wings or buildings on campus. The Revit project can be linked in and even allows for copies of the link to be created (all instances will update if reloaded). Links also have project-wide controls under Manage Links. Here you can reload, unload, or entirely remove the link from the host project.

In the following exercise, you will create two Revit links from existing geometry by first creating groups and then converting the group instances to a link.

Exercise 14.6: Create Revit Links

To begin, open the file c14-ex-14.6start.rvt.

The most straightforward method to insert a Revit link is to use the Link Revit tool on the Insert tab. This exercise will take a different approach by instead using existing geometry in the project and converting it to two Revit links.

A link can be copied, mirrored, rotated, or further modified. There can also be multiple instances of the same link.

1. Open the exercise file to the Level 1 floor plan view. Take note of the RVT Link A and RVT Link B labeled areas of the floor plan.

2. First select all the walls and text around RVT Link A, and click Create Group from the Create ribbon panel. In the Create Model Group dialog, specify **RVT Link A** for the name and click OK.

3. Next, select all the walls and text around RVT Link B, and click Create Group from the Create ribbon panel. In the Create Model Group dialog, specify **RVT Link B** for the name and click OK.

4. At this point you have created two groups, but you need to convert them to Revit links. Select the group RVT Link A and click Link from the Group ribbon panel. When prompted by the Convert To Link dialog, choose Replace With A New Project File. Browse to the location where you saved the Chapter 14 exercise files and save the Revit link there.

5. Repeat the same process for the RVT Link B. Then open the default 3D view and note that you now have two Revit links created and inserted into your project (Figure 14.15).

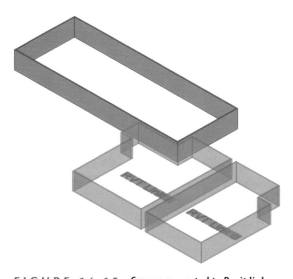

FIGURE 14.15 Groups converted to Revit links

6. Next, let's pretend there are identical—but mirrored—buildings on the other side of the existing building. Select both of the Revit links and click the Mirror - Pick Axis tool from the Modify panel on the ribbon. Click on the reference plane in the center of the building (left image in Figure 14.16) to mirror and copy both Revit links (right image in Figure 14.16).

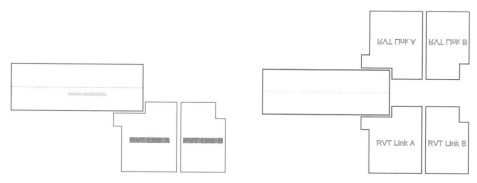

FIGURE 14.16   Mirror Revit links

7. For the last step, you need to edit one of the Revit links to add some geometry, similar to how you might edit a group type. From the Project Browser, expand Revit links. Right-click on RVT Link A.rvt and choose Open (And Unload). Answer OK to the Unload Link dialog.

8. When the link opens, add some interior walls, and then save and close the model. This will take you back to the c10-ex-14.6start .rvt model.

9. When you open a Revit link for editing, the link is unloaded. To reload the link, and the changes you just made to all instances, right-click on RVT Link A.rvt again from the Project Browser. This time, choose Reload.

10. Notice that all link instances are visible again and have updated to reflect any changes you made while editing the Revit link.

A link can be bound into the project (which will place all geometry into a new group). Simply select the link instance and choose Bind Link on the ribbon.

Utilize Tips and Shortcuts

Before we conclude this final chapter, let's review some additional quick tips and shortcuts to utilize in your Revit project work:

Close your views   Close windows you're not using to help minimize the drain on your resources. It's easy to lose track of how many views are open, even if you're concentrating on only a few views—and the more you open, the more information you will load into active RAM. If your main view is maximized, you can use the Close Hidden Windows tool to close all the windows but your active one; on the View tab, click the Close Hidden Windows button (it's also conveniently located in the Quick Access toolbar). You can also assign this command to a keyboard shortcut such as XX.

Use the Purge Unused tool   You won't use every family and every group you create in your model. The Purge Unused tool lets you get rid of those unused elements to help keep your file sizes at a reasonable level. This too can be found on the Manage tab on the Settings panel. If a file is very large, the tool can take several minutes to run, but eventually you'll be presented with a list (Figure 14.17) of all the unused elements in your file.

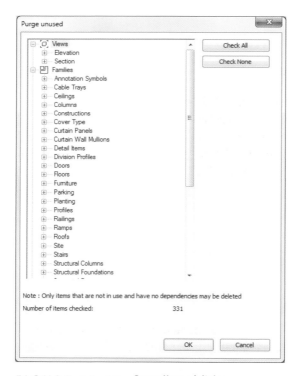

FIGURE 14.17   Purge Unused dialog

Use Reveal Constraints mode   Reveal Constraints is a new temporary view mode that first appeared in the 2015 R2 release. Reveal Constraints is an easy way to see all explicit dimension constraints in a specific view (such as elements that were aligned and locked or dimensions that were locked). Another nice feature is that you can select the red constraint object and Revit will show the constrained objects as selected (Figure 14.18).

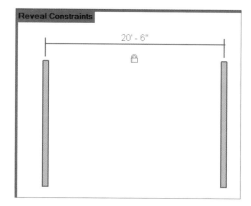

FIGURE 14.18 Reveal Constraints

Use the Selection Box tool New for the 2016 release is the Selection Box tool. This is an easy way to isolate selected elements in the current view and switch over to a 3D view with only these elements visible (it also works in a 3D view to isolate elements). The tool enables the 3D view section box, which will be set to reflect the selected objects only (Figure 14.19).

FIGURE 14.19
Selection box

Filter your selection You can filter selection behavior by customizing any combination of links, underlay elements, pinned elements, the ability to select elements by face, and the ability to drag elements on selection. For example, on a large project, you may want to disable link selection to prevent accidental selection of linked models. These options can be toggled on the fly and are available in several locations, such as under the Modify arrow and on the lower-right corner of the status bar (Figure 14.20).

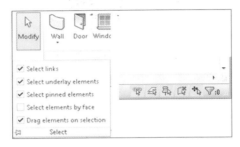

FIGURE 14.20   Selection filters

Customize your double-click behavior   If you navigate to Application ➤ Options ➤ User Interface ➤ Double-Click Options, you can customize the action for the element types (Figure 14.21). The available actions will vary based on the element type; however, each type has a Do Nothing option. For example, if you find yourself accidentally double-clicking to edit families, you can change the default behavior.

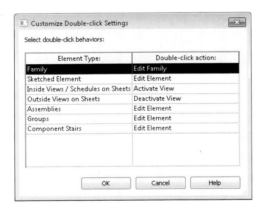

FIGURE 14.21   Double-click settings

Make elevators visible in your plans   Suppose you want to create a shaft that will penetrate all the floors of your building and put an elevator in it that will show in all your plans. To do this, you could use an elevator family and cut a series of holes in the floors by editing floor profiles, but sometimes those holes stop aligning on their own recognizance. Fortunately, you can do both things at once using the Shaft tool on the Opening panel of the Architecture tab.

Here, not only can you cut a vertical hole through multiple floors as a single object, you can also insert 2D linework (using the Symbolic Line tool when editing the shaft opening sketch) to represent the elevator in plan view (Figure 14.22). Every time the shaft is cut, you're certain to see the elevator linework.

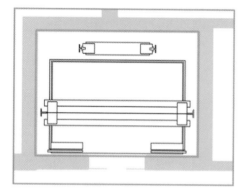

FIGURE 14.22 Adding elevators to a shaft

Orient to view Creating perspective views of isolated design elements can be quick and easy in plan view or in section view, but let's say you want to see that same element in 3D to be able to work out the details.

1. Create a callout or section cut isolating the area in question. If you're using a section, make sure to set your view depth to something practical.

2. Open the default 3D view or any other 3D orthographic view of the project.

3. Right-click the ViewCube, select Orient To View, and select the callout or section from the context menu.

4. Your 3D view looks identical to your section or plan region, but by rotating the view, you can see that portion in 3D.

Customize your shortcuts To edit your keyboard shortcuts, choose Application ➢ Options. Choose the User Interface tab, and then click the Keyboard Shortcuts Customize button. You can also access this command on the View tab in the ribbon under the User Interface flyout button. The Keyboard Shortcuts dialog box (Figure 14.23) allows you to edit those shortcuts. Consider making common shortcuts the same letter. One good example for this is the Visibility/Graphic Overrides dialog box, where both VV and VG are set by default as shortcuts (VV can be used for quicker access).

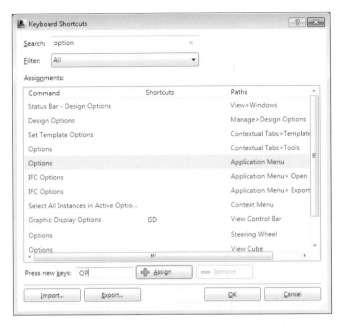

F I G U R E   1 4 . 2 3   Editing your keyboard shortcuts

Copy a 3D view between projects   Suppose you made the perfect 3D view in your last project, and you can't figure out how to get it into your current project. Fortunately, there's a way to copy views from one project to another. Open both files in the same instance of Revit Architecture, and then do the following:

1. In your perfect view, right-click the 3D view in the Project Browser, and choose Show Camera from the context menu.

2. Press Ctrl+C to copy the selected camera.

3. In your new model, press Ctrl+V and click in the view to paste the camera. The view and all its settings are now there (alternatively, you can use the Modify ➢ Paste Aligned To Current View to paste the view).

Disallow joining for walls   By default, Revit Architecture will join walls that intersect; however, you will eventually run into a condition where you need to override this behavior. First select a wall and hover over the Drag Wall End grip. Then right-click and choose Disallow Join. This will unjoin the wall and give you additional control to drag the wall end without it automatically jumping and joining to the intersecting wall.

Join geometry on parallel walls   If you have two parallel walls and there is an opening hosted on one wall (such as a door or window), you may want to automatically cut an opening through the second wall as well. If the walls are close enough, with around 1'-0" (300 mm) between them, you can use the Join Geometry tool between the two walls. After that, an opening will be cut in the other parallel wall and it will move with the original family (Figure 14.24).

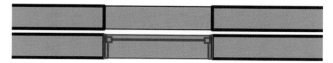

FIGURE 14.24   Join geometry

Prevent room numbers from shifting on cut/paste   By default, when you cut and paste rooms in a project, the room numbers will shift to the next available numbers. There is a trick to maintain the room numbers when cutting and pasting. Select the rooms you will be cutting to the Clipboard and create a group. Once the rooms are in a group, they can be cut and pasted without changing the room numbers. Then they can be ungrouped, and the group can be deleted from the Project Browser.

Copy objects from a Revit link   Need to copy an object from a Revit link and paste it into the host project? No problem; simply hover over the object in the link you want to copy and press the Tab key until the object is highlighted. Then click to select the object and use the standard copy and paste commands. The element will be copied from the link and pasted directly into the host project, where it can be directly manipulated (Figure 14.25).

Show annotation from a Revit link   Some annotation objects can be displayed from a Revit link. If the link contains annotation (such as room tags, dimensions, and so on) and you want to display it in the host project, set the Visibility/Graphic Overrides properties for the Revit link to By Linked View or Custom. You can further customize which view is displayed by adjusting the Linked View name on the Basics tab.

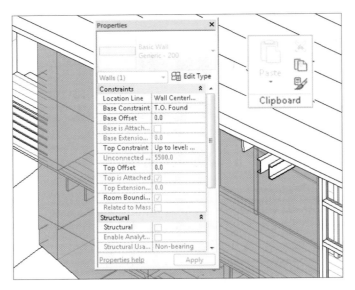

FIGURE 14.25   Copying from a link

Now You Know

This chapter tackled the four primary methods for repetition in Revit Architecture (component families, groups, assemblies, and Revit links). Every project you work on will utilize at least some of these repetition methods. Rounding out the chapter are some tips and shortcuts to take advantage of along the way.

Autodesk Revit Architecture 2016 Certification

Autodesk certifications are industry-recognized credentials that can help you succeed in your design career, providing benefits to both you and your employer. Getting certified is a reliable validation of skills and knowledge, and it can lead to accelerated professional development, improved productivity, and enhanced credibility.

This *Autodesk Official Press* guide can be an effective component of your exam preparation. Autodesk highly recommends (and we agree!) that you schedule regular time to prepare, review the most current exam preparation road map available at www.autodesk.com/certification, use *Autodesk Official Press* books, take a class at an Authorized Training Center (find one nearby at www.autodesk.com/atc), and use a variety of resources to prepare for your certification—including plenty of actual hands-on experience.

To help you focus your studies on the skills you'll need for these exams, the following tables show objectives that could potentially appear on an exam and the chapters in which you can find information on them.

Table A.1 is for the Autodesk Revit 2016 Certified User Exam and lists the topic, exam objectives, and chapter where the information is found. Table A.2 is for the Autodesk Revit 2016 Certified Professional Exam. This book will give you a foundation for the basic objectives covered on the Certified User exam, but you will need further study and hands-on practice to complete and pass the Certified Professional exam.

These Autodesk exam objectives were accurate at press time; please refer to www.autodesk.com/certification for the most current exam road map and objectives.

Good luck preparing for your certification!

TABLE A.1   Certified User exam topics and objectives

Topic	Learning Objective	Chapter
User Interface: Definitions	Identify primary parts of the user interface (UI): ribbon tabs, Application menu, InfoCenter, status bar, View Control bar, Project Browser, context/ right-click menus, ViewCube, Navigation bar.	Chapter 1
User Interface: UI Navigation/Interaction	Name the key features of the ribbon. Define how a split button works. Demonstrate the three ways the ribbon can be displayed: Full Ribbon, Min To Panel Tiles, Min To Tabs. Demonstrate how to detach a panel and move it on the screen.	Not covered
	Describe the hierarchy in the Project Browser for a new project.	Chapter 1
	Define what "context" means when right-clicking in the drawing window.	Chapter 1
	Name the tools found on the Application menu (Save, Export, Print).	Chapter 12
	Demonstrate how to add items to the Quick Access toolbar.	Not covered
	Describe why the Options Bar changes.	Chapter 1
	Describe the function of the status bar.	Chapter 1
	Describe what pressing the Esc key does.	Chapter 1
User Interface: Drawing Window	Describe what double-clicking an elevation view marker does.	Not covered
	Demonstrate how to turn on/off the 3D indicator.	Not covered

Topic	Learning Objective	Chapter
	Demonstrate how to change the view scale.	Chapter 1
User Interface: Navigation Control	Describe the functionality of the ViewCube.	Chapter 1
	Describe what the ViewCube home icon does.	Chapter 1
User Interface: Zoom	Describe how to zoom using the Navigation bar.	Chapter 1
	Describe the quickest way to zoom in or out.	Chapter 1
	Describe the quickest way to pan.	Chapter 1
File Management: Definitions	Define the acronym BIM and why it is important to Revit users.	Introduction
	Define a template file.	Not covered
File Management: Project Files	Identify the filename extension of a project file (.rvt).	Chapter 1
	Identify the filename extension of a template file (.rte). Create a template file for later project use.	Not covered
	Identify the filename extension of a Revit family file (.rfa).	Chapter 5
File Management: Open Existing Revit Project	Locate the Recent Files window.	Not covered
	Demonstrate how to open a Revit file through Projects ➢ Open and through Application menu ➢ Open Documents icon.	Chapter 1

(Continues)

TABLE A.1 *(Continued)*

Topic	Learning Objective	Chapter
File Management: Create New Revit Project	Demonstrate how to create a new Revit project folder and file through Application menu ➤ New ➤ Project.	Chapter 1
	Change to a metric drawing.	Not covered
	Add project information to a new drawing set.	Not covered
	Change system settings to create a new dimension style. Change arrows to architectural tick (obliques).	Chapter 11
Views: View Control and Properties	Navigate and change views using the View Control Bar.	Chapter 2
	Understand the view range of plan views and be able to change it.	Not covered
	Understand the purpose of view templates.	Not covered
	Change object visibility using Temporary Hide/Isolate, Hide Category, and Hide Element.	Chapter 9
Views: View Types	Create section views, including segmented ones.	Chapter 9
	Modify, crop, and place elevation views on a sheet.	Chapter 12
	Create and navigate 3D views.	Chapter 2
	Create callouts for details.	Chapter 11
	Create and annotate a drafting view.	Chapter 11
	Use the section box to create a cutaway 3D view.	Not covered

Topic	Learning Objective	Chapter
Views: Cameras	Create a camera view, and modify its orientation.	Not covered
	Create and edit a walk-through.	Not covered
Levels: Definitions	Describe a level. Describe a use for a non-story level.	Chapter 1
	Understand how levels interact with intersecting views.	Chapter 1
	Create new levels.	Chapter 1
	Understand level properties and characteristics.	Chapter 1
Walls: Architecture tab ➢ Wall	Describe how to place walls.	Chapter 2
Walls: Options Bar	List options available when placing and modifying walls: Height, Location Line, Chain, Offset, Radius.	Chapter 2
Walls: Openings	Create a floor-to-ceiling opening in a given wall.	Chapter 2
Walls: Join	Demonstrate a join on crossing wall elements.	Chapter 2
Walls: Materials	Create a new wall type, and add given materials.	Chapters 2, 9
Doors: Architecture tab ➢ Door	Describe how to place doors.	Chapter 2
Doors: Options Bar	Describe door options: Vertical/ Horizontal, Tag On Placement, Leader, Leader Attachment Distance.	Chapters 2, 5
Doors: Model in Place	Edit existing doors. Use Align to position a door.	Chapters 2, 5

(Continues)

TABLE A.1 *(Continued)*

Topic	Learning Objective	Chapter
Windows: Architecture tab ➢ Window	Describe how to place windows.	Chapter 2
Windows: Options Bar	Describe window options: Vertical/ Horizontal, Tag On Placement, Leader, Leader Attachment Distance.	Chapters 2, 5
Windows: Model in Place	Edit existing windows.	Chapter 6
Component: Options Bar	List options available when placing a component.	Chapter 5
Component: Component Host	Describe how to move a component to a different host.	Chapter 5
Component: Families	Navigate to find component families and load them.	Chapter 5
	Edit a family file and save.	Chapter 6
Columns and Grids: Definitions	Identify the uses of a grid.	Chapter 1
Columns and Grids: Architecture Tab ➢ Grid	Create an equally spaced grid pattern.	Not covered
Columns and Grids: Grid Properties	List the options available when placing and modifying grids.	Not covered
Columns and Grids: Architecture Tab ➢ Column	Place columns on a grid.	Not covered
Columns and Grids: Column Properties	List the options available when placing and modifying columns.	Not covered
Columns and Grids: Modify	List the tools you can use to modify columns and grids.	Not covered
Stairs and Railings: Stair Types and Properties	Set the stair type.	Chapter 4

Topic	Learning Objective	Chapter
	Change the stair tread depth.	Chapter 4
Stairs and Railings: Stair Placement Options	Add a stair.	Chapter 4
Stairs and Railings: Railing Types and Properties	Set the railing to rectangular.	Chapter 4
	Set the railing properties.	Chapter 4
Stairs and Railings: Railing Placement Options	Add a railing.	Chapter 4
Roofs and Floors: Roof Types and Properties	Create a roof.	Chapter 3
	Modify the roof properties.	Chapter 3
Roofs and Floors: Roof Elements	Create a fascia, a soffit, and a gutter.	Not covered
Roofs and Floors: Floor Types and Properties	Set the floor type (sloped and tapered). Create a floor.	Chapter 3
Sketching: Geometry	Sketch geometry and profiles using all sketching tools: lines, arcs, polygons, rectangles.	Chapter 1
Sketching: Fillet, Trim	Fillet objects.	Not covered
	Trim objects.	Chapter 1
Sketching: Snaps	Describe the benefits of using snaps.	Not covered
	List the shortcuts to toggle a snap on and off.	Not covered
Annotations: Text	Add model text to a floor plan.	Not covered
Annotations: Dimensions	Add a dimension to a given floor plan. Create a wall section.	Chapters 11, 12
	Add a spot slope to a roof on a given plan.	Not covered

(Continues)

TABLE A.1   *(Continued)*

Topic	Learning Objective	Chapter
Annotations: Tags	Add tags.	Chapter 11
	Tag untagged elements in a given floor plan.	Chapter 8
Schedules: Schedule Types	Create a door schedule.	Not covered (While there is no specific coverage of a door schedule, creating schedules is covered in Chapter 12.)
	Create a window schedule.	Chapter 12
	Create a room schedule.	Chapters 8,12
Schedules: Legends	Create a legend.	Chapter 11
Schedules: Keynotes	Add keynotes.	Chapter 12
Construction Document Sets: Sheet Setup	Create a title sheet with a sheet list.	Chapter 12
Construction Document Sets: Printing	Create view/sheet sets for printing.	Chapter 12
	Print in scale. Print with percentage.	Chapter 12
Construction Document Sets: Rendering	Render.	Chapter 9
	Place generic lights.	Not covered
Set the solar angle.		Chapter 9

TABLE A.2 Certified Professional exam topics and objectives

Topic	Learning Objective	Chapter
Collaboration	Copy and monitor elements in a linked file.	Not covered
	Use worksharing.	Chapter 10
	Import DWG and image files.	Chapters 7, 13
Documentation	Create and modify filled regions.	Chapter 11
	Place detail components and repeating details.	Chapter 11
	Tag elements (doors, windows, etc.) by category.	Chapter 11
	Use dimension strings.	Chapters 1, 11
	Set the colors used in a color scheme legend.	Chapter 8
	Work with phases.	Not covered
Elements	Change elements within a curtain wall: grids, panels, mullions.	Chapter 2
	Create compound walls.	Chapter 2
	Create a stacked wall.	Chapter 2
	Differentiate system and component families.	Chapter 5
Families	Work with family parameters.	Chapter 6
	Create a new family type.	Chapter 6
	Modify an element's type parameters.	Chapter 2
	Use Revit family templates.	Chapter 5
	Use family creation procedures.	Chapter 6
Modeling	Assess or review warnings in Revit.	Chapter 13
	Create a building pad.	Chapter 13
	Define floors for a mass.	Chapter 7

(Continues)

TABLE A.2 *(Continued)*

Topic	Learning Objective	Chapter
	Create a stair with a landing.	Chapter 4
	Create elements such as floors, ceilings, and roofs.	Chapter 3
	Generate a toposurface.	Chapter 13
	Model railings.	Chapter 4
	Edit a model element's material.	Chapter 9
	Change a generic floor/ceiling/roof to a specific type.	Chapter 3
	Attach walls to a roof or ceiling.	Chapter 3
Views	Define element properties in a schedule.	Chapter 12
	Control visibility.	Chapters 1, 9
	Use levels.	Chapter 1
	Create a duplicate view for a plan, section, elevation, drafting view, etc.	Chapter 9
	Create and manage legends.	Not covered
	Manage the view position on sheets.	Chapter 12
	Organize and sort items in a schedule.	Chapter 12

INDEX